Studying Judaism

STUDYING WORLD RELIGION SERIES

A series of introductory guides, books in the *Studying World Religions* series are designed as study aids for those approaching the world's religions for the first time.

Also available in the series:
Studying Christianity, William H. Brackney
Studying Islam, Clinton Bennett

Forthcoming:
Studying Hinduism, David Ananda Hart

Studying Judaism

The Critical Issues

MELANIE J. WRIGHT

Studying World Religions

continuum

Continuum International Publishing Group

The Tower Building	80 Maiden Lane
11 York Road	Suite 704
London	New York
SE1 7NX	NY 10038

www.continuumbooks.com

British Library Cataloguing-in-Publication Data
A catalogue record for this book is available from the British Library.

PB: 978-0-8264-9719-2

Library of Congress Cataloging-in-Publication Data
Wright, Melanie Jane, 1970-2011
  Studying Judaism : the critical issues / Melanie J. Wright.
    p. cm. – (Studying world religions)
  Includes bibliographical references and index.
  ISBN 978-0-8264-9719-2 (pbk.) – ISBN 978-0-8264-9718-5 (hardcover) 1. Judaism–Study and teaching. I. Title. II. Series.

  BM70.W74 2011
  296.071–dc23
                                                                2011033307

Typeset by Fakenham Prepress Solutions, Fakenham, Norfolk NR21 8NN
Printed and bound in India

Table of Contents

Author Biography

Melanie J. Wright was Academic Director of the Centre for the Study of Jewish-Christian Relations, and a Lecturer in Religious Studies at the Open University, UK. She is the author of numerous articles and books including *Understanding Judaism*, and *Religion and Film: An Introduction*. With Lucia Faltin, she co-edited *The Religious Roots of Contemporary European Identity*, which is also published by Continuum.

Tribute

Melanie Wright (1970–2011) was an exceptionally gifted scholar. Her impressive scholarship had begun to make an impact on the field of Religious Studies, pushing the boundaries of the field to include innovative research in the areas of religion and film and the study of religion through material culture. Within little more than a decade of the submission of her doctorate, she completed four monographs and a sizeable collection of articles (for a list of her publications, see the website dedicated to her legacy: http://www.melaniewright.info/). Her first monograph, *Moses in America: The cultural uses of biblical narrative* (2003), applied cultural studies methods to the study of religion. Her *Religion and Film: An Introduction* (2007) has proven to be highly regarded for the non-theological framework with which she cast light on the making and viewing of films which touch on religion. In the area of Jewish Studies she offered two monographs, *Understanding Judaism* (2003), which was well received, and the present volume, *Studying Judaism: The Critical Issues* (2012). Prominent in all Melanie's work is the commitment to broaden the view from elitist and essentializing constructions of religion, and take seriously the way in which religion is expressed in a wide variety of forms including popular and material culture.

She was highly regarded by her colleagues at Cambridge and the Open University. Her dedication to teaching and learning bore its fruits not only in her relationship with students at Anglia Ruskin and Cambridge Universities, but in particular in her leadership in establishing the MA and then the MSt courses at the Centre the Study of Jewish-Christian Relations, an educational charity of which she was a founding member. At the Open University, which she joined as a member of staff in 2007, Melanie enjoyed working in a department dedicated to the study of religion, proud to be serving at an institution committed to offer education opportunities for all. Her gifts as a scholar and teacher included the ability to see the highest potential in every person she encountered, and to nurture the talent she found in students with generosity and warmth. Melanie was much more than a scholar. She touched the lives of many people through her commitment to friendship and a genuine interest in everyone she met. Her academic legacy will continue to impact on the study of religion.

Series Preface

Religious Studies and Critical Enquiry: Towards a New Relationship.

CLINTON BENNETT

Birth of a Discipline

This new series takes the view that, as a field of studies, the study of religion is multi-disciplinary and poly-methodological and needs to not merely affirm this, but to translate this claim into practice. Religious Studies has its academic, historical roots within faculties or departments of Theology, where it began as a Comparative Study of Religions predicated on the assumption that Christianity was either a model, or a superior religion. The first University appointment was in 1873, when William Fairfield Warren became Professor of Comparative Theology, and of the History and Philosophy of Religion at Boston University. The concept of Christianity as a model meant that anything that qualified as a religion ought to resemble Christianity. Traditional sub-divisions of Christian Studies, almost always called Theology, were applied to all religious systems. Thus, a religion would have a founder, a scripture or scriptures, doctrines, worship, art, sacred buildings and various rituals associated with the human life cycle. These elements could be identified, and studied in any religion. This approach has obvious methodological advantages, but it can end up making all religions look remarkable similar to each other, and of course also to what serves as the template or model, that is, to Christianity. The very terms 'Hinduism' and 'Buddhism' were of European origin, since all religions had to be 'isms' with coherent belief structures. The assumption that Christianity was somehow superior, perhaps uniquely true or divinely revealed to the exclusion of other religions, meant that other religions had to be understood either as human constructs or as having a more sinister origin. Theology was thus concerned with evaluation and with truth claims. The study of religions other than Christianity often aimed to demonstrate how these religions fell short of the Christian ideal. Their strengths and weaknesses were delineated. Some classified religions according to their position on a supposed evaluative scale, with the best at the top and the worst at the bottom. Religious studies, as it developed as a distinctive field of study, quickly distanced itself from Theology even when taught within Theology departments. It would be mainly descriptive.

The Break from Theology

Evaluation would be left to theology. Assessing where a religion might be considered right or wrong, strong or weak, might occupy a theologian, but the student of religion would describe what he or she saw regardless of their own opinion, or lack of an opinion, about whether religions have any actual link with a supra-human reality. In part, this stemmed from Religious Studies' early interest in deconstructing religions; this was the attempt to determine how they began. Usually, they were understood as a response to, or product of, particular social and political contexts. This took the field closer to the social sciences, which remain neutral on such issues as the existence of God or whether any religion can claim to have been revealed, focusing instead on understanding how religions operate, either socially or psychologically. Incidentally, the term 'Comparative Religion' has been used as a neutral term; that is, one that does not imply a comparison in order to refute or evaluate. In its neutral sense, it refers to the cataloguing of religious data under thematic headings, such as ritual, myth and beliefs, without any attempt to classify some as better than others. The field has, to a degree, searched for a name. Contenders include the Scientific Study of Religion and the History of Religion (or *Religionsgeschichte*, mainly in the German speaking academy), but since the founding of the pioneering department of Religious Studies at Lancaster University under Ninian Smart in 1967, 'Religious Studies' has become the preferred description especially in secular institutions. One issue has been whether to use 'religion' in the plural or singular. If the singular is used, it implies that different religions belong to the same category. If the plural is used, it could denote the opposite, that they share nothing in common, arise from unrelated causes and have no more to do with each other than, say, the Chinese and the Latin scripts – except that the former are beliefs about the divine-human relationship or the purpose of life, while the latter are alphabets. Geo Widengren, Professor of the History of Religion at Uppsala, rejected the notion that an *a priori, sui generis* phenomenon called 'religion' existed as breaking the rules of objective, neutral, value-free scholarship. Incidentally, Buddhism and Confucianism were often characterized as philosophies, not as religions because they lacked a God or Gods at their centre. On the history of the field, see Capps (1995) and Sharpe (2006).

Privileging Insidership

The field soon saw itself as having closer ties to the humanities and social science than to theology. It would be a multidisciplinary field, drawing on anthropology, psychology and philosophy, as well as on linguistics and literary criticism, to study different aspects of a religion, what people do as well as what they say they believe, their sacred texts, their rituals, their buildings and how they organize themselves. However, a shift occurred in the development of the discipline, or field of study since it is a multidisciplinary field, that effectively reduced the distance between itself and theology, from which it had tried so hard to divorce itself. While claiming to be a multidisciplinary field, Religious Studies has in practice veered towards privileging a single approach, or way of studying religion, above others. The shift towards what may be called phenomenology or 'insider-ship' took place for good reasons, and was a much-needed corrective to past mistakes and distortions. In the post-colonial space, much criticism has been voiced about how the Western world went about the task of studying the religious and cultural Others. Here, the voice of Edward Said is perhaps the most widely known. Much scholarship, as Said (1978) argued, was placed at the service of Empire to justify colonial rule and attitudes of racial or civilizational superiority. Such scholars, known as Orientalists, said Said, described Others – whether Africans, native Americans, Hindus or Muslims, Arabs or Chinese – who, so that they could be dominated, were inalienably different from and inferior to themselves. However, this description did not correspond to any actual reality. The term 'Other' is widely used in post-colonial discourse and in writing about Alterity to refer to those who are different from us. The term was first used by Hegel. In contemporary use, it denotes how we stigmatize others, so that all Muslims or all Hindus, or all Africans, share the same characteristics, which are radically different from and less desirable than those of Western populations. Cabezón (2006) argues that 'the dialectic of alterity is as operative today in the discipline of Religious Studies as it was in the discipline's antecedents'. This is a sobering assessment (21). The Orientalists portrayed the non-Western world as chaotic, immoral and backward, and as exotic; as sometimes offering forbidden fruits but always offering adventure, riches and the opportunity to pursue a career as a colonial administrator, in the military, in commerce or even as a Christian missionary. Religions were often depicted as idolatrous, superstitious, oppressive and as the source of much social evil.

Admittedly, some scholars, including the man who can be credited as founding the scientific study of religion, F. Max Müller, thought that religions such as Hinduism and Buddhism had become corrupt over time, and that in their most ancient, original form they represented genuine apprehensions of divine truth. Writing in 1892, he remarked that if he seemed to speak too well of these religions, there was little danger of the public 'forming too favorable an opinion of them' since there were many other writers who presented their 'dark and hideous side' (78). It was in his *Chips from a German Workshop* (1867) that Müller used the term 'scientific study of religion'. Supposition about the human origin of religion, perhaps excluding Christianity, resulted in a range of theories about how religions began. T. W. Rhys-Davids, Britain's first professor of Comparative Religion, at Manchester,thought that his work on the classical texts would help to separate the rational, ethical core of Buddhism from the myths and legends that surrounded its contemporary practice. Often, the social–political and cultural milieu in which a founder type figure could be located were regarded as significant contributory factors. In the case of Hinduism, the 'lack of a founder' was often commented upon almost as if this alone detracted from the possibility that Hinduism was a *bone fide* faith. Even such a careful scholar as Whaling says that Hinduism lacks a founder (1986: 43). In the case of Islam, Muhammad was invariably depicted as the author of the Qur'an and as Islam's founder, neither of which reflect Muslim conviction. Of course, for Christian polemicists, Muhammad was a charlatan and worse, Hinduism was a tissue of falsehood and Buddhism, if it qualified as a religion at all, was selfish! The result of this approach was to de-construct religion, to reduce religion to something other than revealed truth. Instead, religion was a psychological prop or a sociological phenomenon that helps to police societies or a political tool used by the powerful to subdue the poor. Another aspect was that ancient or classical rather than contemporary religion was the main subject matter of religious studies.

The Personal Dimension

Even before Said, in reaction to the above, a different approach began to dominate the field. Partly, this was motivated by a desire – not absent in Müller – to right some of the wrongs committed as a result of what can only be described as racial bias. One of the most important contributors to the new approach was Wilfred Cantwell Smith who, in 1950 in his own inaugural lecture as Professor of Comparative Religion at McGill, spoke of the earlier generation of scholars as resembling 'flies crawling on the surface of a goldfish bowl, making accurate observations on the fish inside … and indeed contributing much to our knowledge of the subject; but never asking themselves, and never finding out, how it feels to be a goldfish' (2)[1]. Scholars such as Gerardus van der Leeuw (1890-1950), influenced by the philosophical concept of phenomenology, had already applied its principles to religious studies, arguing that the field should move beyond description, 'an inventory and classification of the phenomena as they appear in history' to an attempt to understand 'all the experiences born of what can only become reality after it has been admitted into the life of the believer' (1954: 10). This introduced what Smith called a 'personal element' into the study of religion an element that has always played a part in theology, which deals with matters of faith, with people's most cherished and deeply held convictions. Smith suggested that all religions should be understood in personal terms: religion is 'the faith in men's hearts'; it is 'a personal thing, in the lives of men' (1959: 42). Thus, the student will make progress when he or she recognizes that they are not primarily dealing with externals, with books and rituals that can be observed but with 'religious persons, or at least with something interior to persons' (1959: 53). In the past, the study of 'other men's religions' had taken the form of an 'impersonal presentation of an "it"' (1959: 34). Now, instead of an 'us' talking about 'them', it would first become 'us' talking 'to them', then a '"we all" talking with each other about "us"' as Religious Studies took on the task of interpreting 'intellectually the cosmic significance of life generically, not just for one's own group specifically' (1981: 187). The Religious Studies' professor now wrote for the Other as well as for outsiders, since they would also read what he wrote. 'The day has long past', said Smith, 'when we write only for ourselves' (1981: 143). Phenomenology, applied to the study of religions, is the effort to penetrate to the essential core, to the *eidos*, of religion, by bracketing out assumptions, theories or preconceptions, so that we see the phenomenon for what it really is, in its own terms. Instead of imposing categories, theories and value judgments from outside, like the Orientalists did, we enter into the religion's worldview. We all but become the Other. Instead of decrying what we write as a mockery, as inaccurate, as belittling what he or she believes, the Other ought to voice their approval (1959: 44).

Leaving aside the problem that not all Muslims, all Hindus or all Buddhists believe identically, and that what one believer finds acceptable another may not, the criterion that believers should recognize themselves in what gets written, has nonetheless become a generally accepted principle within Religious Studies. It is also widely embraced in anthropology. Certainly, effort is made to represent religions as diverse, to counter the impression given by earlier writers that Islam, for example, was more or less the same everywhere and, for that matter, throughout history. Smith himself insisted that there is actually no such thing as Hinduism, as Christianity or as Islam, only what this Hindu or that Muslim believes. At the deepest level, this is undoubtedly true. However, Religious Studies would not survive if it took this too literally, so pragmatically it accepts that while no abstract reality called 'Christianity' or 'Islam' may exist, believers also believe that they belong to a religious tradition, and share beliefs with others who belong to that tradition. They believe that these are not merely their own individual personal opinions, but are 'true' – that is, according to the teachings of the religion itself. The phenomenological approach, or methodology, tries to depict a religion in terms that insiders recognize. Thus, when explaining how a religion began, it describes what believers themselves hold to be true. An outsider writing about Islam might attribute its origin to Muhammad's genius in responding to the need for political unity in seventh century Arabia by supplying a religion as the unifying creed that bound rival tribes together. The phenomenologist will write of how Muhammad received the Qur'an from God via the Angel Gabriel, in a cave on Mt Hira in the year 610 of the Common Era. The phenomenologist does not have to ask, unlike a theologian, whether Muhammad really did receive revelation. However, by neglecting other explanations of Islam's origin they veer, if not towards theology, then at least towards a type of faith sensitivity that is closer to that of a theologian than to a Freudian psychologist or a Durkheimian sociologist.

Faith Sensitivity: A Paradigm Too Far

From at least the mid-1970s, what has been taught in most college and university departments of Religious Studies, or on world religions courses within departments of Theology or Religion, is the phenomenology of religion. Most popular texts on the religions of the world depict their subject matter in what can be described as an insider-sensitive style. Indeed, there is a tendency to employ Hindus to teach about Hinduism, Muslims to teach about Islam, so what gets taught represents a fairly standard and commonly accepted Hindu or Muslim understanding of these faiths. Hinduism does not get described as having kept millions of people in bondage to the evils of the caste or class system, nor is Islam depicted as an inherently violent religion, or as misogynistic. This tendency to appoint insiders has meant, in practice, little of the type of collaboration, or 'colloquy', that Smith anticipated (1981: 193), but also much less misrepresentation. Partly, the trend stems from the suspicion that it takes one to know one. In anthropology, Clifford Geertz has spoken of an 'epistemological hypochondria concerning how one can know that anything one says about other forms of life is as a matter of fact so' (1988: 71). There is a reluctance to depict all religions as basically the same, or to imply that the same fundamental truths can be found in all of them – if differently expressed – because this sounds like theology. However, a similar pedagogical approach to teaching each tradition is commonly practiced. While this approach is more sophisticated than the early model, which simply used Christianity as a template, it is not so radically different. Here, the work of Ninian Smart and Frank Whaling, among others, has been influential (see Figure 0.1). Sharpe's 'four modes of religion' model is worth examining, but is less easy to translate into the classroom (see Figure 0.2). Smart and Whaling say that most religions have elements such as beliefs, scriptures, histories, sacred sites and worship and that, without imposing too much from the outside, an examination of each of these provides a common framework of investigation. Smart's term 'worldview', too, easily includes Marxism as well as Buddhism, and is less problematic than religion because no belief in the supernatural is implied. Flexibility is possible because some traditions place more stress on certain elements, and therefore these can be discussed in more detail. The role, for example, of a seminal personality in Islam, Christianity or Buddhism is very significant, while less so in Judaism and absent in Hinduism. One very positive development associated with this personal understanding of religion was that the field started to take an interest in contemporary religion, not only in ancient texts. Observation and field work, alongside knowledge of languages and literary analysis, became part and parcel of studying religion. If anything, the trend may have gone too far in the other direction, to the neglect of texts. It is just as mistaken to think that you can learn all about a religion by visiting a place of worship as it is to claim that everything can be learnt from reading its texts. It is not insignificant that when Smart proposed his original six dimensions it was in the context of a lecture on the 'Nature of Theology and the Idea of A Secular University', thus his concern was with the 'logic of religious education in a secular or religiously neutralist society … with the *content* of what should be taught' rather than with the 'question of *how* religion should be taught' (1968: 7).

This series takes the view that phenomenology or insider-sensitivity dominates the field today at the expense of other ways of studying religion. This series also takes the view that this dominance has cost Religious Studies its ability to engage with critical issues. The reality of what a student experiences in the field may be different, less pleasant, than what they learn in the classroom. From what is taught in the classroom, religions are all sweetness and light. True, the darker side of religion may indeed be a distortion, or a misrepresentation, or the result of the manipulation of religion for political or for other ends. True, the earliest strand of the religion may not have contained these elements. However, to say nothing about how a religion has been used to sanction, even to bless violence, or to subjugate women, or to discriminate against outsiders or certain designated groups, simply reverses the mistakes of the past. If the Orientalists rarely had anything good to say about religions other than Christianity, the contemporary student of religion appears blind to anything negative. One of the most popular Religious Studies texts, at least in North America, is Huston Smith's *The World's Religions* (1958; 1991; originally

Table 0.1 Comparison of the models of Smart and Whaling.

Smart's seven-fold scheme of study (initially six; see Smart, 1968: 15-18).	Whaling's eight inter-linked elements, behind which lies some apprehension of ultimate reality. (Whaling, 1986:37-48).
1. Doctrinal	1. Religious community
2. Mythological/scriptural	2. Ritual
3. Ethical	3. Ethics
4. Ritual	4. Social involvement
5. Historical	5. Scriptures/myth
6. Social	6. Concepts
7. Material (added in his 1998 text)	7. Aesthetics
	8. Spirituality

Note: Smart categorized 1-3 as 'para-historical' and 4-6 as 'historical'.

Figure 0.2 Eric Sharpe's 'four-modes' (based on diagram on Sharpe, 1983: 96).

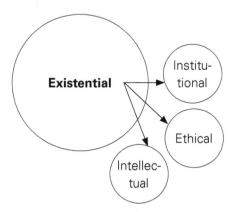

Sharpe sees these as interlinking. Each can be represented by an adjective: Existential = faith; Intellectual = beliefs; Institutional = organizations; Ethical = conduct. A believer or a community may use any of the four as the 'dominant element'; that is, as a 'gateway' to the others (97). On page 96, he has four diagrams, substituting the dominant dimension in each.

The Religions of Man). For all its merit, this deliberately set out to present religions as sweetness and light, or, as the author put it, to show religions 'at their best' (5). Smith himself winced to think how someone closing his chapter on Hinduism and stepping 'directly into the Hinduism described by Nehru as "a religion that enslaves you"' would react (4). He excluded references to the Sunni-Shi'a and traditional-modernist divisions in Islam (3) because he chose instead to note 'different attitudes towards Sufism' by way of taking Islam's diversity seriously. Yet this also avoided discussing some less rose-colored aspects of religion, the full story of which is 'not rose-colored' but 'often crude' (4). What Smith set out to achieve may be said to characterize Religious Studies' agenda; he wanted to 'penetrate the worlds of the Hindus, the Buddhists, and Muslims' and to 'throw bridges from these worlds' to his readers. His goal was 'communication' (10). He wrote of aiming to see through 'others' eyes' (8). Towards the end of his 'Points of Departure' chapter explaining his methodology, he gives an eloquent description of phenomenology, which, although he does not call it that, is worth repeating:

> First, we need to see their adherents [World religions' adherents] as men and women who faced problems much like our own. And second, we must rid our minds of all preconceptions that could dull our sensitivity or alertness to fresh insights. If we lay aside our preconceptions about these religions, seeing each as forged by people who were struggling to see something that would give help and meaning to their lives; and if we then try without prejudice to see ourselves what they see – if we do these things, the veil that separates us from them can turn to gauze (11).

Smart describes the process as one of 'structured empathy', a crossing over of 'our horizons into the worlds of other people' (1983: 16).

Avoiding the Less 'Rosy'

Yet by ignoring such problematic an issue as the Sunni-Shi'a division in Islam, Smith's book, as admirable as it is, provides no tools that could help someone trying to make sense of events in the Lebanon, in Iran and in Iraq. Arguably, this reluctance to deal with critical issues results from oversensitivity to insider sensibilities. A theologian may justify elevating faith sensitivity over all alternatives, but if Religious Studies is a social science, other, less faith-sensitive explanations and content should also be given space on the curriculum. A faith-sensitive treatment of Christianity, for example, would depict Jesus as the son of God and as the second person of the Trinity, who died and rose again, replicating what Christians believe. The implication here is not that it can be stated as fact that Jesus died and rose again, but that this is what Christians believe. However, a critical approach might take Jesus' humanity as a starting point and try to understand the process by which belief in his divinity developed. Christian scholars themselves explore the degree to which the words of Jesus in the Gospels may reflect the convictions of the primitive Christian community, rather than what Jesus really said. Yet this rarely intrudes into a Religious Studies class on Christianity. The volume on Christianity in this series, however, examines the problem of canonicity and discusses the existence of later gospels and epistles as a case for a variegated Christian tradition in the first three centuries. Similarly, a faith sensitive explanation of Muhammad's career depicts him as the sinless prophet of God, who contributed nothing to the content of the Qur'an, replicating what Muslims believe. Again, the implication here is not that it can be stated as fact that Muhammad received the Qur'an from God but that Muslims believe that he did. However, an alternative view of Muhammad might regard him as someone who sincerely believed that God was speaking to him, but whose own ideas and perhaps those of some of his companions found expression, consciously or unconsciously, in Islam's scripture and teachings. Such an alternative view does not have to follow the pattern of past anti-Muslim polemic, in which Muhammad was a charlatan, an opportunist, insincere and self-serving. Kenneth Cragg, who has contributed much to helping Christians form a more sympathetic view of Islam, sees Muhammad as a sincere servant of God, but he does not think that the Qur'an contains nothing of Muhammad's own ideas. Cragg, though, may be regarded as a theologian rather than belonging properly to Religious Studies, which begs the question whether it is useful to maintain a distinction between these two fields. Suggesting how outsiders, who wish to remain committed members of a different faith, can approximate an insider-like view without compromising their own could be part of the agenda of Religious Studies. Currently, this role appears to be undertaken by practitioners of interfaith dialogue, such as Hans Küng (see Küng, 1986) and by theologians such as Cragg, rather than by Religious Studies specialists. In many instances, the distinction is blurred because of the different roles played by people themselves. Frank Whaling is a Religious Studies specialist but also an ordained Methodist minister. W. C. Smith was a Religious Studies specialist (although he preferred the term Comparative Religion) but was an ordained Presbyterian minister. Methodist minister, Kenneth Cracknell had contributed significantly to thinking on how to understand the relationships between religions, but it is difficult to say whether his academic credentials identify him as a theologian or as a Religious Studies specialist (see Cracknell, 1986; 2006). The same can probably be said of this writer. Cabezón discusses the acceptability of scholars today declaring their faith allegiances in relation to the 'us' and 'them' divide, pointing out that some scholars 'self-identify as belonging to multiple religious traditions' and so a simplistic 'us' and 'them' polarity is problematic; 'the Other is problematic when *we* claim to BE-THEM' (33). The author of the volume on Hinduism regards himself as a Hindu but continues to be a licensed priest of the Church of England, a fact that has attracted some criticism in the British press. How will Religious Studies deal with such complexities?[2]

Discussion of some alternative explanations and critical theories can be problematic, given that believers may find them offensive. Some scholars who have challenged the Muslim consensus on Islam's origins have received death threats, so replicating insider views is less risky. A teacher who wants to attract insider approval may find it expedient to ignore other views. The possibility that material from the Gnostic gospels can be identified in the Qur'an, for example, runs contrary to Muslim conviction, and is ignored by almost everyone except Christian polemicists. A Muslim in the classroom may be offended if the teacher alludes to this type of source and redaction critical approach to the Qur'an. Such an approach, if it is pursued, may take place elsewhere in the academy. What has been described as shattering the 'consensus of scholarly opinion on the origins of Islam' came from outside the corridors of any Department of Religion or Religious Studies (Neuwirth, 2006: 100). The Aryan invasion theory is increasingly unpopular among Hindus, who dismiss it as imperialist. This Euro-centric theory, it is said, denies that India's heritage is really Indian. Yet to ignore the relationship between Indian and European languages and the similarity of some ideas and myths could be to overlook important facts about a more inter-connected human story than is often supposed. On the one hand, the term 'Hinduism' is now accepted by many Hindus. On the other, its appropriateness can be challenged. Smith commented that 'the mass of religious phenomena we shelter under that umbrella is not an entity in any theoretical let alone practical sense' (1963: 64). As taught, Hinduism arguably owes more to the theosophist Annie Bessant, who may have been the first to design a curriculum based around the four aims in life, the four ages, the four stages of life and the four classes and their duties, than to any classical Indian text, even though all these can be found in the texts. The elevation of a great tradition over the myriad of smaller traditions needs to be critiqued. Western fascination with Hinduism's esoteric system, Tantra, has attracted criticism that this elevates what is actually quite obscure to a seemingly more central position. Since sex is involved, this revives a certain Orientalist preoccupation with the East as alluring and immoral, offering possibilities for pleasure denied by the West. Wendy Doniger O'Flaherty, a former President of the American Academy of Religion, has been criticized for over-stressing sensuality in her work on Hinduism (see Ramaswamy, 2007).

What has been described as Protestant Buddhism, too, developed as a result of the efforts of theosophist Henry Steele Olcott, among others. A type of 'philosopher's abstraction' (Gombrich, 1988: 50), it set out to present Buddha's teaching as a coherent, systematic system, beginning with the four noble truths followed by the noble eightfold path. These were taught by the Buddha, but he loved lists, and these are two among many. This is not to suggest that Buddhism is unsystematic, although use of the term 'systematic' here could be another example of transposing a European concept into non-European space. In fact, believing that people at different spiritual stages require different teachings, the Buddha sometimes gave different advice on the same issue. Teaching that may appear contradictory, as the 14th Dalai Lama put it, prevents 'dogmatism' (1996: 72). It could be argued, then, that the somewhat dogmatic way in which what the Buddha taught is presented in many Religious Studies classrooms, misrepresents what he actually taught. Kitagawa (1959) observed, and arguably not much has changed, that 'despite its avowed neutrality and objectivity', Religious Studies 'has been operating with Western categories' (27). More recently, Cabezón has said that Religious Studies is still dominated by Western terms, theories and paradigms. Theory parity, says Cabezón, is a long way off; 'for example, it is hard for us to even conceive of the day when a "Theories of religion" course might be taught with a substantial selection of readings from nonwestern sources' (31). How long are Western views of religion, and of what is to be included and excluded as religiously interesting, going to dominate? Cabezón identifies at least the start of a much needed paradigm shift in which non-Western theologies are getting some exposure (34). Cabezón also argues that some non-Buddhist scholars, despite the insider-ship bias of the discipline, 'still construct their identity in contradistinction to the Buddhist Other' which effectively emphasizes the distance between themselves and the 'object (Buddhism)' they choose to study (29 n22). The volume on Judaism discusses problems associated with the very definition of Judaism as a religion, and the relationship between Judaism and the Jewish people, often assumed to be identical. It asks whether such a significant thinker as Freud, who was secular, can be located within a Jewish religious framework. The same question could be asked of Marx.

Another issue, relevant to studying and teaching all religions on the curriculum, is how much should realistically be attempted. If a degree is offered in Islamic Studies, or Buddhist Studies, or Jewish Studies, this issue is less relevant. However, more often than not what gets taught is a survey course covering five or six religions. If a traditional course in Christian Studies covers scripture, history, philosophy of religion, theology and languages, the student usually has three or four years to master these. On a survey course, they have perhaps a day to master a religion's scripture, another day to study its historical development, another to gain an understanding of its rituals. It is widely recognized that in order to understand another world view, some grasp of language is necessary, given the difficulty of translating meaning across languages. Muslims, indeed, say that the Qur'an is untranslatable, that it is only God's word in Arabic. How much Hebrew, how much Arabic, how much Sanskrit, can students be expected to learn in a few days? If the answer is 'hardly any', are they really able to achieve anything that approximates insidership? It is often claimed that students learn more from attending a service of worship than they do from books. This writer has taken students to Mosques where quite hostile attempts to convert them to Islam left them with a less positive view of Islam than they had taken away from the classroom. Yet can any course on Islam neglect a mosque visit? This author has chosen to leave one out on the basis that no such course can cover everything anyway! Another issue, also relevant to studying all traditions covered on the curriculum, is how different interpretations of texts are to be dealt with. For example, the Qur'an can be read by militants as permitting aggression, and by others as prohibiting aggression and sanctioning only defence. Can both be right? Is it the business of so-called neutral Religious Studies scholars, who may well be located in a secular and possibly public (State) school, to say what is, or is not, a more authentic version of Judaism, Islam or Christianity? In some contexts, this could even raise issues of Church–State relations. How seriously should a Religious Studies specialist take the postmodern view that all texts have multiple meanings and no single reading can claim to be exclusively or uniquely true? This certainly challenges some religious voices, which claim infallibility, or at least to speak with special, privileged authority! Far from being fixed objects, or subjects of study, religions are often in flux. The Christian volume in this series, for example, shows how ethical thinking on such issues as war and peace, justice, economic distribution and human sexuality has changed over time and varies across Christian communities.

Reviving Critical Enquiry

If Religious Studies is to live up to its claim to be a social science, it cannot afford to ignore other approaches and critical issues, even if these are less-faith sensitive. Otherwise, it must resign itself to merely describing what believers themselves hold to be true. Only by placing alternative approaches alongside insider perspectives can Religious Studies claim to be treating religious beliefs and practices as subjects of serious and critical investigation. This is not to suggest that faith sensitivity should be abandoned. One reason why students study religions other than their own, or any religion for that matter, is to understand what believers really believe, often as opposed to how their beliefs are popularly or commonly portrayed. A Religious Studies student may be agnostic or an atheist, but he or she will still want to know what a Hindu or a Jew believes, not what some prejudiced outsider says about them. Stripping away misconceptions, overcoming bias and prejudice, presenting a religion from its believers' perspective, will remain an important goal of any Religious Studies programme. On the other hand, the privileging of insider-ship to the exclusion of other ways of seeing religion reduces Religious Studies to a descriptive exercise, and compromises any claim it makes to be a critical field of academic enquiry. Religious Studies will be enriched, not impoverished, by reclaiming its multidisciplinary credentials. This series examines how issues and content that is often ignored in teaching about religions can be dealt with in the classroom. The aim is, on the one hand, to avoid giving unnecessary offence, while on the other hand to avoid sacrificing critical scholarship at the altar of a faith-sensitivity that effectively silences and censures other voices. Since critical issues vary from religion to religion, authors have selected those that are appropriate to the religion discussed in their particular volume. The Smart–Whaling dimensional approach is used to help to give some coherency to how authors treat their subjects, but these are applied flexibly so that square pegs are not forced into round holes. Each author pursues their enquiry according to their expert view of what is important for the tradition concerned, and of what will help to make Religious Studies a healthier, more critical field. Each author had the freedom to treat their subject as they chose, although with reference to the aim of this series and to the Smart–Whaling schema. What is needed is a new relationship between religious studies and critical enquiry. A balance between faith-sensitivity and other approaches is possible, as this series proves. These texts, which aim to add critical edge to the study of the religions of the world, aim to be useful to those who learn and to those who teach, if indeed that distinction can properly be made. Emphasis on how to tackle critical issues rather than on the content of each dimension may not make them suitable to use as introductory texts for courses as these have traditionally been taught. They might be used to supplement a standard text. Primarily aids to study, they point students towards relevant material including films and novels, as well as scholarly sources. They will, however, be very appropriate as textbooks for innovative courses that adopt a more critical approach to the subject, one that does not shy away from problematical issues and their serious, disciplined exploration.

References

Cabezón, Josè Ignacio (2006), 'The Discipline and its Others: The Dialectic of Alterity in the Study of Religion', *Journal of the American Academy of Religion*, 74, 1, 21–38.

Capps, Walter H. (1995), *Religious Studies: The Making of a Discipline*, Minneapolis, MN: Fortress Press.

Cracknell, Kenneth (1986), *Towards a New Relationship: Christians and People of Other Faith*, London: Epworth.

Cracknell, Kenneth (2006), *In Good and Generous Faith: Christian Responses to Religious Pluralism*, Cleveland, OH: The Pilgrim Press.

Dalai Lama, 14th, and Robert Kierly ed. (1996), *The Good Heart: A Buddhist Perspective on the Teaching of Jesus*, Boston, MT: Wisdom Publications.

Geertz, Clifford (1988), *Works and Lives: The Anthropologist as Author*, Stanford, CA: Stanford University Press.

Gombrich, Richard (1988), *Therevada Buddhism*, London: Routledge.

Kitagawa, Joseph (1959), 'The history of religions in America' in M. Eliade and J. Kitagawa (eds) *The History of Religions: Essays in Methodology*, Chicago, IL: Chicago University Press, 1–30.

Küng, Hans (1986), *Christianity and the World Religions*, London: SCM.

Leeuw, G. van der (1954), 'Confession Scientique', *NUMEN*, 1, 8–15.

Müller, F. Max (1867), *Chips from a German Workshop*, London: Longmans & Co.

Müller, F. Max (1882), *Introduction to the Science of Religion*, London: Longmans & Co.

Neuwirth, Angelika (2006), 'Structural, linguistic and literary features' in Jane Dammen McAuliffe ed., *The Cambridge Companion to the Qur'an*, Cambridge: Cambridge University Press, 97–113.

Ramaswamy, Krishnan (2007), Antionio de Nicholas, and Aditi Banerjeei (eds), *Invading the Sacred: An Analysis of Hinduism Studies in America*, Delhi: Rupa & Co.

Said, Edward (1978), *Orientalism*, New York: Pantheon.

Sharpe, Eric J. (1983), *Understanding Religion*, London: Duckworth.

Sharpe, Eric J. (2006), *Comparative Religion: A History* (new edition), London, Duckworth.

Smart, Ninian (1968), *Secular Education and the Logic of Religion*, New York: Humanities Press.

Smart, Ninian (1983), *Worldviews*, New York: Macmillan.

Smart, Ninian (1998), *The World's Religions*, Cambridge: Cambridge University Press.

Smith, Huston (1958; 1991), *The World's Religions*, San Francisco, CA: HarperSanFrancisco.

Smith, Wilfred Cantwell (1950), *The Comparative Study of Religion: An Inaugural Lecture*, Montreal: McGill University.

Smith, Wilfred Cantwell (1959), 'Comparative Religion: Whither and Why?' in M. Eliade and J. Kitagawa (eds), *The History of Religions: Essays in Methodology*, Chicago, IL: Chicago University Press. 31–58. Available online at http://www.religion-online.org/showchapter.asp?title=580&C=761h.

Smith, Wilfred Cantwell (1963), *The Meaning and End of Religion: A New Approach to the Religious Traditions of Mankind*, New York: Macmillan.

Smith, Wilfred Cantwell (1981), *Towards a World Theology*, Philadelphia, PA: Westminster Press.

Whaling, Frank (1986), *Christian Theology and World Religions: A Global Approach*, London: Marshall, Morgan & Scott.

Acknowledgments

Many people have played important roles in the development of this book. Clinton Bennett invited me to contribute to the Critical Issues series and has provided encouragement and support, as have the patient staff of Continuum. I would like to thank my former colleagues in The Open University's Religious Studies department, and the Centre for the Study of Jewish-Christian Relations in Cambridge. I am grateful to members of the University of Cambridge, especially the trustees of the Bethune Baker fund, and members of the Faculty of Divinity, particularly Nicholas de Lange, my dissertation students, and the candidates for paper B14: The Life, Thought and Worship of Modern Judaism, with whom I was privileged to work first as a supervisor, and then as a lecturer between 1998 and 2009.

The friendship and intellectual engagement of James Aitken, Lucia Faltin, Jon Gifford, Graham Harvey, David Herbert, Naomi Hetherington, Hannah Holtschneider, Jerry Toner, George Wilkes, Isabel Wollaston, and my partner, Justin Meggitt, have in different ways stimulated my thinking about studying Judaism. Sasha Anisimova and Dan Avasilichioaie deserve mention for their willingness to endure the extra mile, or twenty, on the road in Romania in summer 2008. Without the National Health Service, specifically Luke Hughes-Davies and the Oncology department at Addenbrooke's Hospital, Cambridge, I would not have lived to complete this manuscript.

This book is in memory of Robert Joseph Isle (1928-2008) who told me never to assume anything.

* * *

All references to the Jewish Bible are drawn from *The Jewish Study Bible* (Philadelphia: The Jewish Publication Society, 1988). Since Adin Steinsaltz's English translation of the *Talmud* is as yet incomplete, I have used I. Epstein, ed., *The Babylonian Talmud*, 35 vols (London: Soncino Press, 1935-52). With the exception of a few names and words that are commonly used in English, transliterations of Hebrew generally follow the *Encyclopaedia Judaica* (Detroit: Macmillan Reference USA, ²2007) with modifications to avoid the use of diacritical marks. Terms are translated the first time they appear in the text (identifiable using the book's index).

Addendum to Acknowledgments

Melanie Wright completed all but one chapter of this book before cancer took her life. She was deeply committed to the project. Before her death, she asked Hannah Holtschneider if she would write the missing chapter and assist in seeing the book through to publication. Hannah agreed. Her own enthusiasm for the book and desire for it to honor Melanie's memory proved invaluable during the final stages. As series editor, I am profoundly grateful for her dedication and contribution toward finishing the book.

Clinton Bennett,
Series Editor.

1

Introduction

The Jews are a scattered people. They live in many different countries, and with one exception they are a numerically insignificant minority in all of them. They belong to many different ethnic and linguistic groupings, and many different cultural backgrounds. Even within a single country these differences divide the Jewish communities from one another. So what is it that binds them all together, and allows us to speak in general terms about 'the Jews'? One superficially attractive but actually misleading answer is that they are united by a common religion.[1]

Judaism is a religion, so we begin by asking what we mean when we define religion in general, and one religion in particular. In general, people treat religion as a set of beliefs about God, and such a philosophical definition sets forth what a religion believes. A definition of Judaism would, therefore, begin with the statement that Judaism believes that God is one, unique, and concerned for us and our actions, thus 'ethical monotheism'. But the philosophical definition leaves out much that religion accomplishes within the social order. Religion transcends belief, because it shapes behaviour.[2]

The *mezuzah* consists of a container of wood, metal, stone, ceramic or even paper containing a parchment with Deut. 6.4–9 and 11.13–21 lettered on the front and the word *Shaddai* (Almighty) on the back. Usually the container has a hole through which the word *Shaddai* can be seen. Otherwise the container should have the word *Shaddai* or the letter *shin* displayed on its front.[3]

How to begin the task of *studying Judaism*? Judaism, as the first of these quotations illustrates, is associated with a group of people, the Jewish people. So we might start by looking at demography – population size, distribution, structure, etc. – and then attempt to locate Judaism amidst the different aspects of that people's experience. Israel is home to the world's largest Jewish population, but only overtook the United States in that regard in 2006. The opening extract, taken from the 2010 edition of Nicholas de Lange's *Introduction to Judaism*, positions Israel as the 'one exception' and presents dispersed, minority status as normatively Jewish. Moreover, his text notes that Jews are a multicultural community, a consequence of historical and present day factors such as adoption, conversion, intermarriage and migration. This kind of starting-point is likely to produce an account of Jews' religious cultures – of Judaism – that emphasizes diversity, or even fracture, as the final sentence in the passage hints.

An alternative strategy is apparent in the second quotation. Initially, its author, Jacob Neusner, seemingly privileges the prioritization of belief in accounts of Judaism. But this approach is quickly dismissed. The targets of Neusner's critique are the unnamed 'people' who characterize Judaism as 'ethical monotheism': first used by Christian biblical scholars to describe the religion of the Hebrew prophets, this label became popular amongst late nineteenth- and early twentieth-century Jewish reformers who wished, in the wake of the Enlightenment,[4] to stress that Judaism was a religion of reason, whose object was to guide people towards right conduct as desired by the one God.

Despite their different emphases, de Lange's and Neusner's texts have some common elements. Both reference the collective or social aspects of Judaism; Neusner's words 'behaviour' and 'order' signal that the study of Judaism needs to embrace both particular actions, and the frameworks that shape and are shaped by them. Both also participate in the discourse of academia. What they say and how they say it reflects the fact that they write primarily for students or teachers in modern, western(ized) colleges and universities. They assume positions of neutrality or open-mindedness, and little or no prior knowledge of Judaism on the reader's part.

The final quotation, although also highly formal in its language, takes a different approach. It does not begin with general statements about the Jewish people, or about the definition of religion, but with a description of the *mezuzah*, the encased piece of parchment that many Jews fix to their home's outer door-post, and in some cases, to the post of every room in the house, save the bathroom. Michael Strassfield and Richard Siegel's aim is to reawaken American Jews' interest in religious ritual, food and art. *The Jewish Catalog* introduces a plethora of traditions and suggests how its readers might re-cast them in personalized, politicized terms. In this context the decision to begin, *in media res*, with the *mezuzah*, is understandable. The scriptural passages referred to in the quotation are the first two elements of the *Shema* ('hear!/listen!'), Judaism's most important prayer. Its opening phrase, 'Hear, O Israel! The Lord is our God, the Lord alone', is often regarded as the quintessential statement of Jewish faith, while subsequent verses remind Jews of the obligation to follow God's words or commandments (*mitzvot*) and to teach them to their children – in other words, to engage in the kind of activity that Strassfield and Siegel wish to promote. Examples of *mezuzah* cases and a scroll are shown in Fig. 1.1.

Together, these quotations, each one taken from the opening pages of an introductory book, suggest something of the diversity of ways in which the study of Judaism may be arranged. They also underscore the extent to which any account of Judaism (or of Buddhism, Christianity, Paganism, etc.) is just that – an account or construct, which only imperfectly reflects religion as its adherents experience and live it. Even writers who strive, as does each of those above, to refrain from imposing an essentialist, normative, or otherwise overly simplistic definition of Judaism at some point find themselves system- atizing their material in the effort to explain and inform. The task, then, is to resist the arbitrary, to offer an account of Judaism that is serious and critical, while acknowledging that 'every project...is, more or less explicitly, a working out of experience and value in the world, the search for a personal point of view and a contribution, however modest, to wider ethics and politics.'[5]

Studying religion, studying Judaism

The publication of *Studying Judaism* in the *Critical Issues* series is itself an intervention in ethics and politics. As Bennett's preface explains, the series seeks to renew Religious Studies by recovering its polymethodic character and thereby honing its critical edge. In writing this book, I attempt to balance clear, wide-ranging information for the reader who has little knowledge of Judaism with analysis and interpretation informed by a number of disci- plinary perspectives. In particular, I draw on approaches in cultural studies, whose impact on religious studies has noticeably grown over the past two decades.

Cultural studies examines the practices and objects of everyday life, and the uses and meanings that people attribute to them. It analyses the ways in which individual and shared meanings and identities are produced and circulated. In considering these things, it emphasizes occasionality – that is, the precise moment or context in which a phenomenon is manifest. Cultural studies is relevant to the study of religion since religion is partly, or entirely, depending on one's viewpoint, 'what humans do, the texts and other cultural products they produce, and the statements and assumptions they make'.[7]

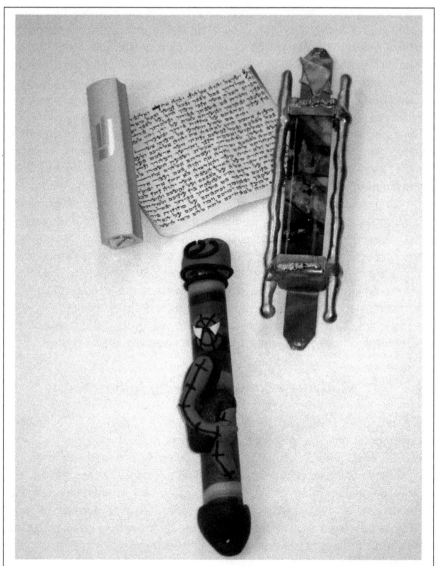

Figure 1.1: A Mezuzah Scroll and Cases, © K. Hannah Holtschneider

According to Jewish religious law, the *mezuzah klaf* (parchment) must be made from the skin of a *kosher*[6] animal. The texts must be written in Hebrew by a scribe (trained religious copyist) and regularly checked for errors or damage. In theory, the case is secondary in importance to the *klaf*, but nevertheless a myriad of designs is available today. These examples are made from aluminium; glass and copper; and a clay-like polymer. Each bears the Hebrew letter ש (*shin*), the first letter of *Shaddai*, a name given to God in the Torah (Hebrew Bible).

An illustration of what the questions and concerns of cultural studies might mean for the study of religion is provided by Nye, who is one of several scholars of religion to argue that what the Academy often conceptualizes as the discipline, or multi-disciplinary field, of 'religious studies' ought to be renamed, and thereby repositioned, as 'religion and culture'. To study Christianity, he suggests,

> one can of course study the Bible, high Christian art, and great thinking, but that does not tell us everything about the traditions of Christianity. For many centuries Christian people have been practising their religions in other ways, through producing less 'great' works of art, music, and literature, which could also be studied as forms of Christian culture.[8]

Two key aspects emerge here. First, the meeting of cultural studies and religious studies is associated with a democratizing definition of religion. It implies an interest in non-elite expressions ('less "great"', in Nye's words) as well as elite ones ('high Christian art and great thinking'). Second, it entails a broadening of the traditional activities of religious studies, to encompass the study not just of sacred texts, but also of other literary and art forms, and, as scholars of religion increasingly emphasize, of actions, objects and the body. As Cort writes of Jainism:

> Jainism, as with any religious tradition, is in part a vast historical enterprise of trying to find, realize, and express the values and meanings of human life. The study of texts alone is insufficient for an adequate understanding of that enterprise. To the extent that human life is by its very nature embodied, physical, and material, the study of religions therefore must involve itself with the study of the material expressions of religion.[9]

One might readily substitute 'Judaism' for 'Jainism' in this quotation.

It is important to stress, especially for readers whose academic home is a religion department, that my referencing of cultural studies does not necessarily imply a wish to dismantle existing institutional structures. Rather, it is intended to underscore the necessity of deploying multiple tools in the effort to do justice to a religious tradition as a diverse, living phenomenon. For non-specialist readers, and particularly for students who major in other subjects but have opted for a single module or course in Judaism, this book's engagement with other disciplines and fields including, but not only, cultural studies, should, I hope, facilitate the drawing of links between the familiar and the new. If I have been successful then the result is a work that makes few assumptions about its readers, but credits them with interested, interesting minds.

Reflecting these goals, the book is 'critical' in two respects. First, it *explicitly* relates Judaism to a set of conceptual and analytical frameworks and second, it addresses matters commonly perceived by 'insider'/adherent and 'outsider'/non-adherent commentators alike to be of critical import, like gender, geo-politics and the growing commodification and 'museumization' of Jewish religious cultures. Influenced by cultural studies, the texts, practices and objects discussed have been selected on the basis of a wish to explore the realities of the everyday and ordinary as much as artefacts deemed to be of aesthetic or intellectual excellence.

Consequently, *Studying Judaism* is structured slightly differently than other introductory books. The chapters are as follows:

What is Judaism? discusses the problems associated with the definition of Judaism as a 'religion'. It considers the relationship between Judaism and the Jewish people, and offers an outline sketch of the major contemporary Jewish religious movements.

Authority looks at the importance of Jewish legal tradition and custom, describing key types of Jewish religious literature and the individuals and institutions associated with their authoritative interpretation. It also considers other types of authority within Judaism, such as the charismatic authority of the *rebbe* in Hasidism.

Worship, Festivals and Mysticism focuses on prayer, the Sabbath and festivals, and considers 'time' in Judaism. The chapter also looks at Jewish mystical tradition, *kabbalah*.

Beliefs examines the role of belief in different movements and historical and geographical contexts. It discusses ideas concerning God, revelation, theodicy, post mortem existence and messianism, and asks whether the work of ostensibly secular thinkers can be located within a Jewish religious framework.

Gender discusses constructions of masculinity and femininity in Judaism, looking at such topics as rites of passage, the family and modesty. It considers the impact of feminism on the practice and study of Judaism.

Politics addresses ideas about holiness, particularly in relation to the land of Israel. It touches on the Israel–Palestine conflict and on ideas about Jewish theocracy; it also considers Zionism and other political ideologies, assessing how far they are derived from Judaism.

Culture attends to Judaism's material dimension, including synagogue architecture and artefacts associated with personal piety. It also looks at food and at 'culture' as it is more popularly conceived, including film.

Memory considers the place given to individual and collective memory within Judaism. It discusses mourning. It also focuses on pilgrimage and memorialization of the *Shoah* or Holocaust.

Jews and Others discusses attitudes within Judaism to inner-Jewish diversity and to other religions. It considers topics such as assimilation and challenges models of religions as discrete, boundaried entities.

Finally, **Studying Judaism: the critical issues: the future** touches on a range of issues vital for the future of Judaism and Jewish life (and for their study), including demography and sexual politics. It discusses how existing forms of Judaism are being challenged by, and are colonizing, new media and technologies.

Religious diversity is one of this book's key themes. I do not want to suggest that the story of Judaism is overwhelmingly one of fragmentation, but as is true of other religions in the *Critical Issues* series, there exist within Judaism a number of different movements. I take account of well-known positions such as Orthodoxy, Conservative and Reform, and of some lesser-known ones like Karaism, Reconstructionism and Renewal. In utilizing these labels, I also remain mindful of the fact that '"Judaism" is an abstract noun. Jews, not Judaism, believe and do things'.[10]

As suggested previously, cultural and religious pluralism are intertwined in Jewish experience, so while it is impossible for me to produce a study free from Eurocentricism, I attempt to keep this in check. Most English language textbooks focus on the religious life of Ashkenazi Jewry. Ashkenazim constitute approximately 80% of the world Jewish population and trace their genealogical and/or spiritual origins to Germany and northern France, where Jews first settled in Roman times. Various factors including violent persecution and poverty prompted Ashkenazi migration eastwards during the medieval period, and then westwards again from the seventeenth century onwards. Today, the Jewish communities of the United States, Britain, continental Europe, Canada and other Commonwealth countries are predominantly Ashkenazi. However, the Middle East was the Jews' principal home for over two-thirds of documented history. Well into the medieval period, most lived under Muslim or Eastern (Orthodox) Christian rule, and it was only after the expulsion of Jews from Spain in 1492 that Western and Central Europe (contexts dominated religiously by Catholic and, later, Protestant forms of Christianity) became major sites of Jewish population, scholarship and religious authority. Accordingly, *Studying Judaism* includes Sefardi Judaism, which spread from the Iberian Peninsula (Spain and Portugal – also home to Jews from Roman times) to the Balkans, north Africa, Amsterdam in Holland, and parts of the Middle East and the Americas. Sefardi Judaism has its own linguistic and liturgical traditions, and its historical significance is such that, in much academic and popular discourse, all non-Ashkenazim are sometimes referred to as 'Sefardim'. It also attends to numerous Jewish communities whose cultures have not been influenced significantly by either German or Iberian Judaism (or, at least, were not until recently). In Israel these are sometimes called *edot ha-mizrah*, 'communities of the Orient/East'. Mizrahi Jews trace their roots to the biblical exile of Jews from the land of Israel to Babylonia (modern Iraq), and to other ancient migrations of Jews to Africa, especially Morocco and Ethiopia, and parts of the Middle East (such as Yemen) and Asia. It must be stressed, however, that like Ashkenazi and Sefardi Judaism, Mizrahi religion exhibits considerable inner diversity, to the extent that in Israel some people reject the broad umbrella terms and prefer to identify themselves with reference to their, or their parents', country of origin (as an 'Iraqi Jew', for example).

The relative absence of Sefardim and Mizrahim, from introductions to Judaism reflects their doubly 'Other' status (as Jews *and* non-Europeans) in Orientalist discourses – discourses that Ashkenazi Jews are sometimes accused of perpetuating, especially in Israel. Yet knowledge of Sefardi and Mizrahi experience is not only necessary for a full picture of the situation there, where these groups form about 50% of the Jewish population. It is also vital for an understanding of 'western' Judaism. The first Jews in America were Sefardim; Sefardim were also quick to settle in England following official readmission in the 1650s, and in 1840 formed the overwhelming majority of members of the country's first Reform congregation, the West London Synagogue of British Jews.

I write this book not just as a European, but also as someone who is not an adherent of Judaism but who has engaged with, studied, and taught Judaism in a variety of settings over many years – a datum pertinent to this series' *raison d'être*. Undoubtedly, Judaism suffered badly at the hands of outsider scholars in decades past. This was previously the case in many Christian theological settings, where a general interest in demonstrating how 'other religions' fell short of Christian ideals was bolstered in Judaism's case by a long history of Christian anti-Judaism. Post-1945 shifts in many churches' theologies of Jews and Judaism have led to a weakening or dismantling of negative presuppositions, but the fact remains that, at least initially, most people – Christian or otherwise – tend to view the religion of others in ways conditioned by their own experiences of religion. In a different vein, in 1930s Europe, Nazi scholars deliberately attempted to discredit the work of Jewish ones, while claiming objectivity and neutrality in their own writings on Judaism, which were created in support of a racist ideology.[11] Given such history, it is particularly vital that outsiders attend carefully to adherents' experiences and articulations of Judaism. But as Clinton Bennett indicates, the need for what he terms 'faith sensitivity' does not dictate that one must therefore be Jewish, or an adherent of Judaism, in order to study Judaism. Nor does 'insidership' or personal commitment to Judaism guarantee accurate, unbiased scholarship on a writer's part.

Take, for example, the work of Heinrich Graetz (1817–1891), one of the first modern Jewish historians. His popular, influential eleven-volume *History of the Jews* (published between 1856 and 1870) was distinguished from works produced by his non-Jewish contemporaries by its author's sympathetic tone and his attempt to give a comprehensive history from the biblical period to the modern era. But Graetz's personal situation within the newly enfranchised Jewish community of Breslau (now Wrocław, Poland) clearly affected his work. In pre-modern Europe, Jews generally lived as a tolerated minority, subject to legal and social restrictions and discrimination. In many countries, they did not have a clearly defined status as individuals in law. The government recognized and dealt with the *kehilla* or community – that is, with Jews as a collective (see Chapter 7). This changed when, in a process beginning in post-revolutionary France, and continuing across Europe throughout the nineteenth and early twentieth centuries, Jews were emancipated or granted full political rights as citizens of the countries in which they lived. But the path to equality was not a single, straightforward one. As late as 1840, the Breslau community joined other Prussian Jews in lobbying the Emperor Frederick William III to demand that they be given the rights granted to them on paper by an 1812 edict of emancipation. Reflecting such struggles for political and social recognition, Graetz presented Judaism as 'high culture'. He focussed on the experiences of religious and other elites, dismissing popular religious movements and impulses like *kabbalah*.

Graetz's history is representative of the *Wissenschaft des Judentums* ('Science of Judaism') school, an intellectual movement which strove to establish the systematic study of Judaism on a secure critical footing. By translating and editing religious manuscripts, and tracing the evolution of ideas and rituals over time, its practitioners sought to counter not only bias in Christian scholarship, but also what they regarded as the failings of the *yeshivah*, a traditional institution of Jewish religious learning. In *yeshivot*, young men were – and are today – not occupied with the study of 'Judaism' as it is described in this and other textbooks, but in the detailed study of the Torah (the first five books of the Hebrew Bible), the Talmud (the foundational text of rabbinic Judaism) and related commentaries, and major works of ethics and *halakhah* (practical religious law). The *yeshivah* curriculum does not aim to stimulate theological questioning, conversation about the reality and nature of God or God's relationship with the world. Nor does it examine how contextual factors impact Jews' religious beliefs and practices in different places and periods. The goal of the *yeshivah* is study for its own sake, and for the purposes of inculcating a desire for and ability to keep the *mitzvot*, the observance of which is traditionally understood to be the primary means by which Jews can acknowledge and enter into a divinely mandated, unique relationship with God.

Although admittedly somewhat polarized cases, the different approaches of the *Wissenschaft* movement and the *yeshivah* to studying Judaism illustrate the extent to which a wholly insider perspective on a religious tradition may generate a very partial account. An individual's or group's own interpretation of a tradition may be naturalized or enthroned as *the* tradition itself, although of course one cannot assume a distorting partiality on the part of adherents, just as one cannot assume reliability on an outsider's part. In *Studying Judaism*, I have attempted not to privilege any one kind of insider, any single voice within Judaism, but to be more broadly insider-sensitive, to develop and model the kind of empathetic approach advocated by Ninian Smart and his successors.

In dialogue with Smart: empathy, and the dimensional approach

The cultivation of empathy is widely recognized as vital for the non-adherent and for the adherent who seeks to approach religion in a manner both critical and faith sensitive. If religious studies are to be critical, empathy cannot be regarded simply as a synonym for sympathy, sharing or agreeing with another's emotions. Instead, it functions as an analytical tool. Deployed in this way it entails not approval but understanding or comprehension. Empathy involves the difficult task of deploying one's imagination and one's intellectual faculties, in order to understand why someone thinks, feels and acts in the way they do. Its maturation takes time – perhaps it is always a work in progress. The goal is to be able to defend an other's religious position as if it was one's own, which is *not* the same thing as endorsing or sharing that position. At its best, empathy allows for a transcending of the simple binaries of the 'insider'/'outsider' debate in the study of religions. As a blend of aspects or qualities that we might (stereo)type as 'insiderly' or 'outsiderly', its aim is akin to that envisaged by Clifford Geertz who, in his comments on anthropological method, speaks of the desire to:

> produce an interpretation of the way a people lives which is neither imprisoned within their mental horizons, an ethnography of witchcraft as written by a witch, nor systematically deaf to the distinctive tonalities of their existence, an ethnography of witchcraft as written by a geometer.[12]

This kind of balance is, of course, advocated more readily than it is achieved. And whereas Geertz's emphasis in describing the fruits of research is on the production of 'an interpretation of the way a people lives', it is also important to be aware of other outcomes. No scholar is completely unchanged by her or his experience of study. For example, the work of Robert Friedmann (1891–1970) who was raised as a liberal Jew, on Anabaptist history and theology was an important factor behind his becoming a Mennonite Christian.[13] Conversely, research activity may influence the lives of its subjects and their descendants. When Yirmiyahu Yovel visited Belmonte, Portugal in 1985, he found that the Marrano Jews' historically secretive, oral tradition had been displaced by a written liturgy. The community's new prayer book was a compilation of prayers and chants published 60 years earlier by an ethnographer. 'Inadvertently, the scholar had … provided their religion with its canonical book.'[14]

The intellectual aspect of empathy implies the deployment of some kind of analytical apparatus. As Bennett's preface describes, for Ninian Smart, who played a pivotal role in securing the place of religious studies as a higher education subject in Britain and the United States, attending to religion's interrelating 'dimensions' or aspects served as an important tool for the structuring of empathy – that is, for the cultivation of balanced description and interpretation of his subject matter.[15] Smart identified the dimensions of religion as follows: practical and ritual, experiential and emotional, narrative or mythic, doctrinal and philosophical, ethical and legal, social and institutional, and material.[16]

The chapters in this book are not straightforwardly congruent with Smart's seven dimensions of religion. Smart's model is important in offering a way of thinking about our subject matter that avoids the pitfalls of the type of reductionist definition and one-sidedness decried by Neusner in the text at the start of this chapter. It calls attention to its character as a *system* of beliefs and practices, an aspect of *human experience*. But the model's use-value lies in the extent to which it has been, and is, able to function as a stimulus to balanced inquiry – it cannot, and was not intended to by Smart, serve as a determining formula or template.

In Smart's own work, the identified dimensions or noteworthy features of religion are contingent and capable of revision; they are not *givens*. His initial list, for example, numbered six dimensions. The addition of a seventh 'material' dimension, embracing architecture, art, books, dress and other objects, in the late 1980s reflects the extent to which religious studies, like many other academic disciplines and fields, had by then taken something of a cultural turn. Towards the end of his life, Smart incorporated a chapter on 'The Political *Effects* of Religion' (my italics) into a book organized around the dimensional approach.[17] A decade or so later, mapping this book's chapters on to the dimensions as Smart stated them in the mid-1990s proves increasingly difficult and even undesirable, particularly as one shifts away from the format of the now 'traditional' religious studies textbook and towards an agenda structured by both insiderly and outsiderly perceptions of critical issues in Judaism and the study of Judaism.

The form and content of Judaism – or rather, of the beliefs and practices of those Jews (and some non-Jews) who identify with Judaism – is constantly evolving. In the early twenty-first century there is, on the one hand, a growing plurality of Jews in North America, Europe and Israel, who, both within and apart from traditional religious institutions, articulate spiritualities typical of those emerging in the contexts of postmodernism or late capitalism (an emphasis on personal autonomy; a blurring or overturning of defined boundaries and structures in favour of porous boundaries and *ad hoc* smaller scale, more fluid alliances) with insights and practices related to a sense of connection with the Judaism of the pre-modern era and/or the 'East', especially the *Kabbalah*. On the other hand, a wide variation in the birth-rates of members of the different modern Jewish religious movements, and the new prominence and increased activity of *ba'al teshuva* movements ('returnees' to Judaism) mean that the number of *Haredi* ('ultra-Orthodox' or very carefully observant) Jews is increasing markedly, both in absolute numbers and as a proportion of the Jewish population as a whole.[18] For their part, those who would study Judaism also bring ever-changing agendas and assumptions to the project. While continuing to eschew the confessionalism associated with theological study, the religious studies of today are characterized by a much greater degree of reflexivity – by an acknowledgement and scrutiny of the scholar's commitments, and an admission of the extent to which they may be risked in the course of inquiry – than is found in Smart's writing. Inevitably, then, and like each of its companions in the *Critical Issues* series, *Studying Judaism* seeks dialogue with the 'classical tradition' of religious studies, as exemplified by Smart, but is not beholden to it.

How to use this book

The chapters of this book may be read in any order. For example, you could read Chapters 3–11, and then consider your own responses to the question, 'What is Judaism?' before turning to Chapter 2. Reflecting the cultural studies influenced approach, the photographs are intended to be regarded as equal or complementary to the written text, and not as supplementary to it. Text boxes may be found in each chapter and serve a variety of functions. Some deliver key facts, or present a case study or example that would otherwise interrupt the flow of the main text. Others include practical guidance on making field visits, for example.

Exercises are optional, and are intended to provide you with additional opportunities to reflect critically on the task of studying Judaism, and religion in general. The text that follows them will often suggest the contours of possible answers, but is not intended to be comprehensive.

The word *studying* in this book's title is intended to indicate an ongoing activity.

EXERCISE

Edward Said suggests that 'a beginning' is not a point of absolute origin, but 'already a project underway'.[19] When we begin to study something, we make a set of choices about where and how to start, which draw together intentions, methods, needs and theories. This chapter has described a variety of ways of beginning the study of Judaism. What are they, and do you find some of them more or less plausible or attractive than others? How far does your answer to the previous question reflect your previous or current interests and experience of the study and/or of religion?

2

What is Judaism?

EXERCISE

Take a couple of minutes to write your own response to the question, 'what is Judaism?' After reading this chapter, reflect on your answer, and consider whether or not you wish to revise it.

If you have attempted the exercise, you may have discovered that, while initially the answer to the question 'what is Judaism?' seemed obvious, you soon encountered difficulties. If you answered, 'Judaism is the Jews' religion', for example, you may have found yourself needing to qualify or gloss the word 'religion', just as Neusner does in the extract reproduced in Chapter 1. In fact, the use of the term 'Judaism' has a controversial history. For many pious Jews, the suggestion that 'Judaism is a religion,' and therefore one example of a wider category of phenomena collectively describable as 'religions,' would be bizarre, even insulting. From their standpoint, Judaism is unique. Unlike other things conventionally labelled as 'religions' Judaism is the embodiment of divinely revealed teaching, mediated to the Jewish people, 'the people Israel', through a covenant agreement with one God. Even for those who do not share this traditional religious perspective, other evidence seemingly undermines any easy definition of Judaism as a religion. For centuries, the very terms 'Judaism' and 'religion' were strikingly absent from 'Judaism's' core texts, and even from the Hebrew language – the main language of the Bible, of prayer and of the *halakhah* (practical religious law) – itself. Reflecting this history, some books avoid the term 'Judaism' in their titles, while acknowledging that alternative labels like 'the Jewish religion' and 'religion of the Jewish people' are not problem-free.[1]

Etymology is not always a helpful starting point in attempting to determine current meanings of a term, but in the case of the English word 'Judaism' an investigation of origins yields some helpful clues.² 'Judaism' derives from a Greek term *Ioudaïsmos*, which emerged in the context of ancient Jewish encounters with Greek-speaking or Hellenistic culture. Specifically, it first appears in 2 Macc., a second century BCE text that describes a successful revolt of Jews, led by Judas Maccabeus, against the Seleucid emperor Antiochus Epiphanes, who ruled a vast empire extending from parts of modern day Greece and Turkey eastwards to Afghanistan:

> The story of Judas Maccabeus and his brothers...who strove zealously on behalf of Judaism ... (2 Macc. 2.19–21).

> ... he had been accused of Judaism, and for Judaism he had with all zeal risked body and life (2 Macc. 14.38).

Ioudaïsmos or Judaism refers here to the condition or state of being a Jew – to an identity distinct from, and in the case of the Maccabees, in conflict with, the Seleucids' imposition of a greater degree of Hellenization (of Greek language and culture) on the ancient Near East.³

It was apparently only in the medieval period, in the context of discussion and polemic with Christianity and Islam, that Jews began to consider 'Judaism' a 'religion' – something distinct from but also bearing some similarities to the traditions of belief and practice articulated by their neighbours. The Hebrew terms they used were *Yahadut* ('Judaism', still in the sense of referring to the entirety of Jewish culture) and *dat*. *Dat* originally referred to 'law' in the sense of particular prescriptions for behaviour, but over time it came to denote 'religion' in a more abstract sense. From the perspective of figures like the philosopher and legal scholar Moses Maimonides (1135–1204) Judaism possessed many of the same characteristics as other religions (*datot*) but it was *dat ha-emet*, 'the true law' or religion revealed by God. Today, *dati* is the modern Hebrew word for a religious Israeli Jew.⁴

As noted in Chapter 1, emancipation and the Enlightenment affected Jewish self-understanding. Whereas previously, a raft of internally and externally imposed social and political restrictions had inhibited contact with non-Jews, increased levels of interaction and integration into wider European society in the eighteenth and nineteenth centuries meant that older markers of Jewish identity were challenged and eroded. New articulations of Jewishness were needed. Emphasizing rationality and empiricism, Enlightenment thinkers tended to approach religions as systems of beliefs. Through the rigorous study of these systems, especially of authoritative textual sources and archaeological sites, one could, they believed, eventually strip away superficial differences and discern a religion's 'essence', paving the way for its comparison with other religions. Influenced by these concepts and a need to demonstrate that Judaism was compatible with legal and social equality and acceptance, many European and European-influenced Jews (most notably in North America) began articulating their identities in similar terms. In his 'Judaism' entry for the 1904 *Jewish Encyclopedia* Kaufmann Kohler (1843–1926) noted that it was very hard to give 'a clear and concise definition of Judaism', but went on to describe 'The *Essence* of Judaism', claiming that '*Judaism is above all the religion of pure monotheism*' and later, that 'the *most characteristic and essential distinction of Judaism from every other system of belief and thought* consists in its ethical monotheism' (my italics).[5] In this respect,

> Judaism is but one example of a more general phenomenon, in which the new scholars of 'religion' defined religious communities in their own terms, only to see the members of those very communities come to see themselves in that way.[6]

These illustrations of the origins and shifting meanings of Jewish uses of the term 'Judaism' reveal several things fundamental to the task of studying Judaism. It is clear, for example, that Jewish self-understanding and expression are not static, but dynamic. Moreover, they have developed in response to encounters with non-Jewish cultures, both popular and academic: identity is *negotiated*. More generally, as Satlow notes, while these *first-order* (insiderly) accounts of Judaism are interesting pointers to the self-perception of individuals and groups, they do not provide an adequate basis for a *second-order*, 'academic and value-neutral' definition.[7] This is because, like many of the traditional definitions of Judaism offered in the study of religions, they tend to be essentialist and normative – they are created by communities for the purpose of defining themselves in relation to other groups.

In reality, Jewish religious life, now and in the past, is so diverse that the adoption of any such definition risks investing what is simply the self-definition of one particular subgroup with normative status. The previous chapter, for example, introduced the *Shema*, noting that its opening phrase ('Hear, O Israel! The Lord is our God, the Lord alone') is often regarded as a declaration of fundamental Jewish beliefs. In emphasizing 'ethical monotheism', Kohler placed belief in one God at the heart of his insider account of Judaism. But it would be misleading to define Judaism purely in such terms. Kabbalistic theology envisages an unknowable Godhead (*Ein Sof*) manifest in the cosmos through the emanation of a series of powers known as *sefirot*. Reconstructionist Judaism is non-theistic, preferring to speak of God as a 'process' rather than as a 'person'. Indeed, while the *Shema* is today widely interpreted as a declaration of monotheism, from a historical perspective this is an anachronistic reading of a biblical verse that does not make a statement about the number of deities, but about the nature of the relationship between the people Israel and its God. It would, then, be hard to establish any particular belief as normatively Jewish (see Chapter 5). Equally, it would be hard to make such claims for any rituals, not least because for many contemporary Jews ritual practice is not a matter of consistency and absolutes, but of occasional distinctions and performances that are subject to ongoing renegotiation. Today's meaningful and popular innovation may, tomorrow, be seen as an unforgivable deviation from tradition, or as a trite cliché. Or as Eleanor Nesbitt puts it, 'real life individuals often do not fit neatly like the smallest of a set of *madrioshka* dolls inside successively larger dolls (the membership groups and tradition or "faith community")'; it is more accurate to think in terms of 'endlessly diverse patterns of innovation, compromise and conservativeness within a single lifespan as well as from generation to generation within a family.'[8]

While neither abandoning the use of the term 'Judaism', nor ignoring what Jews themselves say about Judaism, studying Judaism requires, then, that we find new ways of conceptualizing and defining our subject matter.

'Judaism' as a family term

One alternative way of conceptualizing 'Judaism' (or, indeed, 'religion') is to see it as a 'family term'[9] or 'family of traditions'.[10] This idea is adapted from Ludwig Wittgenstein's notion of family resemblance:

> Think of a family ... whose members are related by blood. One brother may share his father's temperament, and his hair and eye colour. Another brother may be more like his mother in terms of hair colour but not eye colour. A third brother might have his mother's smile and his grandfather's eyes. There is probably no single distinctive feature that runs through the whole family of genetically related individuals, but nevertheless when we meet members of this family we can instantly recognise them as being related to one another. What allows us to do this is a pattern of overlapping and criss-crossing resemblances.[11]

Jews are sometimes referred to (by themselves and by others) as a 'race', but this quotation should not be thought to imply that all Jews are biologically related. Conversion or proselytization into Judaism has always been possible and is traditionally understood as entailing adoption of a religious tradition and peoplehood, as in Ruth 1.16 ('"your people shall be my people, and your God my God"'). Nevertheless, employing Wittgenstein's metaphor, and thinking in terms of a range of phenomena, which each possess their own personalities and characteristics, while also sharing some broad characteristics or family resemblances, allows us to begin to answer the question, 'What is Judaism?' in a way that takes account of commonalities and differences, and allows for the possibility of 'new arrivals'.

Locating the commonalities or resemblances that unite diverse communities into 'Judaism' is much harder than identifying the differences, as Michael Satlow, who has provided the fullest such treatment of the topic to date, admits. He lists three resemblances, 'Israel' (self-identification as part of the people Israel, that is, as Jews); 'textual tradition' (dialogue or engagement with the Hebrew Bible and the rabbinic texts), and 'religious practice' (practices that are passed on through the generations, sometimes in accordance with, and sometimes in spite of, the texts that attempt to ritualize and interpret them). While different communities articulate these aspects differently to create 'unique and distinctive systems of meaning', each one is 'tied to the next through a family resemblance'.[12] A sketch of the origins and key features of some modern Jewish religious movements amplifies and illustrates the point.

Judaism as a world religion

In books, courses, and conversation, Judaism is often presented as a 'world religion'. How appropriate and meaningful is this label?

Judaism might be deemed a world religion by virtue of its *global distribution*. Since at least the sixth century BCE, there has been a Jewish *diaspora* (communities of Jews 'dispersed' in places other than the land of Israel). But missionary activity, colonialism, trade and globalization mean that many religions have an international presence today, rendering the designation 'world religion' somewhat superfluous. Any claim made on the *number* of adherents is also weak: the *CIA World Fact Book 2007* estimates that the number of Jews worldwide (not all of whom practice Judaism) approximates 0.23% of the total population.

Stronger claims for Judaism's status may be made with reference to its *historical significance*. Judaism is widely regarded as the 'parent' tradition of a 'family' of monotheistic religions (together with Christianity and Islam) described by interfaith activists as 'Abrahamic religions'. But this idea is also problematic: it may fail to value Judaism on its own terms, and many Jewish religious beliefs, practices and institutions developed after the emergence of, and were influenced by, Christianity and Islam.

In educational settings, the teaching of world religions is sometimes presented as an instrument for the advancement of toleration and inclusivity. But approached simplistically, it ends up reifying religions, presenting them as a series of discrete, somewhat static phenomena. Ultimately, the concept of a 'world religion', like the Enlightenment idea of 'religion', struggles to deal with variations within traditions, blurred boundaries between 'religions' and the often idiosyncratic, shifting nature of individual's and group's actual commitments.

Reform Judaism

In 1810, Jews in Seesen, northern Germany, dedicated a new synagogue. The services held there began and concluded at set times and included organ music, and sermons and prayers in German as well as Hebrew. As is traditional, men and women sat separately, but no *mehitzah* (partition) divided them. The building was the Seesen Temple, its name reflecting a view that the synagogue and its services had truly replaced – and did not mourn the loss or anticipate the restoration of – the ancient Jerusalem Temple and the sacrifices offered there until its destruction by Roman troops in 70 CE.

In this way, after decades of theoretical debate, 'reform' of Judaism began. Influenced by the Enlightenment, and keen to demonstrate to their neighbours that being Jewish did not imply attachment to an alien, impoverished culture, early European and American reformers developed new forms of public, corporate Jewish expression that they hoped would reflect and cement their new status as citizens of the lands in which they lived.

A series of rabbinical assemblies in 1840s Germany attempted to formulate shared statements on the principles and goals underpinning these changes. In the same decade, German Jewish emigration to the United States gave additional momentum to reform there. (Members of the Beth Elohim congregation in Charleston, South Carolina requested prayers in English as early as 1824; in 1841, the synagogue became the first in America to use instrumental music.) By the late nineteenth century, American Reform Judaism was ascendant. Its changing approach to liturgy and belief, often more radical than that of its European counterparts, is articulated in a series of 'platforms' or programmatic statements on religious issues.

In the first platform, adopted at Pittsburgh in 1885, Enlightenment thinking in the form of rationalism, and a confidence in the reality and goodness of human progress are prominent. Judaism is affirmed as 'the highest conception of the God-idea as taught in our holy Scriptures and developed and spiritualized by the Jewish teachers in accordance with the moral and philosophical progress of their respective ages'. The yoking of development with spiritualization is linked to a rejection of many rituals relating to diet, dress and purity, since these 'obstruct … modern spiritual elevation'. Above all, the Pittsburgh participants, reflecting Kohler's leadership, stress that as citizens of a modern nation-state, Jews are 'no longer a nation but a religious community'.

A hundred and twenty-five years later, today's Reform Jews have revived some previously rejected liturgical practices and other rituals, influenced

Figure 2.1: Menu for the 'Trefa Banquet' held at Highland House, Cincinnati, in July 1883. Courtesy of The Jacob Rader Marcus Center of the American Jewish Archives, Cincinnati, Ohio

This menu describes the dishes served at a banquet celebrating the graduation of the first rabbinical students from Hebrew Union College, Cincinnati. Notoriously, it violates many of the Jewish dietary laws (see Chapter 8) by serving seafood (clams, crabs, shrimp and lobster), non-*kosher* wines and meat ('grenouiles' or frogs' legs) and mixing meat with dairy products. At the time, many American Jews avoided pork but otherwise ate a diet similar to that of their non-Jewish neighbours. The Pittsburgh Platform formalized a more radical approach by explicitly rejecting 'all such Mosaic and rabbinical laws as regulate diet'. The Platform, and the so-called 'Trefa Banquet', divided Reform Jews from the more traditionally minded amongst the non-Orthodox, contributing to the development of Conservative Judaism as a separate religious movement.[13]

in part by an influx of more traditional Eastern European immigrants in the late nineteenth and early twentieth centuries and the revival of the Hebrew language in the State of Israel. The 1999 statement issued by Reform's Central Conference of American Rabbis says:

> We are committed to the ongoing study of the whole of [the] *mitzvot* and to the fulfilment of those that address us as individuals and as a community. Some of these ... have long been observed by Reform Jews; others ... demand renewed attention as the result of the unique context of our own times.

Reform Judaism claims to be the largest Jewish movement in America, with 900 synagogues and 1.5 million adherents.[14] In Israel, there are around 30 congregations,[15] while in Britain, a more cautious Movement for Reform Judaism (formally organized in 1942) exists alongside, and cooperates with, Liberal Judaism (founded in 1902), which is closer in belief and practice to its American Reform counterpart. The emphasis on personal autonomy in spiritual matters, and a characterization of Judaism as a religion offering justice and equality to all, regardless of affiliation, gender or sexuality, appeals to many. Openness to the families of Jews who are married to non-Jews also means that Reform congregations offer a home to those excluded by more traditional groupings.

Orthodox Judaism

The term 'Orthodoxy' percolated from Christian into Jewish cultures in the nineteenth century, when reformers used it in denouncing their traditionalist opponents. Strictly speaking, Orthodoxy does not then pre-date other modern Judaisms. Nor is it monolithic. Some traditionalists (whose contemporary heirs describe themselves as 'Torah-true') responded to emancipation by attempting to resist any accommodation to non-Jewish society, while others took a different stance. In *Nineteen Letters About Judaism*, Samson Raphael Hirsch (1808–1888) argued for a revitalization of traditional Judaism.[16] His position, sometimes termed 'modern Orthodoxy', championed the notion of *Torah im derekh eretz* ('Torah with the way of the world'). From this perspective, modernity presents Jews with opportunities, including religious ones, and these can be embraced so long as the primacy of Torah or Jewish teaching is not subverted. For example, Hirsch believed that it was permissible to hold weddings in the synagogue, rather than out of doors as is traditional; to deliver sermons in the vernacular; and for rabbis to wear clerical-style robes. But he differed crucially from reformers in rejecting the kind of modern textual criticism developed by the *Wissenschaft* school (described in Chapter 1) and emphasizing the importance of belief in *Torah min ha-Shamayim* ('Torah from Heaven'), the divine origin and nature of the Torah.

For much of the nineteenth and twentieth centuries it seemed that, as other movements gathered momentum, Orthodoxy was in decline: by 1900, fewer than one fifth of German Jews identified as Orthodox. More recently, numbers are rising. In America, in the late twentieth century, figures like Joseph B. Soloveitchik (1903–1992) reiterated modern Orthodox principles, describing ways in which *ish ha-Halakhah* ('halakhic man') could achieve a balance between the scientific, rational drive and a sense of religious pathos or yearning for God.[17] As head of Yeshiva University's rabbinical school in New York for over 40 years, he popularized the phrase that became the university's motto, *Torah u-Madda* ('Torah with secular knowledge'), and in articulating the idea that study, observance and repentance were responses to a divinely assigned task of self-creation, Soloveitchik gave Orthodox observance an air of creativity that it was commonly felt to lack.

The most significant growth within Jewish Orthodoxy, both in terms of population and influence is, however, amongst the *Haredim* or 'ultra-Orthodox', a family of religious groups including the *Hasidim* (mystically-oriented revivalists), the *Mitnaggedim* ('opponents', originally of the Hasidim) who try to preserve intact a way of life associated with the *yeshivot* of pre-modern Europe, and various Sefardi and Mizrahi groups who are committed to patterns of religious and cultural life in pre-modern Africa and Asia. While the differences between Haredi groups are significant, they have formed alliances in order to fight what they perceive to be Judaism's 'decline': indeed, the emergence of the shared label 'Haredim' illustrates the extent to which older disputes between groups have been superseded by their perceived need to cooperate in the wake of challenges posed by modernity.[18] Haredim typically emphasize the importance of careful observance of the commandments, and to a greater or lesser extent espouse a degree of separation from non-Haredi society. These traditionalist positions are not, however, untouched by modernity. Whereas Enlightenment thinkers and policy-makers often hoped to speed the assimilation of Jews to non-Jewish norms, Western societies today tolerate – even 'celebrate' – difference, implicitly validating Haredi Judaism as a 'lifestyle choice'. Postmodernism's denial of the existence of the normative, and of the overarching metanarrative, is seemingly radically opposed to the spirit that animates this kind of Jewish religious expression, but has helped shape contexts that facilitate it. At the same time, even the most segregationist groups use modern technologies and methods to further their interests, as is explored in Chapters 3 and 11.

Figure 2.2: Hasidic men at the grave of Elimelech of Lizhensk (Leżajsk) in south-east Poland. © Anna Ordyczyñska, 2007

The iron cage or *ohel* (literally, 'tent') around the grave of this Hasidic *rebbe* or *tzaddik* dates from 1776; the building housing it is a late twentieth-century construction. The original gravestone can be seen on the wall at the left-hand side of the picture, with lit candles in front of it. There is a side room for female pilgrims.

The clothing worn by these men, and their pilgrimage to the grave of Elimelech of Lizhensk (1717–1768) reflect the status accorded to eighteenth-century Jewish religious culture within contemporary Hasidism, and more specifically, belief in the doctrine of the *tzaddik*, which Elimelech himself developed (see Chapter 3). These pilgrims are visiting Poland on the *yahrzeit* (anniversary) of their *rebbe*'s death, to pray and place *kvitlach*, written requests for guidance or aid, on his grave. According to Hasidic theology, the *rebbe* is a powerful conduit between God and his followers, and the *yahrzeit* is an auspicious time to seek such help since it is a moment at which the *rebbe*'s soul is simultaneously drawn close to both God and his gravesite.

Conservative Judaism

The rabbinical assemblies of the 1840s did as much to highlight the differences between early reformers as they did to formulate shared principles and practices. Radical reformers like Samuel Holdheim (1806–1860) advocated an end to circumcision (see Chapter 6) and the moving of the Sabbath to Sunday, while Abraham Geiger (1810–1874) wanted some modifications to prayers but was also willing to make some compromises with traditionalists for the sake of communal unity. A third wing was represented by Zacharias Frankel (1801–1875) who left the 1845 Frankfurt assembly when a majority of the participants voted that it was not obligatory to pray in the Hebrew language. While accepting that there was no legal requirement to do so, he argued that the language had acquired a sacred status by virtue of its historic use by previous generations of Jews. This position, which Frankel called Positive Historical Judaism, formed the basis of today's Conservative Judaism. In contrast to Orthodox teachings, Conservatives typically hold that the critical study of texts and rituals possesses religious value, and argue that Jewish religious expression has changed over time; they also reject the anti-traditionalism of radical reformers:

> There are those who would think that we have but two alternatives, to reject or to accept the law, but in either case to treat it as a dead letter. Both of these alternatives are repugnant to the whole tradition of Judaism … Jewish law must be preserved but … it is subject to interpretation by those who have mastered it, and … the interpretation placed upon it by duly authorized masters *in every generation* must be accepted with as much reverence as those which were given in previous generations.[19]

Early conservatives did not regard themselves as initiating a discrete movement; their institutions and identity only really began to crystallize in North America as a response to the radicalism of the 1885 Pittsburgh Platform. Numerically speaking, Conservative Judaism remains primarily a North American movement. However, many of its founders were European. Solomon Schechter, who elaborated the concept of *klal Yisrael* ('Catholic Israel') – communal consensus as a source of authority in Judaism – was born in Romania and worked in England before settling in New York, where he led the movement's Jewish Theological Seminary and oversaw the creation of its communal umbrella organization, the United Synagogue of America (now United Synagogue of Conservative Judaism). Today, there are small communities of Conservative Jews, often known as *Masorti* ('traditional') worldwide, particularly in Israel, Europe and Latin America.

Conservative Jews have been reluctant to issue platform statements, reflecting their emphasis on community consensus (Reform platforms are primarily drafted and debated by rabbis). Widely varying attitudes and practices can be found amongst Jews affiliated to Conservative synagogues today. For some, the label 'Conservative' implies a position close to that of Modern Orthodoxy. For others, the emphasis on tradition as its own authority entails a de-emphasis on God and permits quite radical, atheistic approaches to religion. This flexibility, the prominence of figures like Abraham Joshua Heschel (who combined a scholarly career with work as a civil rights and interfaith activist) and the development of institutions that support organized religious activity in suburban settings – particularly the 'Synagogue Center' which houses not only worship but a range of activities and facilities designed to foster a sense of community amongst Jews who live and work at some distance from one another – contributed to Conservativism's attractiveness in mid-twentieth-century America.

More recently, numbers have declined: many Jews who were raised as Conservative affiliate with Reform or are religiously unaffiliated in later life.[20] At the same time, the emphasis on the authority of communal consensus implicitly validates groups who wish to break away and develop their own interpretations of tradition. Founded by Mordecai Menahem Kaplan (1881–1983), Reconstructionism formally became a movement in 1968, when the Reconstructionist Rabbinical College was opened under the leadership of Ira Eisenstein (1906–2001). Drawing on sociological discourse, Reconstructionists often refer to the *mitzvot* or commandments as 'folkways' – norms or conventions of behaviour shared by a particular group of people; 'God' is understood not in supernatural terms, but as a power or process that makes for the enrichment of human life. More recently, the 1990 decision to train women as Conservative rabbis led another group of members to suspend their affiliations and found a Union for Traditional Judaism, which now has its own seminary and congregations in the United States.

Critical reflections on 'religious movements'

Although their adherents differ in terms of belief, practice and organization, these modern religious movements discussed in this chapter possess a set of family resemblances that enable us to identify them as 'Judaism'. Those who identify as Reform, Orthodox and Conservative Jews all engage with the Hebrew Bible and rabbinic religious texts (see Chapter 3 of this book), although they do not share a common view of their origins and authority. They all perform rituals which have been, or are believed to have been, passed down through generations, although they differ in their understandings of the function of particular practices and of practice generally, and of the accept-ability of ritual innovation. They also all identify themselves, and for the most part accept each other, as Jews.[21]

Finally, it is important to note that accounts of different Jewish religious movements are just that – accounts – that may be far removed from what actual Jews believe and do, and the motivations for those ideas and actions.

Miri Freud-Kandel and Hannah Holtschneider are amongst several writers who recognize that studies of modern Jewish movements often tend to emphasize the contributions of elites, and to privilege theory over practice.[22] Outside Germany, many European communities, especially those in Austria, Britain and Hungary, modernized the style of their worship in the nineteenth century, but were not ideologically motivated. To an even greater extent, writing on modern Judaism also largely overlooks Mizrahi experiences. The Enlightenment was a largely European(ized) phenomenon, and Jews in Africa and the Middle East generally encountered modernity and its challenges at a later date than their Ashkenazi and European Sefardi counterparts did, often as a result of the expansion of Western influence. For example, many were first exposed to critical study of Jewish history and religion, to secular subjects, and western dress and languages at schools established by the Alliance Israélite Universelle, an organization founded in Paris in 1860 with the aim of emancipating and enlightening – and 'Europeanizing' – eastern Jews. For the most part, there has been no 'Mizrahi Reconstructionism' or 'Mizrahi Orthodoxy', for example, although recently some such groups have emerged in Israel. *Shas*, a political party that seeks to promote Judaism's role in the modern state and advocates Sefardi rights, was founded in 1984 with the help of Ashkenazi Haredim. Its name is an abbreviation of 'Sefardi Torah Guardians', with Sefardi being understood in the earlier, all-embracing sense described in Chapter 1. Its spiritual leader is Iraqi-born Ovadiah Yosef, a former Sefardi Chief Rabbi of Israel.

Ultimately, many insiders' and outsiders' identifications of discrete religious movements are, like the 'world religion' concept, an extension of the Enlightenment construction of religion. As such they share in its weaknesses. 'Orthodoxy', 'Reform' and other such labels can be used in critical scholarship, however, provided that their limitations are recognized. Like 'Judaism' they, too, are family terms. The attitudes and behaviours of those who identify with a particular movement may have some similarities but also exhibit significant diversity, and the boundaries between movements, while sometimes clear cut (traditional Orthodox authorities do not, for example, accept the validity of Reform, Conservative and Reconstructionist Judaism, although they do regard most of their adherents as Jews)[23] are often fuzzy or permeable. For example, research in Florida has documented the phenomenon of '*shul*-shopping': many newcomers to a district visit a different *shul* (synagogue) each week, basing their eventual membership decision on such factors as the congregation's friendliness, the rabbi's personal qualities and financial costs.[24] In other words, a host of pragmatic factors may influence behaviour and affiliation.

Other religious trends cannot readily be regarded as the property of one movement rather than another. The popularity of the *Jewish Catalog* (mentioned in Chapter 1) stimulated a growth in Jewish Renewal. Renewal is an approach to Judaism that is particularly associated with the institution of the *havurah* or fellowship, a small group of people who support each other in worship, study and celebration. The *havurah* movement emphasizes ritual and liturgical creativity, and social and political inclusivity and engagement. In some instances *havurot* have become distinct congregations in their own right, but in many respects Renewal is transdenominational, with participants remaining affiliated to their Conservative, Reform, Reconstructionist and Orthodox synagogues.

3

Authority

From the perspective of many – even most – of its adherents, the ultimate authority in Judaism, as reflected in the words of the *Shema*, is divine. God's rule and the Torah, the sacred teachings revealed by God to Moses at Mount Sinai, stand behind and authenticate all other forms of authority or legitimate power.

In a religious studies context, the task is not to judge the claim that God exists and spoke to the Jewish people through Moses. Instead, this chapter offers a critical study of the *concept* of divinely revealed teaching and the human structures – physical (Smart's social-institutional dimension) and metaphysical (doctrinal, and narrative-mythological dimensions) – associated with its acceptance and practical implementation. It introduces some of the texts traditionally regarded as authoritative in Judaism, and the offices or roles attached to their interpretation, before discussing the figure of the *tzaddik* in Hasidic Judaism, and the impact of new technologies on the operation of authority.

Torah

So far in this book, the word *Torah* has been applied to Jewish religious teaching as a whole (Chapter 2) and to the first five books of the Hebrew Bible (Chapter 1). It can also be used to refer to the entire Hebrew Bible, and to a teaching or law on a particular matter. (For example, the Torah of the Nazirite in Num. 6.21 or the Torah of the leper in Lev. 14.2 – the word is often translated into English as 'obligation' or 'ritual'.) If the discussion in this chapter as a whole relates to Torah in the first sense, this section and the next two focus on Torah as more narrowly defined.

The Hebrew Bible is a composite work of 24 books that were produced by a number of different groups and individuals over a period of several centuries. Since the medieval period, it has often been referred to by the name *Tanakh*, an acronym formed from the initial letters of its three main sections. Very broadly speaking, this three-fold division of the *Tanakh* into Law (Torah – five books traditionally attributed to Moses, whom they depict leading the Hebrew people, known in later texts as Israelites and Jews, out of slavery in Egypt and towards a Promised Land), Prophets (*Neviim* – divided into 'former prophets' and 'latter prophets') and Writings (*Ketuvim* – a loose collection of historical and poetic writings) provides a rough guide both to the relative dates at which critical scholarship suggests these collections were regarded as canonical scripture, and to the degree of religious authority later generations of Jews have believed them to possess.

The books of the Hebrew Bible or Tanakh

Torah
Genesis; Exodus; Leviticus; Numbers; Deuteronomy

Nevi'im – prophets
Joshua; Judges; (1 and 2) Samuel; (1 and 2) Kings; Isaiah; Jeremiah; Ezekiel; Hosea*; Joel; Amos; Obadiah; Jonah; Micah; Nahum; Habakkuk; Zephaniah; Haggai; Zechariah; Malachi

* The books Hosea-Malachi are often grouped together as 'The Twelve Prophets'.

Ketuvim – writings
Psalms; Proverbs; Job; The Song of Songs**; Ruth**; Lamentations**; Ecclesiastes**; Esther**; Daniel; Ezra; Nehemiah; (1 and 2) Chronicles

** These books, known collectively as the *Megillot* (scrolls), are read aloud in the synagogue at particular festivals (see Chapter 4). There is in addition a Sefardi practice of reading Job on the eve of *Tish'ah b-Av*, which commemorates the Temple's destruction.

Modern historical-critical scholarship identifies a number of sources, dating from circa 1000 BCE to the time of the Maccabees (160s BCE), behind the biblical text. Between 500 and 1000 CE textual scholars or *Masoretes* worked to produce a reliable and readable *Tanakh*. However, for many centuries religious Jews have believed that the five books of the Torah were revealed to Moses and the people Israel at Sinai, and have regarded them as the primary, most authoritative source of practical religious law or *halakhah*:

> Moses summoned the elders of the people and put before them all that
> the LORD had commanded him. All the people answered as one, saying,
> 'All that the LORD has spoken we will do!' And Moses brought back the
> people's words to the LORD (Exod. 19.7–8).

The ability of human beings to exercise 'consent' in the face of a divine lawgiver
has been long debated, but until the Enlightenment, the vast majority of Jews
was united in the belief that this revelation, and the communal acceptance
of the Torah, marked the beginning of a special agreement or covenant (*berit*)
between God and the Jewish people. By obeying God's revealed laws, this
people, who were once enslaved in Egypt, could be 'a kingdom of priests
and a holy nation' (Exod. 19.6). Although belief in a supernatural deity, in
the divine origins and authority of the Torah, and in the selection or chosenness of the Jewish people is not universal, most modern forms of Judaism
continue in some way to define themselves in relation to these concepts,
as the overviews in Chapter 2 illustrate. Indeed, for contemporary Orthodox
groups belief in Torah *'min ha-Shamayim'* ('from heaven') or *'mi Sinai'* ('from
Sinai') has come to function as a point of doctrine (see Chapter 5).

   The Torah is, then, pivotal to the Jewish legal tradition (*halakhah*) and to
Jewish religious tradition as a whole. From this perspective, observing the
many biblical *mitzvot* or commandments, traditionally numbered as 613,
is not an onerous burden, but the means to and expression of a unique
relationship with God.

   Later authorities in Judaism have typically sought to legitimate their
teachings by somehow linking them to Sinai. However, despite the foundational authority accorded to scripture in much Jewish legal discourse, in
practical terms, later texts are often the more direct, immediate sources of
guidance and instruction.

Kingship and priesthood

The biblical account of the terms of the covenant between God and Israel is
modelled on ancient Near Eastern royal covenants, in which a people, or a
weaker king, accepted the authority of a more powerful figure.[1] In biblical and
later religious traditions, the concept of divine kingship is associated with a
mistrust of similar types of human political authority:

> Then the men of Israel said to Gideon, 'Rule over us – you, your son, and
> your grandson as well; for you have saved us from the Midianites.' But
> Gideon replied, 'I will not rule over you myself, nor shall my son rule over
> you; the LORD alone shall rule over you' (Judg. 8.22).

Here, Gideon, presented in the text as a humble – even cowardly – man divinely appointed to save Israel from Midianite oppression (6.11–24) espouses the doctrine of God's rule and rejects hereditary kingship. Later passages in the book of Judges link the absence of a monarch, human or divine, to illegitimate worship (17.5–6) and opportunistic violence (21.20–25). The eventual institution of a monarchy is described in 1 Sam. 8 as a reluctantly granted divine concession stemming from a pragmatic recognition of the people's rejection of God's kingship and their desire to become like other nations. The creation of the monarchy therefore seemingly opens up a somewhat secularized political realm, at least partially separate from the religious one. As Walzer, Lorberbaum and Zohar (2000) note in their extensive study of Jewish political traditions, conflicts around kingship persist throughout the Bible. In contrast to modern political debate, the tension is not between 'monarchy' and 'democracy' (or the more anarchic arrangements described in Judges) but is instead presented as a conflict between Godlessness ('secularism' in modern terminology) and Godliness ('theocracy').[2] When kings follow Gideon's humble, God-fearing model, their rule is legitimate and acceptable. But the hubris of rulers who deviate from this ideal is linked to the political conquest of and exile from the lands of Israel and Judah, and the destruction of the First Jerusalem Temple in the eighth and sixth centuries BCE.

In contrast to its account of kingship, the Bible describes an institution through which it is claimed God's rule is not rivalled but actualized on earth – the priesthood. Priestly status and authority formally rests on two bases. It is hereditary, carried in the male line by the descendents of Moses' elder brother Aaron. It is also attached to a particular role. The primary function of the priest (*kohen*) is to carry out sacrifices in the Temple, and this service in God's earthly home (Ezek. 44.15–16) is regarded as placing him in a unique position within the religious economy of ancient Israel – that of a mediator between God and the people. Other roles ascribed to priests, all formally derived from the Sinai revelation, include the pronouncement of God's blessing (Num. 6.22–27), sounding trumpets at festivals and in wartime (Num. 10.1–10), making legal judgements and instructing people:

> They shall declare to My people what is sacred and what is profane, and inform them what is clean and what is unclean. In lawsuits, too, it is they who shall act as judges; they shall decide them in accordance with My rules. They shall preserve My teachings and My laws regarding all My fixed occasions; and they shall maintain the sanctity of My Sabbaths (Ezek. 44.23–24; see also Lev. 10.11).

Following the rebuilding of the Jerusalem Temple (circa 520 BCE) the priestly class effectively ruled Judea, subject to the authority of a succession of occupying regimes. This was true even during brief periods of political independence. When the Hasmoneans, descendents of the Maccabees (see Chapter 2) took the royal title, they retained the priestly office on which their legitimacy depended.[3]

Ultimately, the Temple and its associated structures, including priestly ones, were largely destroyed in 70 CE during a failed Jewish revolt against Rome. The *Sanhedrin*, the supreme Jewish court that sat in Israel during the Roman and Byzantine (early Christian) periods, persisted into the fifth century CE, but was no longer housed in the Temple and increasingly became an assembly of rabbis. Priestly identity persists in Orthodox Judaism today where it confers a few privileges (being called first to read the Torah, and delivering the priestly blessing in the synagogue; being invited to say grace after meals) and restrictions (being prevented from marrying a divorcee or convert; avoiding contact with dead bodies). Amongst Reform Jews the concept of priesthood is widely rejected as anachronistic. American Conservative Jewish leaders have tried to balance a *halakhic* orientation with modern concerns by issuing a regulation that temporarily suspends the restrictions attached to priestly status on the grounds that the facilitation of marriages between Jews should take priority in an age of high rates of intermarriage and assimilation.

The Talmud and the rise of rabbinic authority

For Jews who believe them to be authoritative, the practical application of the biblical commandments repeatedly needs to be clarified, especially, but not only, in the light of new events and contexts. This results in an ever-changing body of religious law. Although the notion of a perfect, eternal Torah has long served as a powerful symbol of Israel's relationship with God, this process began in ancient times. For example, Leviticus 27 describes rules for the tithing of agricultural produce and livestock, a system by which priests and other religious functionaries were compensated: 'All tithes from the land, whether seed from the ground or fruit from the tree, are the LORD's; they are holy to the LORD' (27.30). In the book of Numbers, this was qualified or corrected[4] to explain that Levites, who assisted the priests and were barred from land ownership, should receive some of these tithes and in turn, donate one-tenth of what they received to the priests:

> The LORD spoke to Moses, saying: Speak to the Levites and say to them: When you receive from the Israelites their tithes, which I have assigned to you as your share, you shall set aside from them one-tenth of the tithe as a gift to the LORD (Num.18.25-26).

The activities of exegesis and interpretation, and the importance attached to texts and their study, accelerated following the destruction of the Temple and with it the system of sacrificial worship administered by the priests ceased. During the next few centuries the *Tanakh* was canonized, and the 'Oral Torah', a body of discursive material that had grown up around the Biblical text or 'Written Torah', was extended and codified. These developments reflected and contributed to the rise of a new form of authority, rabbinic authority. Initially, the rabbis were a small, scattered body of carefully observant religious teachers and their followers, whose influence on ordinary people was limited. By the sixth century, their religious authority was so pervasive that the label 'rabbinic Judaism' is often used as a catchall description of Jewish religious cultures from the early centuries CE to the beginning of the modern era. Various factors contributed to the rise of rabbinic authority, including the increasing concentration of rabbis in urban centres, and with it the formalization of religious schools and synagogues; the policies of the Sassanian and Roman empires, who regarded the rabbis as community leaders; and the growth of rabbinic literature.

The archetypal rabbinic text is the Talmud or. strictly speaking, the Babylonian Talmud, which was compiled circa 500 CE. (A lesser, in terms of length and authority, but still important Jerusalem Talmud was compiled circa 400 CE.) Implicitly and explicitly, the Talmud answers the question of how the covenant between the Jewish people and its God is to survive by suggesting that in the absence of the Temple cult all Jews are both required and able to live priest-like lives of divine service. Prayer, observance of the *mitzvot*, and study of the dual Torah – that is, adherence to rabbinic Judaism itself – are sufficient to ensure a right relationship with God: 'If two sit together and words of the Law [are spoken] between them, the Divine Presence rests between them' (*m.Avot* 3.2).

Within rabbinic circles, an individual rabbi (the word is derived from *rav*, meaning 'great [man or teacher]') established his authority by their knowledge of religious texts and the rules through which they could be interpreted. As Walzer, Lorberbaum and Zohar note, early rabbinic writers demonstrate both 'understandable insecurity' and 'extraordinary self-confidence' in the legitimacy of their claims.[5] Two quotations illustrate the point:

> Moses received the Law from Sinai and committed it to Joshua, and Joshua to the elders, and the elders to the Prophets; and the Prophets committed it to the men of the Great Synagogue. They said three things: Be deliberate in judgement, raise up many disciples, and make a fence around the Law (*m.Avot* 1.1).

This passage, compiled around 200 CE, links the work of the 'men of the Great Synagogue' – the Second Temple period scholars who are the idealized founders of rabbinic Judaism – to the moment of divine revelation at Sinai. Their task, and by extension that of the rabbis, is presented as one of conservation not revolution. In building 'a fence around the Law' – that is, by clarifying and extending the body of practical law or *halakhah* – they ensure that God's will for and covenant with Israel will not be accidentally infringed. Interestingly, priests are absent from the succession of individuals and office-holders listed.

Another text, compiled circa 500 CE, makes a bold, but different claim. It appears in the context of a discussion about an oven.

> Rabbi Eliezer said: 'If the *halakhah* agrees with me, let this carob tree prove it!' Thereupon the carob-tree was torn a hundred cubits out of its place ... . 'No proof can be brought from a carob tree,' they retorted. Again he said to them: 'If the *halakhah* agrees with me, let the stream of water prove it!' Whereupon the stream of water flowed backwards. 'No proof can be brought from a stream of water,' they rejoined. Again he urged: 'If the *halakhah* agrees with me let the walls of the schoolhouse prove it.' Whereupon the walls inclined to fall. But Rabbi Joshua rebuked them, saying: 'When scholars are engaged in a *halakhic* dispute, what have ye to interfere?' Hence they did not fall, in honour of Rabbi Joshua, nor did they resume the upright, in honour of Rabbi Eliezer; and they are still standing thus inclined. Again he said to them: 'If the *halakhah* agrees with me, let it be proved from Heaven!' Whereupon a heavenly voice cried out: 'Why do ye dispute with Rabbi Eliezer, seeing that in all matters the *halakhah* agrees with him!' But Rabbi Joshua arose and exclaimed: 'It is not in Heaven.'... . Rabbi Nathan met Elijah and asked him: What did the Holy One, Blessed be He, do in that hour? – He laughed and replied, saying, 'My sons have defeated me, my sons have defeated me' (*Baba Metzia* 59b).

The writers of this tale accept the reality of the miraculous. Nathan meets Elijah, the biblical prophet (1 and 2 Kings) whom, it was believed, returned to earth to teach and discuss with the rabbis. Similarly, there is no denial that the tree has moved, or of the other remarkable events. But the story's ending stresses that rabbinic decision-making is independent from the supernatural, even when this is authenticated by the natural senses of sight and hearing. Whereas Moses received instruction from God and then passed this to the people, the rabbis' approach suggests that a now apparently withdrawn or removed God ('the Holy One, Blessed be He') whose own laughter licences the rabbinic declaration that 'it is not in Heaven', has entrusted them with the responsibility for the law's interpretation.

Like the Bible, the final form of the Talmud reflects centuries of editorial activity. At its heart is a vast number of discrete rabbinic sayings, which have been assembled into longer, thematic units. Often, views attributed to scholars who lived in different times and places are presented as if they were debating an issue face-to-face, a strategy that may reflect the earlier, oral transmission of tradition and/or the rabbinic ideology of continuity discussed earlier. In the early third and fifth centuries CE respectively, two large compilations of these traditions – the Hebrew *Mishnah* (from which the quotation about the 'men of the Great Synagogue' is taken) and lengthier *Gemara*, in which the story about the rabbis' argument appears, which is mainly written in Aramaic, were created. These are both divided into six sections or orders, named by later scholars as: *Zeraim* ('seeds' or agricultural laws); *Moed* ('appointed time', i.e. Sabbath and festival laws); *Nashim* ('women' or 'laws of marriage and divorce'); *Nezikin* ('damages', i.e. torts and jurisprudence); *Kodashim* ('holy things', laws relating to Temple sacrifice) and *Torohot* ('purity', dealing with laws of ritual purity) and appear side-by-side in editions of the Talmud.

As both this complex literary history and the quotations given earlier illustrate, it would be simplistic to describe the Talmud straightforwardly as a 'law code'. However, much of the Talmud's contents are legal and it is in the study and application of such material that pre-modern rabbinic authority is formally located.

A final passage illustrates the relationship between *Mishnah*, *Gemara*, Bible and the strategy of building 'a fence around the Law':

Mishnah: If [a Jew] has a house adjoining an idolatrous shrine and it collapsed, he is forbidden to rebuild it. How should he act? He withdraws a distance of four cubits into his own ground and there builds. [If the wall] belonged both to him and the shrine, it is judged as being half and half'... .

Gemara: [But by acting as directed in the *Mishnah*], he enlarges the space for the shrine! Rabbi Hanina of Sura said: He should use [the four cubits] for constructing a privy! – He should make a privy for use at night. But behold a Master has said: Who is modest? He who relieves himself at the same place where he relieves himself by day! And although we explain that [in that statement] the phrase 'in the same place' is to be understood as 'in the same manner', still it is necessary to safeguard modesty! – He should, then, make [a privy] for children; or let him fence in the space with thorns or shrubs (*Avodah Zarah* 47a-47b).

The springboard for this debate is a biblical commandment against idolatry in Deut. 7.26. By *Mishnaic* times this law was deemed to require not only that Jews refrain from worshipping alien deities, but also that they avoid deriving benefit from, or from offering support to, idolatrous worship. If the Jew in the hypothetical case rebuilds the shared wall he will infringe the law by helping to reconstruct a pagan temple. So the *Mishnah* says that he must rebuild the wall 'four cubits into his own ground'. The *Gemara* identifies a problem with this answer: it inadvertently benefits the shrine, since room is created for its expansion. Another solution is then explored; the land could be used for a night 'privy' or toilet, i.e. one without walls. An objection to this solution is raised – it conflicts with other laws concerning modesty. Finally, a new answer is offered. The land may be used as a privy for children, who are not subject to the same rules as adults concerning modesty, or it can be made unusable by planting it with thorns or other shrubs. Either of these solutions enables the Jew to avoid infringing the law.

Medieval rejection of rabbinic authority

Not all religious Jews regard rabbinic tradition as authoritative. The Karaites, a religious community originating in eighth-century Iraq, argue that an individual's careful reading of scripture is sufficient in order to understand God's will. This Karaite critique of rabbinic literature was composed in Jerusalem around 930 CE:

We believe firmly that the Written Law
Was in truth given to Israel by the right hand of the Almighty
According to the testimony of the whole congregation of the Lily [Israel],
Who are scattered in every land.
All of them, believers as well as unbelievers,
Divided as they are by language and tongue,
All Israel, from the east to the westernmost ends of the world,
Testify to the sanctity of the written Law, all of them, little and great.
...
I have looked again into the six divisions of the Mishnah,
And behold, they represent the words of modern men.
There are no majestic signs and miracles in them,
And they lack the formula 'And the Lord spoke unto Moses and unto Aaron.'
I therefore put them aside, and I said, There is no true Law in them.
... And I saw that they are very contradictory in content,
Thus one Mishnaic scholar declares a thing to be forbidden to the people
Israel, while that one declares it to be permitted.[6]

For the passage's author, Salmon ben Jeroham, divine miracles underpin scriptural authority, whereas rabbinic texts are illegitimate, human innovations. Note how, although Karaites generally place a greater emphasis on individualism than did rabbinites, communal consensus also plays a role in establishing scripture's legitimacy.

In Salmon's day ten percent of Jews were Karaites; many medieval rabbinic texts were shaped by the conflict with Karaism. Today, there are 20–25,000 Karaites in Israel, with smaller communities in America and Europe (especially Lithuania, Poland and Turkey).

Rabbinic authority extended and challenged: codes and responsa

The medieval period witnessed the development of two literary genres associated with the institutionalizing of rabbinic authority, responsa (in Hebrew, *she-elot u-teshuvot*, 'questions and answers') and codes. Codes – structured accounts of rules and regulations, usually with an emphasis on issues relating to everyday life – began to develop in the eighth century, particularly in Spain and North Africa, which were then emerging as major sites of Talmudic study. They take one of two main forms. Books of *halakhot* give brief discussions of and conclusions on the *halakhah* currently in force, while books of *pesakim*, which became more prominent from the early twelfth century onwards, give decisions only. Although their authors often ostensibly sought to stimulate more advanced legal studies, codes became increasingly popular, their status more elevated, and their aims more ambitious as the medieval period progressed. The codes of Isaac Alfasi (1013–1103), Moses ben Maimon ('Maimonides'; 1135–1204) and above all Joseph Karo (1488–1575) established, or sought to impose, normative observance amongst large sections of the Jewish world.

Karo was born in Spain, but lived in Greece, Turkey and Israel after the expulsions of Jews from the Iberian peninsula in the 1490s. His *Shulhan Arukh* ('prepared table', first printed in 1565) is a book of *posekim*, intended as a guide to daily ritual, personal status (marriages, divorces) and civil laws. It quickly gained authority amongst Sefardim – partly because its appearance coincided with the new technology of printing – and, following Moses Isserles' (died 1572) addition of notes (known as the *mappah* or 'tablecloth') detailing distinctive Ashkenazi customs and regulations, secured broader acceptance. Today the *Shulhan Arukh* remains a widely studied and influential code. In the twentieth century, Ovadiah Yosef championed the view that Israeli Jews should set aside their differing *halakhic* traditions in order to adopt a single Sefardi culture based on Karo's work.[7]

Complementing the conservative impulses at play in codification, responsa were, and remain, the means to innovation in the *halakhah*. Responsa, answers to questions submitted by a rabbi to a specialist *posek* ('decider'), emerged in Babylonia, where Muslim legal scholars were developing *shari'a* through similar legal devices known as *fatwas*. Responsa tend to follow a common format. The question is set out and the *posek* replies by discussing relevant legal sources, highlighting analogies and precedents, and then offering an opinion on the issue. A *posek*'s authority rests in his knowledge of religious texts and his skill in reasoning. Crucially, it also depends on communal recognition, which may be linked to a range of factors including the *posek*'s moral stature, his performance in teaching or leadership roles, and the degree of fit between his answers to specific questions and publicly accepted values.[8] Some *posekim* attain significant international reputations, their responsa serving as precedents consulted by others, although there is no concept of strictly *binding* precedent in the *halakhah*. Questions from prominent contemporaries, and the passage of legislation in some rabbinic courts requiring *halakhic* problems to be decided in accordance with the decisions in his law code, the *Mishneh Torah* ('second Torah'), evidence Maimonides' considerable authority (particularly amongst Sefardim and Mizrahim), but his unconventional practice of not citing his sources or detailing the reasoning behind decisions was controversial.

EXERCISE

Suggest reasons why: 1) numerous law codes were produced during the medieval period; and 2) no such widely accepted codes have been produced since Karo's *Shulhan Arukh*.

Maimonides was *naggid* (secular and religious leader) of the Jewish community in Fostat (Old Cairo), Egypt, and physician to the Vizier who ruled there in Salāh ad-Dīn Yūsuf ibn Ayyūb's absence during the Crusades. In many parts of Europe, North Africa and the Middle East at this time, the policies of civil authorities (the crown or other government structures) were important influencers of Jewish attitudes towards particular religious offices and office-holders.[9] For example, Jewish settlement was often restricted to approved rural areas or urban districts, known in Europe as ghettos and in Morocco as *mellahs*. State policy obliged them, if they wished to live as Jews, to be subject to the *halakhah* and rabbinic authority: voluntaryism or choice only became a significant aspect of religious observance after emancipation. In many instances senior rabbis were directly or indirectly appointed by non-Jewish authorities. This was true of the Egyptian *naggid*, who, in addition to exercising authority in legal cases and appointing rabbis,

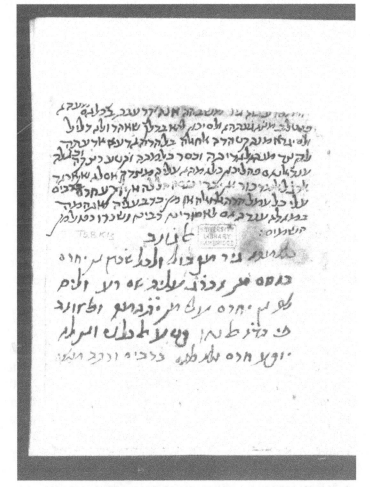

Figure 3.1: Moses Maimonides' responsum concerning an accusation of sexual impropriety. Reproduced by kind permission of the Syndics of Cambridge University Library (T-S_8K13.8,r.).

According to the question, an aged widow has accused a respected teacher of expressing a wish to sleep with her. There are no witnesses and she cannot provide evidence for her claim. Should the man, who wishes to clear his name, publicly ban or excommunicate anyone who tells lies about him?

Maimonides answers that the woman's testimony is not legally acceptable. The man has the right to excommunicate his slanderers but the correct procedure in this case is to silence the gossip, not to pronounce a ban, and not to discuss the matter further. The responsum, written in Judaeo-Arabic (Arabic written in the Hebrew script), is short and the reasoning is not given. It ends with the words, 'Moses wrote this'.

was required to enforce conditions attached to the Jews' status as *dhimmi* (non-Muslim subjects in an Islamic state), collecting taxes and ensuring that no new synagogues were constructed.

In the pre-emancipation era, rabbinic authority was, then, typically sustained by intertwining, if not always mutually supporting, factors:

- the exercising of power in deciding legal questions in responsa and *battei din* (religious courts), supervising institutions (for example, the *mikvah* or ritual bath) and procedures such as *shehita* (slaughter of animals and birds) and acting as agents of civil authorities;

- civil authorities' confirmation of the rabbinic office and particular office-holders, through the ratification of appointments and recognition as community representative;

- ordinary people's acceptance of the *halakhah*;

- popular belief that rabbis were, by virtue of their training and personal qualities, legitimate interpreters of *halakhic* rules and norms.

As Jewish identity and religious belief and practice has diversified in the wake of Enlightenment and emancipation, it has become impossible for any new codifier or *posek* to produce a book or responsum acceptable to all. As described in Chapter 2, not only do religious Jews interpret the law differently, but they also differ significantly in their beliefs concerning its authority. The Conservative position that the consensus-tradition of the Jewish community (*klal Yisrael*) is in itself revelatory of God's will, and therefore authoritative, is evident in the style of Conservative responsa, which are drafted by a rabbi and then voted on (by the Committee on Jewish Law and Standards (CJLS) in America) and often refer to historical and contextual factors alongside legal sources. A Reform responsum attempts to persuade its readers, in theory at least, that the final decision on an issue is ultimately a matter for an individual's own conscience.

The pre-modern figure of the 'communal rabbi', whose judicial authority extended over a particular urban or rural territory, has over time given way to the synagogue rabbi, whose activity is mostly pastoral and whose authority, in the absence of formal powers of coercion, has become more personal.[10] Yet the rabbinical office remains important across the spectrum of Jewish religious movements. While in the early nineteenth-century liturgical changes were often requested by lay people, the rabbinate gradually assumed the driving seat within the developing institutions of Reform Judaism. Influenced by Protestant Christian models in Europe and North America, the Reform rabbinical role emphasizes pastoral care, and leadership in prayer and worship, changes that are reflected in the development of auditorium-style synagogues (see Chapter 8). Reconstructionism has advocated a third approach, in which the rabbi is neither a *halakhic* authority nor a model of Jewish ethics and spirituality. Instead, the Reconstructionist rabbi aims to function as an educator and facilitator, helping members of the congregation or *havurah* (see Chapter 2) to build 'Judaized lives'.[11] The situation differs in Israel. Reflecting the *millet* system[12] introduced by the Ottoman Empire and retained subsequently by the British, who ruled the region from 1920–1948, legal authority over matters of personal status rests with religious authorities (there is, for example, no civil marriage for Israeli Jews)[13]. A dual Sefardi and Ashkenazi Chief Rabbinate is sovereign in matters of personal status – births, weddings, divorces, burials – which are conducted and registered in line with Orthodox *halakhah*.

The Tzaddik

German sociologist Max Weber (1864–1920) argued that there are three types of authority in society.[14] *Traditional authority* is derived from customs or habits that have been handed down from the past and are believed to confer legitimate power on particular individuals. Hereditary monarchies are traditional authority structures, but in Judaism's case, the priesthood provides a clearer example. Priestly status is inherited regardless of aptitudes or skills; it is traditionally believed to have been divinely instituted. In contrast *rational-legal authority*, grounded in the application of a system of written rules and regulations, is exemplified by the *halakhah* and the rabbinical office, whose incumbents derive their authority from technical knowledge and impersonal application of religious law.

Much sociological analysis of religion has concentrated on *charismatic authority*, the third Weberian type. Charismatic authority is linked to the personal appeal of a leader who is able, by virtue of distinctive gifts or abilities, and inspires the obedience of his or her followers. The term 'charisma' is derived from early Christian literature and charismatic leaders often, but not always, emerge in religious settings. Within Judaism, one such example is Israel ben Eliezer (1669–1761), also known as the *Baal Shem Tov* ('Master of the Good Name'), or Besht.

Born in Tłuste (north-east Poland), ben Eliezer was an itinerant wonder-worker who used prayer and wrote amulets to achieve healings and other miracles. His combination of instrumental techniques with a life of intense prayer and reliance on the teachings of the *Zohar*, the most important work of Jewish mysticism (see Chapter 4) placed him at the forefront of the emerging Hasidic movement. This approach to Judaism challenged dominant religious aspirations, countering the traditional rabbinic ideal with that of the *Hasid* or pious person who, without the privilege of a lifetime's textual studies, could achieve intimacy with God through ecstatic prayer, ritual observance and mystical discipline. Over time, Hasidism dominated southern Poland and Ukraine, while rabbinic Judaism retained the upper hand in Lithuania and northern Poland.

Ben Eliezer's success developed in a context of religious and social ferment, resonating with Weber's claim that charismatic leaders are particularly likely to emerge in times of crisis, when the more stable or rigid systems associated with traditional and rational-legal authority struggle to cope. Between 1648–1667, tens of thousands of Jews had been killed in a series of military conflicts that accompanied the decline of the Polish–Lithuanian Commonwealth. *Shabbateanism*, a popular messianic movement, had also left many European and Middle Eastern diaspora communities in disarray following its leader, Shabbetai Zvi's (1626–1676), conversion to Islam.

Pure charismatic authority is short-lived. Charisma must be routinized, in other words, a set of norms and rules must be established, if a movement is to survive the death of its founder and attain long-term viability. In Hasidism, this process resulted in the creation of new concepts and structures focused on charismatic leaders known as *tzaddikim* ('righteous men').[15] Following Israel ben Eliezer's death, one of his followers, Jacob Joseph of Polonnoye, published a book containing many of the founder's teachings. Another, Dov Baer of Mezirech, organized a group of disciples to spread Hasidic ideas. Although his approach was not unopposed, these men came to be regarded as *tzaddikim* in their own right, commanding the obedience of followers in different regions of Central and Eastern Europe. (One of the most influential was Elimelech of Lizhensk, whose grave is shown in Fig. 2.2 on p.23). Further mechanisms developed for the transfer of power to future leaders. Early *tzaddikim* were succeeded by their most prominent disciples, but later dynasties of *tzaddikim* developed, many of which persist to the present day. Over time, the practice of hereditary succession has become sacrilized: the *tzaddik*'s holy thoughts during sexual intercourse are said to bring down a special soul into the male child then conceived, so that the son inherits something of his father's charisma. Additional mechanisms have developed, which provide Hasidism with a stable economic base. A Hasid visiting the court of his *tzaddik* or *rebbe* presents him with a written statement or *kvittel* detailing his name and his material or spiritual needs (the *tzaddik* is believed to be able to provide both spiritual guidance and healing or other miracles – even after his own death) and a sum of money, the *pidyon nefesh* ('redemption of soul'). The *pidyon nefesh* pays for the maintenance of the *rebbe*, his family and his assistants, but it is often rationalized in spiritualizing terms. While the *tzaddik* is believed to have no real need of material comfort, gift-giving is understood as something that he permits so as to enable his followers to feel a sense of connection to their leader. Some dynastic successions are hotly disputed, with rival factions championing the cause of one candidate over another, until consensus is, or is not, reached. But ostensibly a *tzaddik* or *rebbe* derives neither his livelihood nor his authority from the will of his followers: it is the *duty* of those whom he addresses to recognize him as their charismatically-qualified leader.

The Weberian tripartite classification of authority is an analytical tool, intended to help the researcher understand how power, the ability to have others do what one wishes, is institutionalized and affects individual and group relationships. Traditional, rational-legal and charismatic authority are ideal types, abstractions existing only in the realm of ideas. In any given example, authority may stem from several sources, as illustrated by medieval discussions of *yeridat ha-dorot*, 'the decline of the generations'. According to this idea, generations are successively religiously inferior to their predecessors, 'the fingernail of the former generations is worth more than the belly of the later ones' (*Yoma* 9b). For Rabbanites engaged in anti-Karaite polemics, *yeridat ha-dorot* reinforced their argument that the Talmud, a record of earlier scholars' deliberations, remained authoritative. The concept was elaborated in rational-legal terms: previous generations were closer in time to the Sinai revelation, and they lived in contexts supportive of intensive study. It was also articulated in charismatic terms. Some medieval writers suggested that early rabbis possessed unique gifts or qualities that set them apart from, and enabled them to make decisions that were binding upon, Jews in later ages.[16]

Weber's approach is not without its weaknesses. As Pierre Bourdieu notes, reflecting the more populist interests of contemporary cultural studies, the account of pure charisma emphasizes the nature of the individual leader and downplays the religious interests and needs of the public to whom s/he relates.[17] Writing a century ago, Weber was also profoundly shaped by modernism: he believed that traditional and charismatic forms of authority were destined to wane, as rational-legal authority and its associated impersonal, bureaucratic culture increasingly came to the fore. In the early twenty-first century, the progressive disenchantment of the world may no longer be regarded as a given.

The impact of information and communications technologies

EXERCISE

Visit one or more of these websites. Based on an examination of their contents, what impact do you think information and communications technologies are having on authority in Judaism?

http://www.chabad.org/ – Chabad-Lubavitch, a Hasidic group.

http://www.aish.com – a website run by *Aish haTorah*, a non-Hasidic Haredi organization.

http://www.opensourcehaggadah.com/siteuse.php – an open source version of a religious text for Passover (note: a Hebrew font is needed to access parts of this site, but the sections most relevant to this exercise ['Building a Haggadah' and 'Contribution Guidelines'] are in English).

http://www.israelforum.com/blog_home.php – a gateway linking to several hundred Jewish blogs.

Contemporary Judaism has been significantly impacted by information and communications technologies. Many religious texts have been digitalized and are more widely accessible than was previously the case. The internet also facilitates new forms of interaction and organization, offering new opportunities for participation in different kinds of 'online' or 'virtual' Judaism. For example, in Second Life, a virtual world launched in 2003, members' avatars can study in a virtual *yeshivah*, and pray at several synagogues.

Such developments remain comparatively little studied. It is far more common for online environments to be mined by students of religion as sources of information *about* a religious culture than for them to be admitted and analyzed *as* religious cultures in their own right. Teaching activity reflects this emphasis, concentrating on the skills needed to make use of the Internet for university and college assignments. (For an example of an online tutorial of this kind, see 'Internet for Religious Studies', published by Intute.[18]) These skills are necessary, but to think exclusively in such terms neglects an important aspect of Jewish religious experience in late modernity. In some respects, these developments constitute a radical extension of the voluntaryism and individualism associated with religion in modernity, and so might be thought to challenge or overturn existing rules and hierarchies. It is possible, for example, for a female non-Jew to construct an avatar (representation of herself) as a male Jew, and participate in a virtual *minyan* (group of ten adult males required for corporate worship) in a Second Life synagogue. Many people now create their own rituals and celebrations using materials adapted from the internet, a development that some longer established institutions and their leaders find disturbing. Blogging allows ordinary people to have public voices on religious issues, and online social networks like Facebook can be used to foster virtual communities or to advocate a particular cause internationally.

In 2006, the head of the Haredi *Agudath Israel* organization in the United States, argued that:

> In recent years ... the authority of *daas Torah* ['knowledge of Torah'] has been significantly undermined, even within our own *chareidi* circles. Most troubling has been the proliferation of Internet 'blogs' where misguided individuals feel free to spread every bit of *rechilus* and *loshon hora* [gossip and harmful speech] about rabbonim and roshei yeshiva [rabbis and *Yeshivah* Principals], all with the intended effect of undermining any semblance of Torah authority in our community.[19]

Despite such visions of anomie, however, many virtual or online materials, and the practices associated with them, largely mirror those of 'real' or offline Judaism. The past decade, for example, has seen the emergence of the e-*kvittel*: rather than visit a particular *rebbe* or site in person, it is possible to submit a prayer or religious question electronically. Indeed, the online presence of Haredi groups is particularly noteworthy; www.aish.com logs around 3 million visits each month, which suggests an appeal extending far beyond its roots in a *mitnaggedic yeshivah*. *Agudath Israel*, although it does not have a website, uses email, and its views are disseminated via a number of online Haredi publications. Belz, one of the larger Hasidic groups, reversed its 1999 ban on the internet in 2008.[20] Writing on Haredi book publishing companies, Stolow has suggested that through their bestselling prayer books and guides to ritual, the Haredim have acquired a status as 'the most legitimate bearers of tradition, and purveyors of the greatest knowledge of "correct practice", even among those who do not subscribe to their belief system.'[21] Similar dynamics are at play when readers consult Haredi websites for *the* Jewish approach to an issue.

Further examples illustrate how new technologies may possess the potential to extend the reach of current authority structures and foster a more authoritarian approach to religious observance. In 2010, a 'mitzvah app' was launched for the Apple iPhone.[22] By visiting synagogues and other Jewish communal centres (activities logged by a series of electronic sensors), users would, it was announced, be able to accumulate points redeemable against the expenses associated with synagogue and burial society membership. Conversely, points would be lost for activities such as shopping on *Shabbat* and religious holidays, when the app would also disable the iPhone, with the exception of emergency calls. Such an app raises a number of questions. Is it a useful encouragement to an *halakhically* observant lifestyle, particularly suited, perhaps, to young adults? Or, does it foster an overly mechanical approach to observance, and threaten individual liberty if, for example, use of the app is a requirement for synagogue membership?

While the use of new technologies is not always radical or democratizing, and can sometimes serve to extend existing authority structures or perhaps implement new ones, some change is inevitable. From the Orthodox *posek*'s perspective, prayer in a virtual *minyan* is no better than praying on one's own, and adopting a Jewish avatar does not make one in any sense Jewish, or make one's online activities Judaism. But no real life sanctions can be imposed on a Jewish avatar, or on consumers who choose to navigate away from, or simply ignore instructions on a website. In this respect, the nature and limits of authority are in flux. Judaism is colonizing new media and in the process of doing so, is itself transformed.

4

Worship, Festivals and Mysticism

In the past two and a half centuries, as individual Jews have gained civil and political rights, the synagogue has replaced the *kehillah*, or semi-autonomous Jewish community, as the primary site of organized religious life in most countries. Attempts to separate the operation of public institutions and activities from matters of religious belief and practice have encouraged the privatization of religion, and consequently the home's significance as a site of observance and identity has been strengthened. This chapter will look at the rituals associated with home and synagogue, at prayer and at some major festivals. It will close with a discussion of *kabbalah*, a practice based in Judaism that is promoted by and to Jews and non-Jews today.

Prayer

The Bible presents prayer as an activity bound up with the personal outpouring of emotion:

> In her wretchedness, she prayed to the LORD, weeping all the while ... Hannah was praying in her heart; only her lips moved, but her voice could not be heard (1 Sam. 1.10–12).

> And Hannah prayed:
> My heart exults in the LORD;
> I have triumphed through the LORD (1 Sam 2.1).

In contrast, the Talmud and other rabbinic literature, while stressing the importance of *kavvanah* (intention) on the part of someone who approaches God, emphasizes public, corporate worship, fixing times for morning (*shaharit*), afternoon (*minha*) and evening (*maariv*) liturgies that are built around the recital of two key prayers, the *Shema* (said in the evening and the morning, as specified in Deut. 6.7) and the *amidah* ('standing prayer') a series of nineteen *brakhot* (blessings), short paragraphs articulating praise, petition and thanksgiving in the first person plural ('Grant *us*' etc.). On *Shabbat* (Sabbath) and other festivals, hymns and biblical readings also feature prominently in the services. Another liturgy (*musaf*) follows *shaharit* on these days, and on *Yom Kippur* (see later) a fifth service known as *ne'ilah* is added.

Services may take place in a synagogue, at home or other appropriate venue. Polish Hasidim, who were barred from leading prayers in synagogues, partly because they cultivated *kavannah* in prayer at the expense of regulations governing its timing, gathered in a *shtibl* ('small room'). Although an individual may perform much of the basic liturgy, the rabbinic ideal, reflected in the language of the *amidah*, is for prayer in a group or *minyan* of at least ten adult males. Traditionally, some significant elements of the service, including the mourners' *kaddish* (a prayer recited for eleven months after the death of a parent or other close relative) and the reading of scripture cannot take place without such a quorum. However, in the late twentieth-century American Conservative Jewish authorities, while allowing congregations to exercise their discretion on the matter, ruled that women could both count towards a *minyan* and lead prayers. Reform and Reconstructionist Jews often define the *minyan* even more flexibly; six or seven men and women may be deemed sufficient, so as to facilitate 'full' worship in small communities.

How might one study prayer and other forms of religious devotion or worship? Examination of, for example, the liturgies published by different groups, illustrates their theological and cultural differences. Here is the opening passage of the *amidah* as it appears in the *Authorised Daily Prayer Book*, used by most Orthodox Jews in Britain:

> Blessed are You, LORD our GOD and GOD of our Fathers, GOD of Abraham, GOD of Isaac and GOD of Jacob; the great, mighty and awesome GOD, GOD Most High, who bestows acts of lovingkindness and creates all, who remembers the lovingkindness of the Fathers and will bring a Redeemer to their children's children for the sake of His name, in love.[1]

Reflecting the impact of feminism, British Reform Judaism's *Forms of Prayer*, references the wives of the patriarchs who are mentioned in the traditional text, attempts to avoid gender-specific language in its description of God, and speaks of hope for 'rescue' rather than a personal 'Redeemer' in the future:

Blessed are You, our God, and God of our ancestors, God of Abraham, God of Sarah, God of Isaac, God of Rebecca, God of Jacob, God of Rachel and God of Leah, the great, the mighty, the awesome God, God beyond, generous in love and kindness, and possessing all. You remember the good deeds of those before us, and therefore in love bring rescue to the generations, for such is your being.[2]

But what do such textual differences tell us of their users' experiences? Segal has recently suggested that liturgies are 'official or normative' and have 'shaped the religious sensibilities of Jews (not only the males) through daily recitation'.[3] Such a stance is widely implied by other textbooks that posit liturgical texts as keys to the 'meaning' of religious festivals, and informs the decisions of those who revise liturgies to balance the highly masculine imagery in the traditional *siddur*. However, such processes, if they occur, are partial, unconscious, and therefore extremely hard to examine.

General textbooks aside, scholars increasingly emphasize prayer as a human activity,[4] a shift reflecting religious studies' trend away from purely textual analysis and towards a pragmatically- or ideologically-motivated methodological agnosticism. Whereas approaches that focus on liturgy implicitly suggest that there is an essential Judaism expressed in a 'script' that people perform more or less perfectly, writers like Smart (who located worship within the practical and ritual dimension) emphasize 'the luxurious vegetation of the world's religions' and the need to give equal weight to ideas and practices.[5] In this context, it is interesting to note that in the pre-modern era young Sefardi boys were taught [f]*azer tefilá*, 'to *do* prayer'.[6]

Viewed in this way, prayer and worship are practices or *performances* that invoke – play off and create – values. Jewish reformers in nineteenth-century Europe were not only distinguished from their Orthodox counterparts by the contents of their prayer books, they also defined themselves through their use of sound, silence and gesture. The traditional practice at the time, which was for worshippers to arrive and leave at different times, and to pray at different speeds, accompanied by a range of gestures and vocalizations, was regarded by the emerging middle classes (from whose ranks the reformers were overwhelmingly drawn) as an alienating cacophony. In ordering and disciplining sound and movement (by introducing uniform prayer times, discouraging bodily gestures and so on), reformers sought to express and bolster their new self-understandings as sober, mannered citizens of the nations in which they lived.

In contrast to earlier textually-focused studies, recent scholarship on worship also highlights diversity and change. Projects to create new rituals and to redesign familiar ones, particularly in ways that make them more fluid and open-ended, have been a hallmark of much Western religious life since the 1960s.[7] To take one example within Judaism, some couples now personalize or customize the traditional *huppah* or canopy beneath which they are married. In some instances, guests decorate a panel of cloth, and meet before the ceremony to offer the bride and groom their encouragement and advice, and join the pieces together. Vanessa Ochs characterizes this as part of a broader, explicit drive 'to personalize and to create community' within contemporary Judaism.[8] Such ritual developments, and the material culture that is linked to them, are easily overlooked if practice is regarded simply as the execution of a pre-existing script of beliefs and traditions.

The concept of performance also highlights the physical, sensory aspects of religious expression and experience. The wearing of a *tallit* (prayer shawl) and *tefillin* (small leather boxes bound by straps to the forehead and arm, which contain scriptural passages, including the first two passages of the *Shema*) and head-covering are all associated with prayer in Judaism, although the specifics of their usage varies (see Chapter 8). Posture during prayer is also noteworthy. Karaite daily worship consists of a sequence of prayers accompanied by actions such as standing, bowing down and kneeling. In other traditions, especially those of the Ashkenazi, prayerful intention is traditionally associated with *shokeling* (swaying) and closing one's eyes: according to the Talmud, Rabbi Akiva (50–135 CE), popularly regarded as one of the founders of rabbinic Judaism, prayed and swayed so intensely that he would begin in one part of a room and finish in another (*Ber.* 31a). However, simply recognizing prayer's embodied nature does not mean that the interior life of religious adherents is anything other than extremely hard for scholars to access, regardless of whether they, too, identify themselves as religious. Within cultures in which physical movements are interpreted as evidence of prayerfulness worshippers may know how to appear to be immersed in prayer while their minds are elsewhere. Conversely, as one ethnographer of Orthodox Judaism notes, 'the faking may itself intensify one's spiritual state … the acts themselves produce it'.[9]

EXERCISE

Read the statement below by two Reconstructionist rabbis. What explanations do you think Jews who share these views might offer for their continuing practice of prayer? (It may be helpful to re-read 'Conservative Judaism,' in Chapter 2.)

'God neither intervenes in human history to reward, punish, and effect His purposes, nor abides in a celestial realm, listening attentively to prayers.'[10]

There are many possible explanations and justifications for prayer in Judaism. In earlier rabbinic texts, prayer is positioned as a replacement for the sacrificial system of *avodah* ('divine service') rendered impossible by the destruction of the Jerusalem Temple: one Talmudic scholar asks 'What is *avodah* of the heart?' and responds, 'It is prayer' (*Ta'anit* 2a). Here, prayer is a means to communicate with God – to express gratitude and love, confess wrong-doings or request something for oneself or for others. In mystical circles, prayer offers a means to achieving a direct experiential relationship with the divine, a closeness to God known in *kabbalah* as *devekut*. Noting that the Hebrew verb to pray (*lehitpallel*) is reflexive, some modern Orthodox writers like Samson Raphael Hirsch and Joseph D. Soloveitchik have characterized prayer as an opportunity for introspection and moral or spiritual development. 'Prayer changes the world because it changes us,' suggests Jonathan Sacks.[11] Other, sociologically-driven accounts of prayer are possible, and have currency amongst some adherents of Judaism, particularly (but not only) amongst those who identify as non-Orthodox. These may stress prayer's significance for the individual, emphasizing its value as a way of recognizing and expressing experiences and emotions. Alternatively, they may focus on corporate worship. The wording of many prayers, and the act of gathering together to recite them, can, for example, encourage feelings of shared history, fate and community – although such notions again raise questions about the extent and manner of individual worshippers' engagement with liturgy.

The Sabbath

Some form of Sabbath observance is one of the family resemblances discernable across the range of phenomena describable as Judaism. For all religious Jews, the Sabbath (Hebrew, *Shabbat*) is set-apart time. For many, it is symbolically delineated from the rest of the week by candle lighting and *kiddush* (blessing recited over wine) at home on Friday night – the former practice was observed by roughly half of the affiliated Jews (members of synagogues or other communal organizations) questioned in the American National Jewish Population Survey (NJPS) in 2000–2001 – and (less commonly) the ceremony of *havdalah* or 'separation' as the first stars appear on the following Saturday evening. (In the Jewish religious calendar, day follows night.) In fact many Jews who do not identify themselves as religious observe *Shabbat* in some manner. In 1991, two thirds of people surveyed for the Guttman Report on the religious attitudes and behaviour of Israeli Jews, including more than one third of those describing themselves as 'totally non-observant' somehow marked the day.[12]

Formally, the Sabbath's institution is linked to two experiences widely regarded as literally or symbolically foundational for Judaism; the world's creation, and the people Israel's experience of exodus (escape) from slavery in Egypt:

> Gen. 2.2–3: On the seventh day God finished the work that He had been doing ... God blessed the seventh day and declared it holy, because on it God ceased from all the work of creation.

> Deut. 5.12–15: Observe the sabbath day and keep it holy, as the LORD your God has commanded you. Six days you shall labour, and do all your work, but the seventh day is a sabbath of the LORD your God; you shall not do any work ... Remember that you were a slave in the land of Egypt and the LORD your God freed you from there with a mighty hand and an outstretched arm; therefore the LORD your God has commanded you to observe the sabbath day.

The Bible does not elaborate on the kind of activity prohibited. However, drawing on its list of tasks entailed in constructing the tabernacle (a movable tent for meeting [with God] that the former Hebrew slaves carried with them in the wilderness) the writers of the *Mishnah* identified thirty-nine kinds of work prohibited on *Shabbat*. The practical implementation and extension of the *Mishnaic* rules has typically proceeded by analogy, in the light of the principle of 'building a fence around the law' (see Chapter 3). Thus the prohibition on kindling and extinguishing fire is understood by Orthodox Jews to proscribe turning electrical devices on or off. Timer switches are widely used to keep homes, hotels and synagogues heated and lit during *Shabbat*. Keen to exploit a niche market, some appliance manufacturers have developed a 'Sabbath mode', allowing users to leave ovens turned on for long periods of time while disabling all lights and alarms, so that they may keep warm food that has been prepared before the day itself. The permissibility of these products is a matter of contention, with each technical modification requiring rabbinic appraisal. Such processes illustrate not only the demands associated with strict Sabbath observance, but also the creative approach taken to the exploitation of new technologies, and the extent to which observant Jews are not untouched by consumerism.

Ostensibly, the use of timers and the historical practice of hiring a non-Jew, a *Shabbat goy*, to light fires and candles, is not about the circumvention of religious law. Reflecting Isa. 58.13–14, which speaks of the Sabbath as a delight, textual tradition and popular custom in Judaism attach religious value to the cultivation of *oneg Shabbat* (Sabbath joy). The festival is about both the absence of work, and the active presence of pleasure and beauty, manifested in various ways. Liturgically, in the hymn *Lekhah dodi* ('Come, my beloved') its arrival is likened to that of a bride. People generally make an effort beforehand to tidy their homes, and to eat, drink and dress well. The Sabbath is also a popular time to host guests (provided that, in the case of Orthodox Jews, this does not entail prohibited travel) and is traditionally regarded as an apt time for sexual relations. While the day is often home-centred (weekly synagogue attendance on *Shabbat* is a minority activity, with the Friday night service more popular than that on Saturday morning) for some Hasidim, *oneg Shabbat* is also connected with the phenomenon of the *tish* ('table') an event at which the *rebbe* eats, sings hymns and teaches Torah. Some traditions speak of Jews possessing an 'extra soul' on *Shabbat* and for Hasidim, closeness to the *rebbe* at such a time – being present at the *tish* and, for a fortunate few, eating his *shirayim* (leftovers) – is a unique opportunity to experience or participate in their leader's exceptional spiritual qualities or, in Weberian terms, his charisma.

Amongst Jews affiliated to Conservative, Reform and the other non-Orthodox movements, which are sometimes collectively described as 'Progressive', differing understandings of the nature of the *halakhah*, and the emphasis placed on individual choice, result in a proliferation of Sabbath observances. The notion of rest, of 'being-not-doing', and the cultivation of spiritual and physical refreshment, typically takes a degree of precedence over the details of the regulations on work. For example, Orthodox authorities prohibit driving on *Shabbat*, since it entails two forms of proscribed work – burning fuel and travelling. Individual Reform Jews may choose not to drive on *Shabbat*, but are unlikely to hold the view that Jews in general are prohibited from doing so. In the 1950s, the Conservative Committee on Jewish Law and Standards (CJLS) exempted journeys to synagogue services from the usual *Shabbat* prohibition on driving, reflecting Conservativism's emphasis on the promotion of Jewish *community*. In the 1990s, its Israeli counterpart reasserted the ban, arguing that the circumstances faced by suburban Americans, who might live some distance from their fellow Jews, do not apply in Israel, where a *minyan* may be found in every neighbourhood.

Alongside *Shabbat*, other festivals punctuate the year. Collectively, they are significant aspects of Jewish experience. Whether or not they consider themselves to be religious, most Jews will participate in some kind of *Pesach* (Passover) ritual, or remember having done so during childhood; many will attend synagogue at *Rosh ha-Shanah* (New Year) and/or *Yom Kippur* (Day of Atonement). Religious studies must, then, do more than simply reporting first order explanations of festival customs and liturgies, and their origins and meanings (although equally, it should not ignore these things). As with prayer, the study of festivals can highlight the embodied, sensory aspects of observance, and the extent to which ritualized activities can communicate and create ideas and experiences. In Israel, many holidays foster a sense of national unity in addition to their more conventionally religious meanings, and in many respects this holds for diaspora settings too.[13]

The calendar

The Jewish calendar is lunisolar. Each month begins with the new moon, lasting twenty-nine or thirty days, while important festivals are linked to agricultural seasons determined by the sun's position. According to Deut. 16, *Pesach* must fall in the spring month of *Aviv* (also called *Nisan*), *Sukkot* around harvest-time and so on. Since the lunar year takes eleven fewer days than the solar one, adjustments must be made to avoid *Pesach* (for example) moving through the solar year to fall outside the springtime. An extra lunar month is added to seven years out of every nineteen lunar ones, and the new moon date is calculated rather than observed. The current mathematically-derived calendar, replacing one promulgated by the *Sanhedrin* during Temple times, dates from the seventh or eighth century and has near-universal acceptance. Contemporary Karaites have reinstated an observational calendar, and make use of the internet to publish written and photographic reports of the new moon as it appears in Israel.

Pesach

Like *Shabbat*, *Pesach* or Passover is a predominantly home-based festival. The *seder*, a liturgical meal held on Passover eve, is one of a few rituals regularly observed by an overwhelming majority of Jews worldwide.

In origin, the *Pesach* of today is a conflation of two separate festivals mentioned in the *Tanakh* – an agriculturally-oriented feast of unleavened bread and an animal sacrifice offered at the Jerusalem Temple to commemorate the exodus or departure of the ancient Hebrew slaves from Egypt (Deut. 1.6:5–7). Rabbinic Judaism stressed the historical connotations of *Pesach*, seeking to anchor its meanings to the biblical story in which God 'passes-over' or spares the slaves and kills their oppressors' first-born sons (Exod. 12). At the same time, since the destruction of the Jerusalem Temple meant that sacrifices were no longer possible, they shifted emphasis from the lamb to the unleavened bread (*matzah*) as the primary symbol of the holiday.[14]

In Israel, Passover lasts one week. Outside Israel, ancient diaspora communities added an extra day to its observance, and to other festivals, because it took time for confirmation of the new moon, and thus the correct date, to reach them. This was partly because of interference from Samaritans, a neighbouring Middle Eastern people, who regarded, and still do regard, their religion as the true biblical one. The additional day provided a margin for error for diaspora Jews and is maintained in Orthodox Judaism and by most American Conservative and British Masorti congregations. At the Breslau conference of 1846, Reform rabbis rejected the second day of festivals as an anachronism.

According to the Torah, the possession and consumption of *hametz* (fermented grain such as wheat, barley and rye) are forbidden (Exod. 12.15; 12.19; 13.3) during *Pesach*. Thoroughly cleaning the house of *hametz*, ceremoniously hunting for the final crumbs, replacing bread with *matzah* or unleavened bread and, traditionally, specially cleansing crockery, cookware and utensils, or using a set that has been kept separately for the festival, help to demarcate it as a set apart time. While such rituals are largely home-based, their widespread frequency enhances a sense of broader Jewish *communitas*.

An early *seder* (meaning 'order') ritual is described in the Talmud. The event is usually conducted according to a liturgical text called the *haggadah*: the earliest surviving version is found in a prayer-book issued by Saadia Gaon (882–942), the principal of one of the Babylonian rabbinic academies. The *haggadah* sets out what is to be done and, distinctively, gives direction as to the correct mental attitude of participants, who are exhorted to feel that they personally are experiencing the exodus as a living reality. Contemporary versions are elaborate products of a series of transformations that reflect and create changing understandings of the themes of bondage and liberation; they include poems, songs and explanations. Activity always focuses, however, on the *seder* table, typically decorated with a white cloth and candles, and a *seder* plate or tray holding several ritual foods. These include three *matzot* (pieces of unleavened bread); *maror* (bitter herbs, often horseradish) said to symbolize the bitterness of slavery (Exod 1.14); *haroset* (a sweet paste made from almonds, apples and wine) symbolizing the mortar used by the slaves and/or the sweetness of their redemption; salt water (symbolizing tears); parsley (for dipping in salt water); and a roasted bone and egg, reminders of the Passover sacrifice brought in Temple times (and not consumed during the *seder*).

The *haggadah* details a series of actions to be performed including the consumption of four cups of wine, hand-washing, the tasting of each of the symbolic foods, the posing of four questions about the meaning of the *seder* (these are often read by the youngest person present, but in some communities, for example amongst Yemeni Jews, adults question the children) and the responses they elicit, and, after a meal, the chanting of *hallel* psalms (Ps. 113–118) and a final hymn ending with the phrase, 'Next year in Jerusalem!'

At first sight, the *seder* may appear to be historical–commemorative, but in addition to the *haggadah*'s advocacy of a presentist attitude on the part of participants, other aspects of the evening are future-oriented. In one (predominantly Ashkenazi) custom, an extra cup of wine is filled, and the house or apartment door is momentarily opened at the end of the meal. Traditionally, these are marks of hospitality towards the biblical prophet Elijah, who is believed to visit each Jewish home on *seder* night, and who is the forerunner of the *Messiah*, God's anointed one, who will usher in a future age of redemption and peace (see Chapter 5).

No textbook account of *Pesach* can exhaust the range of meanings that Jews individually and collectively may attach to the festival. The variety of distinctive foods consumed, and the use of songs and poems, makes the *seder* a profoundly sensory experience. It can also be physically and emotionally demanding. Fulfilling the commandment to recount the story of the exodus is interpreted by some people as requiring not simply the reading of the *haggadah*, but additional song, debate and discussion of the festival's significance. In an age when many Jewish populations are characterized by high levels of geographical mobility, divorce and inter-marriage, the gathering together of family and friends for the festival, and competing expectations as to the detail of the liturgical meal, can be sources of anxiety and tension. At the same time, more than any other festival in Judaism, Passover celebrations have become increasingly personalized and diversified. Just as each generation of Jews is urged to view themselves as if they had come out of Egypt, so in many instances Jews have narrated their own experiences in the terms of the biblical story of slavery and redemption. It cannot be assumed that each group of *seder* participants performs its text to the letter, but even if this were the case, the publication of several thousand different editions gives a sense of the multiplication of *haggadot*. Some of these directly comment on historical events. In the 1920s *kibbutzim* (Israeli collective settlements influenced by Zionism and Socialism)[15] began using *haggadot* that celebrated Jews' connection with the land of Israel and omitted references to God. Following Israel's victory in the Six Day War, *haggadot* appeared to mark the recapturing of Jerusalem. Images and text in *A Survivors' Haggadah*, created at the end of the Second World War, interweave biblical stories with those of Holocaust survivors.[16] Other versions reflect socio-political concerns, including feminism and vegetarianism. Many more encode textually the denominational differences within modern Judaism, while some attempt to transcend the challenges associated with Jewish diversity or Jewish/non-Jewish relations.

Such diversity, and the *seder*'s continuing ubiquitousness, demands critical analysis. For Emanuel Feldman, writing recently in the journal of the (Orthodox) Rabbinical Council of America, the meal's popularity is linked to

Passover's connections with the origins of the Jewish people. Memory of this foundational moment is part of 'the national soul'; a 'collective unconsciousness' predisposes Jews to commemorate the exodus, even though as individuals they may not be able to articulate why they do so.[17] In positing the existence of a collective unconscious, Feldman is influenced by Carl Jung's psychology of religion. But the Jungian notion that ideas and images rooted in the experiences of the Hebrew slaves lie beneath the individual psyches or souls of Jews today remains at best empirically unverifiable, and at worst speculative and grounded in a problematic discourse of race. Such accounts do not satisfactorily explain Passover's place within contemporary Judaism, but are instead part of the data that falls within the remit of religious studies.

The reworking of the *seder* in relation to recent historical experience, and Feldman's characterization of Passover as 'foundational', are examples of a tendency to subsume new events and concerns within a biblical metanarrative: slavery in Egypt, and liberation leading to entry into the Promised Land, become types of suffering and liberation in relation to which other experiences can be narrated and made sense of. But 'exodus' and 'entry' are not the only Judaic 'fundamentals'. Others might include the concluding of the Sinai covenant (Exod. 19.4–6) and the Torah itself, both of which are commemorated (at *Shavuot* and *Simhat Torah*, respectively). Are there then other factors that have contributed to the *seder*'s preeminence?

The *seder*'s timing, location and infrequency are crucial factors since they enhance the possibility for innovation or flexibility within a broad, traditional rubric.[18] A geographically dispersed family, for example, may make a new decision each year as to the meal's venue, leader and *haggadah*. Since the *seder* is held annually, in the evening and usually in a private, domestic space, it allows participants to express ideas and identities in a way that does not foster social isolation. Any practical or symbolic boundaries which it establishes between Jews and non-Jews are limited, permeable and relatively non-problematic. (For more on this issue, see Chapter 10.) For Jews who live in societies shaped by Christianity, *Pesach* also functions as a Jewish alternative to Easter celebrations in the wider community. Finally, the ostensible orientation of much of the *seder* (songs, stories, the four questions and their answers) to children provides nostalgic, nominally and non-observant adults with a rationale for their own participation.

Mimouna – customs and politics

For many Jews of Moroccan descent, *Pesach* is followed immediately by *Mimouna*, a festival originating in North Africa and now celebrated more widely among Israeli Mizrahim and Sefardim. Explanations of *Mimouna* customs, which include decorating a table with flowers, figs, greenery, coins and a live or uncooked fish, and wishing one another prosperity and good luck, typically link them to events connected with the exodus – the parting of the Red Sea, and the slaves' plundering of treasure from their oppressors. The festival's name has been variously linked to the death of Maimonides' father, to 'faith' (Hebrew, *emunah*) and 'luck' (Arabic, *mimoun*). However, its origins are unclear.

In the 1950s and 60s over 200,000 Moroccan Jews migrated to Israel. Many experienced deprivation due to their low levels of economic and social capital, and discrimination at the hands of Ashkenazi elites. Massed rallies and picnics celebrating *Mimouna* began in the mid-60s, and were visible assertions of Mizrahi identity during an era of ethnic unrest and national debate. Representatives of political parties began visiting *Mimouna* celebrations in their efforts to court a sizeable, somewhat neglected, electorate. Since then, the gulf between Ashkenazim and other Israeli Jews has decreased but not disappeared: Mizrahim remain more lower-class and more traditional-religious than Israelis in general.

Shavuot

In Temple times, a sheaf of wheat (an *omer*) was presented as a harvest offering on the second day of *Pesach*. From that day, a period of seven weeks known as the 'Counting of the Omer' was counted, ending on the fiftieth day with the festival of *Shavuot* or 'Weeks' (Lev. 23.9–21; Exod. 34.22), which rabbinic Judaism later connected to the giving of the Torah at Sinai (*Pesach* 68b.)

No *halakhically* prescribed rituals are attached to *Shavuot*, but customs have developed over time. Emulating the practice of medieval mystics, some Haredim engage in all-night Torah study. Synagogues may be decorated with greenery and flowers, and dairy foods consumed. The latter are sometimes held to recall the Torah's ability to 'nourish' the faithful. It is also customary to read the story of Ruth, whose voluntary obedience to God (see Chapter 2) is sometimes seen as echoing Israel's acceptance of the covenant. Some Liberal and Reform congregations, which have supplemented or replaced *bar* and *bat mitzvah* (see Chapter 6) with Confirmation ceremonies to mark teenagers' acceptance of religious responsibilities, do so at *Shavuot*.

Rosh ha-Shanah and *Yom Kippur*

In Exod 12.2 *Nisan*, the month during which Passover falls, is described as the first month, but in the Talmud (*Rosh HaShanah* 16b) an autumn festival is *Rosh ha-Shanah*, 'the Head [beginning] of the Year'.

Rosh ha-Shanah, commemorated with 'loud blasts' (Lev. 23.24) on a *shofar* or ram's horn, inaugurates a ten-day season of *teshuvah* (repentance) culminating in *Yom Kippur*, 'Day of Atonement', when Jews stand, individually and collectively, before God to confess sins, seek cancellation of unfulfilled vows and, tradition says, God decides one's fate for the coming year. From the standpoint of rabbinic tradition, *Yom Kippur* is a high point of the year. Observance of a full day, 25 hour fast and synagogue attendance is widespread, even amongst those who do not identify themselves as religious, suggesting that, like the *seder*, *Yom Kippur* is an important identity marker for many Jews. To cope with the surge in numbers, many congregations hire special venues at this time of the year, or restrict admission to paying members or those who have reserved seats in advance. The revenues generated in this way are a vital source of income for small synagogues.

Rosh ha-Shanah customs are often held to articulate the ambiguity of the period, for example, consuming *hallah* (sweet bread) and apples dipped in honey or sugar (in the case of Baghdadi Jews)[19] is linked with a desire for a 'sweet' year. Many Orthodox Ashkenazi communities observe *tashlikh*, visiting the seaside or river to throw breadcrumbs into the water, symbolically casting away their sins at the same time (compare Micah 7.19). Amongst Sefardim and Mizrahim, *tashlikh* is less widespread, or carried out in different ways. For example, in India the Bene Israel wave white handkerchiefs over the water, and afterwards children fly white kites, reflecting a wider Indian custom at religious and cultural events.[20] There is also a Sefardi tradition of holding a *Rosh ha-Shanah seder*, in which symbolic food consumption is accompanied by prayers and poems requesting an end to worries and a blessed new year. In September 2009, for example, the *Los Angeles Times* reported that Zebulon Simantov, believed to be the only remaining Jew in Afghanistan, celebrated the arrival of the new year with a meal of lamb, chicken, fruits and vegetables.[21]

Synagogue sermons, New Year messages from leading rabbis and guides to practice all stress the importance of undertaking a period of soul-searching reflection and reparation in the lead into *Yom Kippur*. There is often an attempt to practice stricter standards of ritual purity during this period, perhaps immersing oneself in the *mikvah* (ritual bath). In the custom *kapparot*, a white fowl is swung around the head, slaughtered, and given to the poor. The practice is widely opposed by adherents of most modern religious movements, both on animal welfare grounds and because it appears to be a quasi-magical attempt to transfer sins on to an animal. Haredi leaders have recently attempted, with little visible success, to curb the practice, partly because an overworked slaughterer may fail to kill and examine the birds in accordance with *kosher* food laws.

Traditionally, the *Yom Kippur* fast entails complete abstention from food and drink. Its roots lie in the biblical purification ceremony outlined in Leviticus, as do the other forms of ritual purity observed: no washing, no anointing, no wearing of leather shoes, and no sexual intercourse. As on *Shabbat*, work is prohibited (Lev 16; 23.29). For religious Jews, almost the whole of *Yom Kippur* is spent in the synagogue, in a succession of five congregational services. For them, and for many otherwise secular Jews, the day's opening declaration, *Kol Nidre* ('all vows'), possesses particular appeal.[22]

Sukkot

Beginning five days after *Yom Kippur*, the week long festival of *Sukkot* takes its name from the temporary structures (in Hebrew, *sukkot*) built by the former slaves during their journey to the Promised Land (Lev. 23–42). During *Sukkot* a booth or shelter is built (often from wood or canvas, with a roof made from branches). Some Orthodox Jews begin its construction immediately after the end of *Yom Kippur*, thereby moving from one *mitzvah* (commandment) to another, and strive to make the *sukkah* their 'home', sleeping and eating there during the festival (following *Suk* 2.9). However, this is difficult where space is lacking, where the autumn climate is intemperate, and in contexts where the *sukkah* offers a vulnerable, visible target for anti-Jewish hostility. In many places it is, therefore, customary to build a communal *sukkah* in the synagogue grounds, rather than in individual families' homes, although in Israel the domestic *sukkah* has undergone a revival. Many apartment block and hotel balconies are constructed so as to facilitate the building of a *sukkah*; around half of Guttman Report respondents claimed to do so.[23]

The culmination of the autumnal season is *Simhat Torah*, 'rejoicing in the law', on which synagogue communities complete, and immediately resume, the annual reading of the Torah. Torah scrolls are processed around the synagogue, accompanied by singing, dancing and general celebrations.

Hanukah

The winter festival of *Hanukah* ('dedication') is of comparatively recent origin, first mentioned in rabbinic texts as a response to the second century BCE victory of the Maccabees (see Chapter 1). According to legend, when the Maccabees recaptured Jerusalem, they found only a day's worth of oil with which to fuel the Temple's *menorah* (seven-branched candelabrum) (*Shabbat* 21b). Miraculously, the oil lasted for eight days. *Hanukah* celebrates this by lighting candles or lamps for eight days – one on the first day, two on the second and so on. An additional light is used to kindle the main lights, so the special candle-holder used at this time has nine branches.

While the Talmud's approach to religious practice is usually highly discursive, its editors begin their discussion of *Hanukah* with the question 'What is *Hanukah*?' (*Shabbat* 21b), suggesting that it was little marked or understood at the time. Although authored by Jews, the books of 1 and 2 Macc. which recount the story of the revolt, do not form part of the Jewish scriptures, and have only been preserved in the canon of the Catholic and Orthodox Christian churches. In medieval times, *Hanukah* observance was relatively low-key, centring around the lighting of oil lamps and recitation of Psalms 113–118 (known as *hallel*). But in the modern period, *Hanukah* observance has become more elaborate and more widespread.

EXERCISE

What factors contribute to the increasing prominence given to *Hanukah*? Re-reading the section on *Pesach* may help you to formulate your ideas.

Changing *Hanukah* observance illustrates the malleability and polysemy of ritual. During periods when Jews lived as vulnerable minorities in Christian- or Muslim- dominated cultures, rabbis downplayed the political character of the Maccabbean project and emphasized the miracle of the oil-flask. Post-Enlightenment, the military and nationalistic dimension was newly emphasized amidst widespread debates about nationhood and identity. Zionists recast *Hanukah* as symbolic of Jewish national redemption; in Israel its public commemoration includes the carrying of a torch from Modi'in, the Maccabees' home and final resting place, to Jerusalem.

Other trends in diasporic *Hanukah* observance suggest that, as with *Pesach*, its timing and location make for its popularity. Most people celebrate at home, and since the lighting occurs after dark it is (like the *seder*) a marker of Jewishness compatible with full membership of a largely non-Jewish society. As a winter festival, it also provides an alternative to Christmas for Jews who live in societies shaped by Christianity:

> *Hanukah* ... must be made as interesting and joyful for the Jewish child as Christmas is made for the Christian child. The *Hanukah* festival should be the season for gifts. The children should look forward to gifts from their parents, and parents from their children.... . It should be the season for paying social calls, playing home games, and holding communal entertainments.[24]

While such trends worry some Jews, others see *Hanukah*'s accentuation as the only means of resisting Christmas: some Hasidim promote the erection of large candelabra in public parks and squares (see Chapter 7). Many North American and European Jews have built on the traditions of giving money (*gelt*) to children, special foods (especially ones fried in oil) and exchanging greetings cards in ways that approximate Christmas celebrations. Despite its origins, *Hanukah* has, then, become a key site of acculturation to historically non-Jewish norms.

Purim

According to the *Tanakh*, the sixth century BCE Persian official Haman drew lots (*pur*) to determine the date on which he would exterminate the Jewish people (Est. 3.7–14). Esther was a Jewish woman chosen by the Persian King to be his queen, who successfully pleaded with him to avert both the marriage and the slaughter. Her cousin, Mordecai, instructed Jews to celebrate by 'feasting and merrymaking ... sending gifts to one another and presents to the poor', (Est. 9.20–22).

In synagogues, the *megillah* (scroll of Esther) is read. Particularly, but not only, in Ashkenazi communities, children wear fancy dress to attend the reading and, when Haman's name is mentioned in the text, worshippers make noise to drown it out. Three-cornered cakes filled with poppy seeds or date, and known as *hamantashen*, 'Haman's pockets' or 'ears', also form a traditional part of the celebrations, as do parties and alcohol consumption.

Kabbalah

A Jungian account of the *seder*'s popularity was described earlier in this chapter. Jung's psychology of religion has found support amongst adherents of Judaism and other religions, partly because it suggests that a sense of relationship with God and fellow believers meets fundamental psychological needs and contributes to mental and physical wellbeing. Variations on this idea can be seen in contemporary positionings of religious concepts and practices, amongst them the *kabbalah*, or Jewish mystical tradition, as therapeutic.

Since the twelfth century the term '*kabbalah*' ('received') has denoted an aspect of Judaism that blends mystical practice with textual study. The *kabbalah* has generated an extensive body of literature, most notably the thirteenth-century *Zohar*, a series of complex books – part Bible commentary, part spiritual adventure story – that claim that events on earth are intimately related to those in divine realms, and that observing commandments brings harmony to both of these worlds alike.[25] Lurianic Kabbalah, named after Isaac Luria (1534–72), dominated Ashkenazi Judaism in the early modern period. Luria's work, which argued for a correlation between different aspects of the human soul and the *sefirot* or divine powers (see Chapter 5), influenced the Baal Shem Tov, whose career and significance for Hasidic Judaism was described in Chapter 3. However, while popular Hasidic literature uses *kabbalistic* terminology, the rise of the *tzaddik* as intermediary between God and his followers, helped foster the current situation in which serious *kabbalah* study is often confined to a particular *tzaddik* and his close circle.[26]

Various factors have combined to give *kabbalah* a prominent place within twenty-first-century Western discourses on religion. In the nineteenth and early twentieth centuries, *kabbalah* was one of several 'exotic' traditions referenced, but not always seriously engaged, by European spiritualists, occultists and psychologists, including Jung.[27] *Kabbalistic* concepts were also repackaged for a general Jewish and Christian readership in Hasidic stories and sayings collected by progressive Jews like Martin Buber, Arthur Green and Abraham Joshua Heschel. Heschel's teachings in turn influenced the Renewal movement, whose *Jewish Catalog* further popularized aspects of Jewish mystical tradition. More recently, the perceived appeal of *kabbalah* to spiritual seekers has led to its use in outreach work, especially by Lubavitch and Bratslav Hasidim (worldwide movements originating in Lyubavichi, western Russia and Bratslav, Ukraine respectively). The most high profile example of such activity is the Kabbalah Centre, an international organization headed by Philip S. and Karen Berg, who seek to instruct Jews and non-Jews alike.[28] Funded by donations, the proceeds from classes and the sales of books, water and red string amulets, the Centre promotes itself extensively via the internet and telemarketing and has attracted some high profile followers including Britney Spears, Demi Moore and Madonna. The latter's music videos and stage shows have, in recent years, drawn extensively on Judaism and *kabbalah*. In the video for her 2002 song 'Die Another Day', Madonna wears *tefillin*; the 72 names of God and the Tree of Life, a *kabbalistic* map of creation, were repeatedly projected on a screen behind her during live performances. Unlike traditional *kabbalah*, whose study was formally restricted to married observant males aged 40 or above, the Kabbalah Centre offers its teachings to all married and unmarried men and women. But as students progress, they are expected to adopt Orthodox-style observances.[29] The Bergs' personal wealth, the health claims made for Kabbalah Water, and the practice of encouraging non-Jews and Jews to participate in religious rituals together, has attracted fierce criticism, particularly from Orthodox authorities.

Despite the contemporary visibility of *kabbalah*, it often receives scant coverage in introductory textbooks and courses. To a degree, this reflects the legacy of *Wissenschaft des Judentums*. For Graetz and his peers, *kabbalah*, and mysticism generally, was the preserve of the poor and ignorant, and had no place in a modern, European – or more specifically, German – Judaism. Rejecting this approach as sterile and partial on the grounds that it neglected the crucial experiential and non-rational aspects of Judaism, Gershom Scholem (1897–1982) devoted his career to the academic study of mysticism. In his efforts to prove its place at the heart of both Judaism and Jewish Studies, Scholem over-systematized his materials, which included many manuscripts of unclear provenance. Like other scholars of religion at the time, he emphasized *kabbalah*'s contemplative-theological dimensions over its ritual, practical ones. He also neglected contemporary *kabbalistic* thinkers such as Abraham Isaac Kook (see Chapter 7). Conceptually, Scholem's tendency to explain each new phase in the 'evolution' of mysticism with reference to external social conditions and events also seems less secure today than it did 50 years ago, perhaps reflecting the declining influence of Darwinian paradigms on academic discourse in the study of religions. Nevertheless, Scholem's work, particularly his *Major Trends in Jewish Mysticism* (1946) delineated a new field and continues to be influential in this growing sub-field within the study of Judaism.[30]

5

Beliefs

Approaching belief

For the most part, religious Jews have not traditionally produced creeds or formalized, definitional statements of belief. Neither the *Shema*, nor later formulations such as Maimonides' Thirteen Principles has historically functioned as a test of religious identity or orthodoxy. This contrasts markedly with other religions addressed in the *Critical Issues* series, particularly Christianity, whose comparative emphasis on creeds and confessions provides a starting point for Smart's writing on the doctrinal and philosophical dimension.[1] It is sometimes suggested that the explicit discussion of belief has not been the main, or even one of the main, modes of Jewish religious expression because Judaism lacks a central body with the ability to formulate and impose doctrines. This is, at best, an incomplete explanation. Any religion could have been developed differently, structured around other concerns. Data about the application of the sanctions that *were – are*, in some Orthodox circles – previously available to rabbinic authorities, like the *herem* or ban (a kind of exclusion or shunning) shows that these were principally used to enforce behavioural norms. Beliefs were generally only a factor when they were thought likely to have problematic practical consequences. In other words, ortho*praxy* – right *action*, keeping the *mitzvot* – was more important than assent to particular doctrines.[2]

This does not mean that belief is irrelevant in Judaism – only that it is articulated and functions differently than in Christianity, say. While the *Tanakh* and Talmud do not offer systematic theologies, they contain assertions about God's nature and activities, as do prayer books and other religious writings. In this respect the careers of Maimonides who, in addition to his role as community leader and legal decision maker, was a philosopher, and of Joseph Karo, who was a lawyer and a *kabbalist* who believed he was inspired by the *shekhinah* (divine presence) in the guise of a heavenly guide or *maggid*, are emblematic of a creative tension within rabbinic Judaism between the emphasis on the *halakhic* system as a set of behavioural norms, and the conceptualizing of that system as the expression of a unique relationship between God and the Jewish people.

While Jewish theology is often implicit, manifest in the lived faith of communities and individuals rather than in abstract treatises, there are examples of instances in which debate around belief has been significant for the formation of religious identities and institutions. In the nineteenth century, some German reformers began holding Confirmation ceremonies at which young boys answered questions on belief and recited the Ten Commandments and Maimonides' Thirteen Principles. This catechetical approach, influenced by Protestant Christianity, reflected a desire to downplay Jewish distinctiveness in the early period of emancipation by reconceptualizing Judaism as a confession. More recently, British Orthodox rabbi Louis Jacobs published a book (first edition 1957; revised in 1961 and 1965) in which he argued that the *Tanakh* and Talmud were not the immaculate products of divine dictation, but partly human documents recording 'the divine-human encounter in the history of our ancestors, in which they reached out gropingly for God and He responded to their faltering quest'.[3] Several Orthodox leaders regarded this as an affront to belief in *Torah min ha-Shamayim* ('Torah from Heaven/God'), the revelation of the Torah to Moses at Sinai. Under pressure, Chief Rabbi Israel Brodie vetoed Jacobs' appointment as Principal of Jews' College (now the London School of Jewish Studies) and his reappointment as rabbi of the New West End Synagogue, on the grounds that his views conflicted with traditional Jewish beliefs. Practically speaking, the affair precipitated the creation of new, theologically differentiated institutions within British Judaism. Jacobs and his supporters created the now Assembly of Masorti Synagogues, while the United Synagogue (the largest Ashkenazi Orthodox umbrella organization in Britain) moved away from its centrist position, assuming a stance less tolerant of Jewish religious pluralism. The Orthodox ban on Jacobs as a preacher and teacher persisted until his death. In 2003, Chief Rabbi Jonathan Sacks and the London *Beth Din* (rabbinical court) intervened to prevent him receiving an *aliyah* – the honour of being called up to the reading of the Torah scroll during a synagogue service – during a visit to Bournemouth, on the grounds that had Jacobs recited the customary blessing, 'Our God ... who gave us the Torah of truth ...', he would have made a false statement.[4]

EXERCISE

According to *The Oxford Dictionary of the Jewish Religion*, 'Judaism does have dogmas, in the form of certain common assumptions of faith, but no doctrinal system.'[5] As you read this chapter, consider how far you agree or disagree with this statement.

Studying belief is a far from straightforward task. The consequences of particular beliefs are rarely so evident as during the 'Jacobs Affair', and are often disputed. One might review theological and philosophical writings, exploring their origins, similarities and differences, and considering how these ideas play out in particular cultures. But if, as suggested in Chapter 4, there are difficulties attached to regarding liturgies as repositories of belief or instruments of theological formation, the same must be said for theological treatises, the circulation of which is generally restricted to intellectual elites. While this holds for the study of any religion, the problem is acute in Judaism's case, given a traditional disinterest in defining and defending doctrines.

At the micro level, we can only establish what actual people believe by asking them, but this also presents challenges. Contextual factors influence the ways in which beliefs are articulated, validating some expressions and de-legitimating others. Methodological decisions also affect research outcomes. For example, the Guttman Report's data was gathered from Hebrew-speakers, thereby under-representing the views of recently arrived and largely secularized immigrants from the former Soviet Union. It also largely excluded *kibbutz* residents and responses collected from settlers, religious Zionists living on land captured by Israel in 1967 during the Six Day War. The questionnaire asked for respondents' agreement with, or rejection, of propositions including 'The Torah was given to Moses on Mount Sinai' and 'There is a world-to-come'.[6] But the meanings of concepts like 'God' or 'world-to-come' can vary to the point of idiosyncrasy – and respondents do not have to answer truthfully. Consequently, psychologists of religion often rely on what respondents *do* to confirm hunches about their credibility.[7] This again underscores the importance of methodological pluralism in religious studies.

God and the Jews

'When God began to create heaven and earth ...' (Gen. 1.1): the first line of the *Tanakh* takes for granted the existence of a God. Like the passages from

Judges discussed in Chapter 3, early Jewish literature tends to emphasize the need for *belief in* in the sense of *reliance on* God, rather than *belief that* he exists. For the writer of the Psalms, the fool who thinks that 'There is no God', is not an atheist but someone who believes that 'God does not care' (Ps. 53.2).

The Hebrew term used to express the concept of belief is *emunah* or 'trust'. The biblical character Abraham, whose obedience to God made him ready to undertake implausible and painful tasks, including the near-sacrifice of Isaac, his son (Gen. 22.1–19), is popularly regarded as a model of faithfulness. He is also presented as a patriarch, a father-founder of the Hebrew (or Israelite or Jewish) people, party to a covenant (*berit*) with God symbolized by male circumcision and renewed with the whole people at Sinai, so that they might become 'a holy nation' (Exod. 19.6).

Most writers stress the idea that God's choosing the Jews was not founded on any superiority on their part, spiritual or otherwise: in the Bible, the covenant's terms confer extensive duties (for example, Deut. 6.1-11.32), which they are depicted as regularly failing to honour. Alternative views were advanced by philosopher-poet Judah ha-Levi (1075–1141), who argued that Jews possessed unique spiritual capacities; and, in the kabbalistic idea that Jewish souls yearn for God, are therefore particularly disposed to keep the *mitzvot*, and having done so for many centuries, have cultivated superior qualities. Whichever of these religious positions is taken, Jewish chosenness is not traditionally held to imply lack of divine interest in or power over other peoples. The *Tanakh*, especially *Nevi'im* (Prophets) ridicules those who rely on 'dumb idols' (Habakkuk 2.18). It also describes Israel as 'a light of nations' (Isa. 49.6): in witnessing God's dealings with the Jews, other peoples have the opportunity to know God's sovereignty.

Medieval Rabbinic Jewish contacts with Karaite and Muslim philosophers, and through them, with Greek philosophical tradition, stimulated the development of new theological emphases. Maimonides strove to demonstrate that anthropomorphic passages in the *Tanakh* and Talmud, which describe God as possessing human-like physical and psychological qualities, were metaphorical and did not contradict philosophical understandings of God as an unchanging unity beyond the realms of time and space. In his commentary on the *Mishnah*, he listed Thirteen Principles, affirmation of which he regarded as a positive obligation for all Jews who desired a share in the World-to-Come or afterlife.[8] The first five of these assert that God is creator, is one, is incorporeal, is eternal and is the only being worthy of worship.

This religious rationalism continues to occupy a visible place within Judaism. Maimonides' principles appear in Orthodox prayer books, in prose form (the *Ani Ma'amin*, often recited at the end of morning prayers) and as the *Yigdal*, a fourteenth-century hymn. However, later theological writings and popular piety have also revived and maintained ideas about a more personal deity with whom it is possible to enter into a relationship akin to those between human beings. Kabbalists developed increasingly elaborate mythological-theological systems. Like Maimonides, they conceived of an infinite and perfect entity, beyond description, and only referable to in negative terms as *ein sof*, translatable as 'without end' or 'holy nothingness'. Drawing on biblical and rabbinic terms and concepts, however, they also held that there were ten *sefirot* or emanations through which God was manifest in the universe. In the Bible, the names for these – *keter* (crown), *hokhmah* (wisdom), *binah* (discernment), *hesed* (loving mercy), *din* (judgement), *tiferet* (beauty), *nezah* (endurance), *hod* (majesty), *yesod* (foundation) and *shekhinah* (divine presence) – are descriptions of God's attributes, but in *kabbalistic* thought the *sefirot* are typically (Jewish mysticism exhibits a high degree of internal diversity) regarded as quasi-separate entities.

Just as Maimonides sought to reconcile Judaism with Arabic and Greek concepts, so various modern writers have sought to articulate Jewish beliefs in ways that cohere with Enlightenment ideas. The contents of the Platform statements illustrate the extent to which a lively discussion of belief has been maintained within Reform Judaism (or at least, within its rabbinate). More so than Orthodoxy, Reform has acknowledged that people conceive of the 'God-idea', as the 1885 Pittsburgh Platform phrased it, in different ways, and that traditional conceptions of God, and of the relationship between God and the Jews, have been challenged by events like the Holocaust. Unlike Conservativism and Reconstructionism, it has not seen these factors as reasons to downplay the place of belief and theology in Judaism. For example, in the wake of the Holocaust Ignaz Maybaum (1897–1976) reworked ideas about chosenness, arguing that a Jewish mission to advance the social and ethical condition of humanity was furthered not just through specific activities but by Jewish existence *per se*:

> The conception of the Jewish mission calls up on the Jew to work together with all the noble pioneers who help mankind to make progress. Obeying this call the Jew experiences happiness; he is filled with the satisfaction of a man who is creative in the field of human endeavour and glory.[9]
>
> We Jews are servants of God, reminding the world of God not merely by what we think and do but by being on the spot, by existing as Jews in this world of the Gentiles [non-Jews].[10]

Maybaum was very much a thinker of his time, but these passages exemplify a wider trend away from the formulation of proofs for the existence of God and/or enumeration of divine attributes, towards an interest in the relationship between God, Jews and the world. Some of these dialogically-oriented writings have appealed to non-Jewish readers as much as (and, in some instances, more than) they have to Jewish ones: in the second half of the twentieth-century authors like Martin Buber (1878–1965) and Emmanuel Levinas (1906–1995) acquired the status of public intellectuals in some Western countries.

The language used to describe God remains a source of considerable debate. Recent Reform liturgies have variously attempted gender neutrality by removing references to God as 'He', by alternating 'He' with 'She', or by re-assessing conventional descriptions of God's activity. Such moves reflect a desire to limit the use of anthropomorphisms which, if not recognized as metaphors, might result in prohibited idolatrous worship (Exod. 20.4–5) and compromise the monotheism that, classically, Reform has presented as central to Judaism. (See Chapter 2 on Kohler's description of Judaism's essence.) They also seek to counteract the privileging of the male gender that can attach to understandings of God as father (Jer. 3.19), king (Ps. 10.16) or warrior (Exod. 15.3). For Judith Plaskow, such language reflects and sustains patriarchy, a system operated by and in favour of men. If it was once conducive of (male) religious experience, it is today 'morally suspect and disturbing'.[11] 'Conversely, as new feminist metaphors for God begin to emerge out of a Jewish community already in the process of change, these metaphors support further change in a feminist direction'.[12] Orthodox perspectives value continuity or fixity in public, communal prayer. Commitment to the latter, often yoked to Moses Sofer's (1753–1839) declaration that 'anything new is forbidden on the authority of the Torah',[13] precludes the change Plaskow advocates. Orthodox apologists defend the *status quo* by emphasizing that biblical texts sometimes depict God in feminine terms (Isa. 42.14; 66.13), that several *sefirot* are female and that innovation in religious language inappropriately emphasizes the 'gender' of a God whom the *Tanakh* says is revealed to Moses as '*Ehyeh-Asher-Ehyeh*' (Exod. 3.14) – 'I Am that I Am' or 'I Will Be What I Will Be'.

Judaism and evolution

Christian responses to Charles Darwin's (1809–1882) theory of evolution by natural selection are the subject of considerable popular interest in Western cultures. The rejection of evolution and advocacy of creationism – belief that the universe and everything in it was created by God, as described in the book of Genesis – is today a rallying point for conservative Christians, particularly in the United States. In contrast, views on creation and evolution have not functioned so readily as markers of Jewish religious identity or commitment: when Darwin's *The Origin of Species* appeared in London in 1859, evolution was only one of many ideas that confronted newly emancipated Jews.

In late nineteenth- and early twentieth-century Germany, evolution was used by race theorists to lend an air of scientific plausibility to antisemitism. Meanwhile, some Zionists utilized evolutionary concepts to argue that biological, as well as social and political, benefits would result from Jewish migration to Israel–Palestine. In America, Mordecai Kaplan's understanding of evolution as progressive change influenced his programme for Reconstructionist Judaism.

Christian creationists are sometimes targeted by polemicists who claim that Judaism is more open to scientific advances. But the current rightwards drift of Orthodoxy has been accompanied by the development of anti-evolutionary arguments within Judaism. In 2005, 'Zoo Rabbi' Nosson Slifkin's writings on zoology and Judaism were banned by several Haredi authorities on the grounds that they challenge the literalness, and hence the authority, of the Torah. Most religious Jews, however, integrate evolutionary discourse with the Bible, interpreting the latter as a metaphorical account of the world's origins and humanity's place within it.[14]

Revelation

Chapter 2 suggested that the term Judaism can be conceptualized as a family term, since the study of those who identify themselves as its adherents reveals both diversity and division, and overlapping, criss-crossing resemblances. As illustrated by the 'Jacobs Affair' and the rise of rabbinic authority, differing conceptions of revelation (perceptions of the act and fruits of God's communication with humanity) underpin many of the tensions between the phenomena that constitute the Judaism family.

In the Torah, God's creation of the world is associated with the speech act (Gen. 1.3), and in several passages God appears and speaks to patriarchs and prophets:

The LORD appeared to him [Isaac] and said, 'Do not go down into Egypt ...' (Gen. 26.2).

I [Amos] saw the LORD standing by the altar, and He said ... (Amos 9.1).

Although other verses query or qualify what might be meant by these terms, suggesting that 'you cannot see My face, for man may not see Me and live'

(Exod. 33.20). Standing above all, God's revelation to Moses is presented as superior to other revelations, both in content, because it is fundamental to Israel's formation (Exod. 19.5ff.), and in character:

> When a prophet of the LORD arises among you, I make Myself known to him in a vision, I speak with him in a dream. Not so with my servant Moses; he is trusted throughout My household. With him I speak mouth to mouth, plainly and not in riddles, and he beholds the likeness of the LORD (Num. 12.6–8).

By the medieval period, the Talmudic view that revelation, widely equated with prophecy, had ended in ancient times dominated (see the discussion of *Baba Metzia* 59b in Chapter 3). Mainstream Jewish cultures did not validate claims to individual, direct contact with God, preferring instead to emphasize textual study and interpretation as having replaced the lost system of Temple sacrifices as vehicles for the routinized experiencing of the *shekhinah*, God's presence. By diligently studying, a Jew could receive for himself the gift of divine teaching. Even *kabbalists* at this time tended to write commentaries and sermons, rather than accounts of personal mystical experiences – a clear example of the ways in which theological and literary conventions can structure the articulation of belief.[15]

Maimonides' Principles state that Moses is the greatest prophet, that the Torah was revealed to him by God and that it is immutable. These statements are essentialist claims about the fixed, unchanging character of Judaism's history and texts. But in reality the Principles are relational and reflect the conditions in which they were formed. In asserting Moses' superiority over all those who preceded and followed him, Maimonides, who worked in Egypt, rebutted the Islamic view that Muhammad was the greatest prophet of God, and that the divine word preserved in the Qu'ran is alone perfect and therefore superior to the humanly corrupted version given in Jewish and Christian scriptures. He also dismissed Christian claims that the *Tanakh* (for Christians, the Old Testament) had been superseded by Jesus.

Maimonides' Principles illustrate a tendency to attach increasing significance to the concept of God's revelation at Sinai. As explored in Chapter 3, authorities in Judaism have typically sought to establish their teachings as normative by formally linking themselves to this event. Drawing on early rabbinic homilies on Exod. Orthodox tradition regards the Sinai revelation as all encompassing: all possible questions and their solutions are derivable from what was given to Moses.[16] This idea is manifest in contemporary Haredi discourse on *daas Torah* ('knowledge of Torah') according to which extremely devoted Torah scholars are believed to cultivate intellectual and spiritual qualities that make them able to provide authoritative answers on all matters, even where these cannot be proven from explicit sources.

While some practitioners of Judaism have reacted against the naturalism of the Enlightenment era to the extent that assent to belief in the literal revelation of the Torah at Sinai increasingly functions as a shibboleth of Orthodoxy, others conceive of revelation non-propositionally, as a relationship between two active partners, rather than (in simple terms) one between a divine dictator and a faithfully accurate human scribe. Non-theists deny its reality completely. According to the American Reform movement's 1937 Columbus Platform, 'Revelation is a continuous process, confined to no one group and to no one age.' Rather than being confined to specific moments in the past, revelation happens whenever God reveals aspects of Godself to the world. The Torah was not revealed at Sinai but is the record of human responses to divine revelation, and as such, it is important for, but not the totality of, the Jewish dialogue with God. From this perspective, argued by German-Jewish philosopher Franz Rosenzweig (1886–1929), textual criticism of the *Tanakh* does not undermine the reality of God's revelation to the world. As Louis Jacobs, whose position approximates Rosenzweig's in this matter, put it:

> The Torah which speaks to the Jewish soul is the Torah which is now in our hands and this is so even if the Masoretic Text is not accurate in all its parts and even if the Samaritans, for example, had the better text. The person or persons who were finally responsible, those who sifted the older material and presented it to us as the Torah in its present form, are our teachers of the living Torah.[17]

In such a model, an active, context-specific human response to God is necessary for revelation to take place: 'In all the days of the year,' wrote Rosenzweig, 'Balaam's talking ass [Num. 22–24] may be a mere fairy tale, but not on the Sabbath wherein this portion is read in the synagogue, when it speaks to me out of the open Torah'.[18] While such approaches query the historicity of the biblical account of revelation, and thus its absolute authority, adherents of Reconstructionist and other non-theistic and atheistic forms of Judaism (for example, Humanistic Judaism) reject belief in a personal deity and therefore the possibility of revelation as it is understood by most Orthodox, Reform or Conservative Jews. For Kaplan's followers the Torah, and the beliefs that have developed around it, are examples of Judaic folkways that have acquired a kind of sanctity by virtue of their use as reflections and fulfilments of the needs and desires of Jewish people in specific historical and cultural circumstances. They warrant attention as valuable records of human searching and discovery, but are not the sole resource for the reconstruction of Jewish life, which must be pursued anew by each generation.

Theodicy and the Holocaust

EXERCISE

What do these verses from the *Tanakh* and the *Yigdal* (the hymn based on Maimonides' Principles) suggest about God and God's relationship with the Jews?

Know, therefore, that the LORD your God is God, the steadfast God who keeps His covenant faithfully to the thousandth generation of those who love Him and keep His commandments, but who instantly requites with destruction those who reject Him – never slow with those who reject Him but requiting them instantly (Deut. 7. 9–10).

Behold I am the LORD, the God of all flesh. Is anything too wondrous for Me? (Jer. 32.27).

O LORD, You have examined me and know me.
When I sit down or stand up You know it;
You discern my thoughts from afar.
You observe my walking and reclining,
And are familiar with all my ways (Ps. 139.1–3).

He is Master of the universe to every creature – He demonstrates His greatness and His sovereignty. He scrutinizes and knows our hiddenmost secrets – He perceives a matter's outcome at its inception … He recompenses man with kindness according to his deed – He places evil on the wicked according to his wickedness. (*Yigdal*)

Philosophically speaking, Judaism's adherents face challenges if they seek to reconcile the experience of evil with belief in an all powerful, all knowing, benevolent God. Numerous biblical texts, and following them, Maimonides, stress the notion that God rewards those who keep the *mitzvot* and punishes transgressors, a theme reiterated liturgically at *Rosh ha-Shanah* and *Yom Kippur*. However, other texts highlight the challenges that innocent or disproportionate suffering and the prosperity of wrongdoers pose to this view. Job rejects attempts to attribute suffering to sin, or to otherwise explain it: 'fear of [trust in] the Lord is wisdom' (Job 28.28).

Two Talmudic stories of Rabbi Akiva's death (c. 135 CE) illustrate additional emphases in post-biblical, rabbinic theodicy. In the first, Moses travels through time to visit Akiva in his academy:

Moses said, 'Lord of the universe, You have shown me his *Torah* [Akiva's teaching] – now show me his reward.' 'Turn around,' said God. Moses turned around and saw Rabbi Akiva's flesh being weighed out in a meat market. 'Lord of the universe,' Moses cried out in protest, 'such Torah, and such its reward?' God replied, 'Be silent – thus has it come to My mind' *(Menahot 29b)*.

The second describes Akiva's own response to suffering:

Once the evil kingdom [Rome] decreed that the Jews may not engage in Torah study. Pappus ben Yehudah found Rabbi Akiva teaching Torah in public to large groups. He said to him, 'Akiva, are you not afraid of the authorities?'… When the Romans took Rabbi Akiva to execute him, it was time for the reading of the *shema*. They were tearing his flesh with iron combs, and he was reciting the *shema*. His students said to him, 'Master, must one go so far?' He said to them, 'All my life I was troubled by the verse *'With all your soul,'* [Deut. 6:5] which I understood as 'even if God takes your soul,' and I wondered about when I would have the opportunity to fulfil it? Now that I have the opportunity, shall I not fulfil it? *(Berakhot 61b)*.

The longer extract presents Akiva's death as the fulfilment of a *mitzvah* and an expression of love for God – an example of *Kiddush ha-Shem* (sanctification of [God's] name) or martyrdom, while also hinting at an afterlife. The other appeals to mystery.

Such traditional theodicies have come under pressure in the aftermath of the Holocaust, the persecution and murder of Jews in a programme planned and executed by the Nazis and their allies during the Second World War. This is partly because of the magnitude of suffering: upwards of six million people died, among them one and a half million children. Of these, about half were gassed and about half were beaten to death, shot, starved or died of disease. Another factor is the dehumanizing treatment of the victims, including forced settlement in ghettos and deportation to concentration and extermination camps; slave labour; and the removal of personal effects and body parts such as dental fillings and hair. Existing divisions within modern Judaism have also made it impossible for any single Holocaust theodicy to gain universal acceptance.

Some early theodicies invoked the idea of *mi-penei hata'einu* ('because of our sins', a phrase used liturgically to explain the Temple's destruction). For some Haredim dismayed by the changing character of Judaism in modernity, assimilation to non-Jewish norms, exemplified by religious reform and Zionism, was the sin that invited divine wrath upon European Jewry. In this worldview, Nazism's origin in Germany – the engine-house of Reform Judaism – is far from coincidental. The deaths of carefully observant Jews in the Holocaust were martyrdoms.

This view, particularly associated with *Satmar rebbe* Yoel Teitelbaum (1887–1979) still circulates, but popular Haredi literature – perhaps because such views are regarded as questionable on the grounds of reason or taste – increasingly associates faithfulness with an absence of theological questioning:

> we need not attempt to explain it [the Holocaust] at all. Our staunch faith in the Creator and Master of the Universe also permits us not to understand ... There is no answer ... because God does not wish there to be an answer.[19]

Like the secular and Reform Jews who were Teitelbaum's targets, most present day Haredi and modern Orthodox authorities reject the *mi-penei hata'einu* explanation for the Holocaust. Eliezer Berkovits (1908–1992) advanced a version of what is often, in the philosophy of religion, termed the 'Free Will' theodicy, arguing that evil was possible because God withdrew from the world in order to grant humanity the freedom to enter into a genuine relationship with him. Berkovits claimed a precedent for this view in the biblical concept, *hester panim*, the mysterious 'hiding of the divine face' (Deut. 31.17).

Maybaum also sought to construct a biblically rooted account. For him, the Holocaust was a terrible event that brought to an end Jewish 'medievalism'. Postwar, Jews could newly engage Western civilization, which Maybaum believed would function as the vehicle for humanity to live as God intended, in 'justice, kindness, freedom and peace'.[20] In this sense, the Holocaust might be seen as part of a divine plan and Hitler, as a modern Nebuchadnezzar, whom God describes as 'my servant' in Isa. 52.13. The suggestion that God somehow 'used' Hitler is a difficult one for most Jews (and for many non-Jews), and from an Orthodox perspective Maybaum's equation of a *halakhic* life with medievalism is objectionable. Maybaum's theodicy is also strikingly Eurocentric, equating the West with progress and the East with the past.

For Richard Rubenstein (b. 1924) the logic of Jewish theology similarly points to the conclusion that the Nazis were instruments of God's will. However, he regards such views as untenable, choosing instead to reject belief in an omnipotent God who is active in history and has a covenant with the Jews. Auschwitz marks the 'death of God', a position often interpreted as atheism, although Rubenstein has repeatedly emphasized that he understands the death in sociological or cultural terms (death of the sense or awareness of God) and that 'we shall never know whether it is more than that'.[21]

Rubenstein described God after Auschwitz as 'nothingness'. In this respect, his work is representative of a *kabbalistic* turn in contemporary Jewish theological writings. According to Lurianic Kabbalah, a cosmic tragedy at the beginning of time led to evil's presence in the world. In order to make space for creation, the *ein sof* (holy nothingness) contracted or concentrated itself, and projected light outwards through vessels or vehicles into the vacated space in order to form the universe. The vessels were, however, unable to contain the holy light and shattered. As a result, God and creation are fractured. Evil occurs because of the resulting disruption in the flow of divine blessing to the world. By performing *mitzvot*, Jews can help to reunite the divine shards or sparks with their source, an act of restoration or reparation known as *tikkun*. They can do this because, as human beings, they are created in the divine image, and therefore 'mirror' God.

These ideas have found new currency post-Holocaust. On the one hand, the idea of a fractured, 'exiled' divinity obviates the philosophical problems attached to omnipotence; on the other hand, positive value is attached to human activity in the face of evil. Spiritualizing and secularizing popularizations of the concept of *tikkun* are now widespread. It is used, for example, by youth and community groups, particularly those linked to progressive religious movements, as a synonym for social justice and ecological activism. In relation to the Holocaust, the views of philosopher Emil Fackenheim (1916–2003) who eschewed theodicy, regarding survival as a new *mitzvah* and the State of Israel as a work of *tikkun* that could heal the Jewish people, have enjoyed greater levels of acceptance than those of Rubenstein, et al. This, and the findings of surveys like the Guttman report (which seems to indicate that Israeli Jews are likely to express belief in God, but are less willing to assent to the idea that non-observance of *mitzvot* invites punishment on oneself and others)[22] suggests that articulating an appropriate practical response to the Holocaust generally takes priority over the search for philosophical or theological understanding.

The future

As noted before, Maimonides claimed that Jews who did not assent to the Thirteen Principles had no share in the World-to-Come (*olam ha-ba*). This concept, not found in the *Tanakh*, is articulated in rabbinic literature, including the *Mishnah* and Talmud, where life in the present age is described as anticipating a glorious future: '*olam ha-zeh* [this world] is like an antechamber to *olam ha-ba*. Prepare yourself in the antechamber so that you may enter the palace' (*m.Avot* 4.21–22).

The forward-looking thrust of Maimonides' list is underscored by the subject of the two final Principles, belief in a coming messiah ('anointed [one]') and bodily resurrection. Belief in a messiah who will restore the Jewish people and usher in an age of godly peace has been the subject of much interest, scholarly and otherwise. Most obviously, Christianity appropriated Judaism's scriptures and reinterpreted them as referring to its founder-leader, Jesus of Nazareth.[23] Christian belief that Jesus was the messiah (the word 'Christ' is derived from *Christos*, the Greek translation of the Hebrew *mashiah*) whose appearance on earth to save the world from sin was foretold in the *Tanakh* has often led Christians and others to assume that messianic expectation was, and is, a significant feature of Judaism.

In fact, there is little evidence that messianic expectation was prominent within first-century Judaism. In the Hebrew Bible, 'messiah' refers to kings (especially those of the Davidic dynasty, described in the books of Samuel and Chronicles), priests and objects that are anointed with oil as a mark of their being dedicated for godly use. Generally, such figures are associated with the present, not the future, and they are rarely idealized (see Chapter 3 on kingship). The earliest written references to a future king-messiah are in the *Psalms of Solomon*. This collection of texts, which religious Jews today do not regard as religious scripture, dates from the period after the Maccabean revolt; its contents are critical of the Hasmonean regime's authority claims and look forward to a future Davidic king who will restore correct socio-religious order in Israel (17.21–25). In other words, this future hope constitutes a returning to an idealized past, an age when, according to the *Tanakh*, Israel was able to overcome her enemies and worship God in the Jerusalem Temple. Even so, like Maimonides, the *Psalms of Solomon*'s authors regard the messiah as a human being, rather than a divine or miracle-working figure.

According to the Jerusalem Talmud (*Ta'anit* 4.5, 68d) Akiva, considered to be one of the founders of rabbinic Judaism, proclaimed the leader of the Jewish revolt against Rome (132–135 CE) Simon bar Kokhba, to be the messiah. The revolt's disastrous consequences, which included the expulsion of Jews from Jerusalem, deteriorating relations with Christians and Akiva's own martyrdom, encouraged further new emphases in rabbinic thinking. The messiah's arrival was increasingly described as following a period of great suffering, and, as rabbinic authority developed, was expected to unfold in accordance with the *mitzvot*:

In the footsteps of the Messiah, arrogance will increase; prices will rise; grapes will be abundant but wine will be costly; the government will turn into heresy; and there will be no reproach … (*Sotah* 9.15).

Were Israel to observe two Sabbaths punctiliously, they would be redeemed immediately (*Shabbat* 118b).

He [the Messiah] will not arrive on the Sabbath, since that would require people to violate the Sabbath in welcoming him (*Pesahim* 13a).

Elijah [the prophet whose return is believed to herald the messianic age] will arrive no later in the week than Thursday, leaving room for the Messiah to arrive by Friday (Jerusalem Talmud *Pesahim* 3.6).

Despite its frequent downplaying by rabbinic authorities, messianism is a recurring feature in festivals and liturgy, and has periodically assumed a central place within Judaism. For example, the Talmud suggests that, like sexual intercourse and a sunny day, the Sabbath is a foretaste of the messianic age and the World-to-Come (*Berakhot* 57b), while since medieval times, it has been customary to have a chair for the messianic figure Elijah at circumcision ceremonies, and a cup for him at the *seder*.[24] In eighth-century Persia (Iran), Abu 'Issa Al-Isfahani led a revolt against the Abbasid caliphate, claiming that to be the forerunner of the messiah. In the twelfth century, messianic claimant David Alroy attempted to lead Jews from Iraq to Jerusalem; Chapter 3 intro-duced Shabbetai Zvi, who attracted the support of Jews across the Middle East and Europe in the seventeenth century. Most recently, disagreements concerning the late *rebbe*, Menahem Mendel Schneerson (1902–1994), have led to a rift in Lubavitch Hasidism. Believing the Holocaust to be the time of trial that presaged redemption, Schneerson encouraged and organized his followers, particularly young rabbis and their wives, to undertake a vast programme of *kiruv*, or 'bringing close'. By encouraging non-observant Jews to adopt ten religious observances (including charitable giving, fixing a *mezuzah*, lighting *Shabbat* candles, keeping a *kosher* kitchen and observing laws of family purity), he aimed to reconstruct a form of Jewish life that had been devas-tated during the war, and also to prepare for, and hasten, the advent of the messiah. During the final years of his life, however, speculation increased that Schneerson himself was the messiah. Since his death, many Lubavitch Jews have rejected this idea, or at least its public discussion. Others continue to publicize their belief, variously disputing that Schneerson died – and therefore refusing to visit his grave or commemorate his *yahrzeit* (the anniversary of his death) – or accepting Schneerson's death, but arguing that he will return once his true messianic identity is universally recognized. Such developments are strongly opposed by other Orthodox and non-Orthodox movements and individuals including David Berger, who has written extensively on the topic.[25]

From a religious studies' viewpoint, the dynamics of the Schneerson case markedly resemble those of other messianic movements. For example, some followers of Abu 'Issa and Alroy continued to assert his messiahship after his death, while a small group in Turkey, the Dönmeh, still believes that neither Shabbetai Zvi's conversion to Islam nor his death has invalidated his messiahship. Michal Kravel-Tovi has written recently on Lubavitch messianists' rational, emotional and ritual responses to what might be deemed the failure of their messianic expectations, locating this in relation to other similar phenomena in the history of religions.[26] Within the field of Jewish studies, Berger, Avrum Ehrlich and others have specifically suggested parallels between the claims of early Christians about Jesus' messiahship and Hasidic assertions that the messiah of Jewish religious tradition will experience death, burial and resurrection before returning to complete his mission.[27] Similarities between the content of Lubavitch and first-century Christian messianism, and the means by which their adherents seek to disseminate their message, have also attracted the interest of those who study Christian origins, such as Joel Marcus.[28]

The Schneerson case is not typical of modern Judaism. Orthodoxy generally retains belief in a personal messiah while also emphasizing caution over attempts to identify signs of his imminence. Early Reformers revised their liturgies to reflect a rejection of the concept of a future king, with its strong nationalistic and particularistic overtones, in favour of hope for a messianic age of peace and justice. While the authors of the 1885 Pittsburgh Platform professed to identify the approaching realization of that hope, the 1999 Pittsburgh Principles expresses the idea that Reform Jews are partners with God in *tikkun olam*, and as such help to bring closer a messianic age of peace, freedom and justice. Jews affiliated to Reform Judaism are also more likely than Orthodox and Conservative affiliates to explicitly reject aspects of traditional belief concerning post-mortem existence. While liturgical assent to belief in a bodily resurrection continues to be a defining feature of Orthodoxy, Conservative and Reform liturgies are more open-ended. Many earlier Reform prayer books replaced references to God as reviver of the dead with descriptions of God as a lifegiver, and the Columbus Platform speaks of the immortality of the human 'spirit', but the recent American Reform *siddur* is closer to the Conservative position in offering worshippers the possibility of choosing to use the traditional formula. It is hard to judge, however, whether this reflects a shift in belief amongst Reform Jews, a nostalgia for older liturgical forms, or new metaphorical approaches to religious language about restoration.

Despite the debates that such developments have engendered, discussion of the post-mortem fate of individuals, or of Jews or humanity collectively, is not a prominent feature of Judaism. Traditional sanctions against the taking of life (including non-therapeutic abortion and euthanasia), and stories in which pious figures like the Vilna Gaon (1727–1790, a leading *halakhist* and opponent of early Hasidism) are held to have wept on their deathbeds because they will no longer be able to observe the *mitzvot*, suggest that, although one's existence in an afterlife has popularly been described as a 'reward', it nevertheless lacks the possibilities for right action that are offered in the here-and-now.

Sigmund Freud and Judaism

Sigmund Freud's (1856–1939) ideas are part of the culture created by Jews, but should they be studied as an aspect of Judaism? Reflecting on his development of the psychoanalytical approach to human behaviour and psychology, Freud suggested that,

> because I was a Jew I found myself free from many prejudices which restricted others in the use of their intellect; and as a Jew I was prepared to join the Opposition and to do without agreement with the 'compact majority'.[30]

In *Moses and Monotheism*, Freud used psychoanalytical theory to generate the hypothesis that Judaism originated in the ancient Israelites' guilt at having killed Moses, an Egyptian priest who tried to propagate monotheism. In this respect, Freud's work could be said to manifest two of the family resemblances associated with Judaism in Chapter 2 (Jewish self-identification; engagement with textual tradition).

However, Freud pathologized the third resemblance, religious practice, likening it to obsessive behaviour. In both instances, one acts in a highly circumscribed manner, for no obvious end. For Freud, God is a fantasy arising from the desire for a father figure who will protect us from life's cruelties. Once religion's illusory character is recognized, it can be abandoned in favour of rational, scientific thinking.

Although Freud's claim to be 'completely estranged from the religion of his father' was exaggerated,[29] his scholarship was more obviously influenced by secular and Christian writings, including those of James Frazer and William Robertson Smith on the origin and function of religious ritual in ancient societies. Today, adherents of Humanistic Judaism are amongst those who understand themselves as Freud's successors, but this does not mean that Freudian psychoanalysis may itself be accurately termed 'Judaism'.

6

Gender

Gender emerged as a critical concept in the 1960s amidst efforts to distinguish the biological (or 'sex') differences between women and men from
the social practices and meanings ('gender') attached to those differences.
Although this binary model remains a popular starting point for analysis, it
has subsequently been challenged and modified. Understanding sex as a
set of fixed biological differences can lead to heterosexism, a denigration
of homosexual, bisexual and transgendered people on the basis that their
feelings and behaviours are somehow 'unnatural'. It is also simplistic, since it
is impossible to experience biology outside the realm of culture. In Judaism's
case, male circumcision[1], cutting the foreskin from the penis, is a good illustration of how human bodies are affected by cultural practices and processes.
Other examples include the practice amongst some Orthodox Jewish women
of covering the hair after marriage (or shaving it off, in the case of *Satmar*
women) and numerous *halakhot* on dress.

Critical analysis of the gendering of women and men has potentially far
reaching implications for the study of religions. Gender-aware studies were
first advocated by feminists seeking to expose and overturn unjust discrimination between men and women. But men, too, have been in some senses
'invisible' in past scholarship:

> Studies which are routinely about men, in that men constitute the acknowl-
> edged and unacknowledged subjects, are not necessarily about men in a
> more complex, more problematized, sociological sense. They … are rarely
> about men in the sense that the researchers believe that such studies
> might make any contribution to the sociology of gender or the critical
> understanding of men and masculinities.[2]

From this perspective, as the dominant gender, men's experiences have been
naturalized and placed beyond the realm of critical scrutiny, with the result

that our understanding of both men's and women's experiences is compromised. Yet many scholars in the field acknowledge fears that studies of men and masculinities may, in the context of academic and wider cultures shaped by patriarchy, reinforce older patterns of gender inequality and male power.[3] To combat this possibility, researchers attempt to disrupt and question existing gender roles and relations.

This type of approach to Jewish masculinities has been adopted by Daniel Boyarin. Boyarin's work takes a cue from a story told to the young Sigmund Freud by his father,

> ... 'When I was a young man', he said, 'I went for a walk one Saturday in the streets of your birthplace; I was well dressed, and had a new fur cap on my head. A Christian came up to me and shouted: 'Jew! get off the pavement!'. 'And what did you do?' I asked. 'I went to the roadway and picked up my cap,' was his quiet reply. This struck me as unheroic conduct.[4]

The story can be read autobiographically and historiographically.[5] As a religious man – the fine clothes and hat may be those worn on *Shabbat* and other festivals by Hasidic men (see Fig. 2.1) – oriented towards study, prayer and domesticity, Freud's father represents a pre-modern Jewish ideal. In some such communities, men combined religious study with housework and women worked to support their piety, as reported by the children of late nineteenth-century Jewish migrants to Britain:

> Interviewees [born in Manchester, between 1890 and 1910] sometimes refer to their fathers as dreamy and remote, lacking in practicality, while their mothers appear as resourceful, businesslike and, often, assertive.[6]

But for Sigmund Freud's own generation, raised in the context of modernity, such norms had been overturned and replaced by alternative paradigms emphasizing autonomy, independence and even ruthlessness as hallmarks of masculinity.[7] For Boyarin, these models are drawn from non-Jewish ideals, although the work of Ann Oakley, who argues that in Britain the gendering of public/economic and private/domestic as male and female spaces is a comparatively recent development, suggests their emergence within Judaism may lie in the profound social and political consequences of the industrial revolution, rather than in encounter with non-Jewish values *per se*.[8]

Notwithstanding the contributions of Boyarin and others, much scholarship continues largely to elide 'gender' into 'women's issues'. This was true of Smart's work and of many Judaism textbooks.[9] Chryssides and Geaves' recent textbook on the study of religions also takes this approach, which may perpetuate the problematic idea that religions are essentially gender-neutral.[10]

Viewed more neutrally, it is also unsurprising given gender studies' origins in the problematization of women's position in history and culture.

EXERCISE

'What we describe as "religious studies" is really the study of men's experiences of religion.' Consider, with reference to your own study of Judaism, how far you agree or disagree with this statement.

Studying Judaism, studying gender

Beruriah

Uniquely in early rabbinic literature, Beruriah (second century CE), the wife of Akiva's pupil Rabbi Meir, is presented in the Talmud as intellectually and spiritually superior to her male contemporaries. When her sons die on the eve of the Sabbath, she conceals the fact from Meir, so as not to detract from his enjoyment of the festival, which the Talmudic authors regarded as religiously mandated. Her views on legal questions are on several occasions accepted as authoritative. But the Talmud also refers to Meir fleeing because of 'Beruriah's deed'. Medieval commentator Rashi (1040–1105) explained the remark as follows:

> Some say it is because of the story of Beruria: Because she once made fun of the saying of the sages: "Women are weak-minded." [*Shabbat* 33b]. R. Meir said to her: "By your life, you will end up admitting [the truth of] their words." He then commanded one of his students to seduce her for the purpose of sinning. The student enticed her for many days until she submitted and when she found out, she strangled herself. Rabbi Meir then left Babylon out of shame (*Avodah Zarah* 18b).

EXERCISE

How might this story be interpreted? How are Beruriah and Meir represented? Does Rashi's comment reinforce or challenge a traditional view that women should be discouraged from studying the Torah?

For the most part, women and men are regarded as being obligated to keep the same *mitzvot*, but the Talmud lists a number from which women are exempted (*Kiddushim* 29a). Referred to as 'positive, time-bound command-ments' – instructions to do something at a specific time – these include many festival *mitzvot* (living in a *sukkah*; raising up the *lulav*, a collection of four plant species, on *Shavuot*) and others that attach to specific times of the day or week (reciting the *Shema*; wearing *tefillin* and *tzitzit*). It is partly on the basis of the exemption to perform specific prayers at specific times that in Orthodox Judaism men alone may count towards a *minyan*.

Many positive time-bound commandments relate to public, corporate rituals, with the result that religious studies approaches focusing only on such readily identifiable and observable phenomena tend to neglect aspects of female religiosity, and therefore of Judaism. At the same time, the majority of authoritative textual sources are written by and about men. Like Beruriah, the women who appear in them are objects of male discourse: the responsum in Chapter 3, for example, does not reveal how the unnamed widow reacted to Maimonides' judgement, or how she felt about one of the factors informing his decision; namely, that with few exceptions women are ineligible to serve as witnesses in a religious court.

Drawing on the ideas of Paul Ricoeur, New Testament scholar Elisabeth Schüssler Fiorenza has modelled a 'hermeneutics of suspicion' which does not presuppose the authority or truth of a scriptural source but assumes its androcen-trism, and 'investigate[s] *how and why* the text constructs ... women as it does'.[11] Schüssler Fiorenza identifies as a Catholic, but her approach has influenced confes-sional and non-confessional work on religious texts. Read suspiciously, Beruriah's story reinforces the view that women are innately unsuited to Torah study. Her pride ends in tragedy; no amount of learning can overcome her female nature. This stance finds echoes in the arguments of contemporary Orthodox opponents of the training of women as *halakhic* authorities, which appeal to psychological research into the differences between men's and women's thought-processes.[12] Finally, the textual tradition on Beruriah hints at a shift in attitudes. The Talmud presents her favourably; Rashi, more ambivalently. Through the medieval and into the early modern period, a few women, such as rabbis' daughters, whose fathers and brothers hosted others for study on *Shabbat* afternoons, acquired significant legal knowledge.[13] These included Hannah Rachel Verbermacher, the 'Maid of Ludmir', whose father was a wealthy businessman and a Chernobyl Hasid.[14] But such figures were the exception rather than the rule, at least until the development of cheap printing processes led to the widespread circulation of popular collections of religious stories and ritual handbooks aimed at readers who had little knowledge of Hebrew and lacked formal religious educations.

Gendering Judaism does not just entail new approaches to existing sources. It opens up new lines of inquiry. For example, Sarah Bunin Benor's account of how Orthodox boys in California constructed their masculinity focuses on their use of particular linguistic practices associated with religious learnedness, [15] while Susan Starr Sered's work with elderly, illiterate Mizrahi women in Jerusalem uncovers areas of belief and ritual expertise that 'have little in common with what most of us mean when we talk about Judaism'.[16] Sered's subjects' elaborate manipulation of food – preparing certain foods, abstaining from food, choosing to give more or certain kinds of food to particular people – reflect their investment of everyday tasks with complex religious meanings. And in contrast to the *Tanakh*'s image of powerless, marginal widows (Deut. 26.12; Isa. 1.17) they often experience widowhood as a time of unprecedented independence, during which they deepen and extend their religious activity from the domestic environment into the synagogue, day-centre and cemetery.[17] In a similar vein, Sezgin has used documentary evidence and ethnographic fieldwork with Jews who were children in the Middle East and eastern mediterranean around the time of the fall of the Ottoman Empire in 1922, to construct an account of women's religious lives in the late nineteenth and early twentieth centuries:

> Women's belief systems ... revolved around general Middle Eastern and Mediterranean folk religion. Infant mortality was a constant problem, as was jealously from neighbours, relatives, and friends. There was a belief in the evil eye (*ojo malo*) and its related practices such as amulet (*kameya*) wearing, or the heating of lead in water to break bad luck ... infertility gave rise to many practices. Ottoman Jewish women in Cairo ... stayed overnight in the Maimonides Synagogue and said special prayers.[18]

Mindful of these issues, this chapter now focuses on several public rituals and on more private ones, particularly those surrounding menstruation. *Tzniut* (modesty) is also discussed, and the chapter closes with a section on *agunot*, 'chained' women whose marriages are in *de facto* terms over, but who remain *halakhically* tied to their husbands.

'Indeterminate' gender: androgynous and tumtum

In addition to male and female, classic rabbinic sources categorize some individuals as androgynous or hermaphrodite (person possessing male and female reproductive organs) or *tumtum*, a person whose sex cannot be determined because their organs are sealed or covered by a membrane. According to the Talmud (*Brachot* 61a and *Eruvin* 18a, derived from Gen. 1.27), the first human being was androgynous; Eve's creation (Gen. 2.20–

22) entailed the separation of Adam into two people, male and female. Heterosexual marriage reunites the two and in doing so restores primeval unity, an idea developed in the *Zohar* and other *kabbalistic* literature.

The legal status of both the androgynous and *tumtum* are the subject of much *halakhic* debate. Although intersex conditions are very rare, many *mitzvot* are specific to the male or female genders and rabbinic authors strive to position what they regard as ambiguously or indeterminately gendered individuals in relation to this binary scheme. The *tumtum*'s status is usually seen as temporary: the assumption is that surgery will reveal an individual as male or female. In the meantime, a *tumtum* is regarded both as a doubtful male and a doubtful female. Some texts also regard the androgynous individual as a doubtful male and a doubtful female. Others view the androgynous as a separate kind of being, or as partially male and partially female, or as definitely male. Reflecting the desire to 'build a fence around the Law' (see Chapter 3) the majority *halakhic* position, operative within Orthodox observant circles today, is that an androgynous individual should follow a cautious and maximalist approach to observance of the *mitzvot*. Thus, unlike women, the androgyne is required to observe all positive, time bound commandments, and like women, may not serve as a witness in a *bet din*.

Public prayer and reading of the Torah

While the Talmud describes women as exempt from positive time-bound commandments, over time this has acquired the force of prohibition. As noted earlier, women do not, with the recent exception of a few egalitarian or 'partnership' *minyanim*, count towards the quorum of adults needed for group prayer in Orthodox synagogues. Likewise, the exemption of women from the commandment to participate in the weekly reading of the Torah has come to be understood as proscribing such activity. These practices, together with traditional teachings against women's study of the Torah, preclude women from entering the Orthodox rabbinate.

This situation has been variously rationalized. Forty years ago, Orthodox rabbis Saul Berman and Moses Meiselman offered arguments that remain widespread. For Berman, the exemption of women from positive time-bound *mizvot* reflected the Torah's accommodation of an existing social reality. Most women in the ancient past fulfilled a 'wife-mother-homemaker' role. Accordingly, 'the *Torah* modified the ... demands it made on Jewish women, to ensure that no legal obligation could possibly interfere with her performance of that particular role' by taking her away from the domestic environment.[19]

Segal similarly suggests that 'the assignment of gender roles was ... not a function of the religious traditions' and 'the basic realities of biology and economics' were instead determinative.[20] For Meiselman, such roles are themselves prescribed by Judaism. They reflect divine will and essential spiritual differences between women and men. Women's place in the private social and religious realms reflects the Genesis 2 story, in which Eve is created from one of Adam's ribs, a part of the body which is hidden beneath skin and clothing.[21] Meiselman later argued against women-only prayer groups. These emerged as a modern phenomenon in Orthodox Judaism in the 1970s, although there is evidence of similar practices in medieval Germany; data from the city of Worms suggest that some women prayed regularly in a special synagogue built in 1213.[22] Although such groups are not *halakhically* forbidden, they should, Meiselman says, be avoided because they may lead to transgressions like the desecration of Torah scrolls. Moreover, they dangerously blur the boundaries between Orthodox and Conservative Judaism.[23]

Regina Jonas (1902–1944)

Regina Jonas studied at the *Hochschule für die Wissenschaft des Judentums*, Berlin, completing her dissertation on the question, 'Can women serve as rabbis?' Initially, she was refused *semikha* (rabbinic ordination), but in 1935 she was ordained privately by Max Dienemann, a leading figure in the German Liberal movement.

Jonas' rabbinical authority was not widely recognized. She taught, and lectured at the New Synagogue in Oranienburger Strasse, Berlin, but did not preach until after *Kristallnacht*, a Nazi-coordinated programme of anti-Jewish violence in November 1938. Jonas was deported to Theresienstadt concentration camp (Czech Republic) in 1942, and worked with Viktor Frankl, providing psychological support for fellow prisoners. She died in Auschwitz (Poland).

Jonas' story was neglected for decades. Frankl did not mention her in his post-war writings. Nor did Theresienstadt survivor Leo Baeck, who taught Jonas at the *Hochschule*. Her 'rediscovery' in the 1990s was due to various factors including: a growing emphasis on Holocaust memory (see Chapter 9); the accessibility of archives following German reunification in 1990; and a perceived need on the part of some Jewish feminists to identify a usable past that provides legitimating and inspiring precedents for present-day activities and innovations.[24]

Meiselman's concerns illustrate how the issue of gender and public worship has become a visible point of difference between modern Jewish religious movements. Early reformers internalized Enlightenment values, including universalism. This was translated into a rejection of ascribed or involuntary statuses like priesthood (see Chapter 3) and ultimately, certain differences attached to gender. From the early twentieth-century organizations like the (United States') National Federation of Temple Sisterhoods began lobbying for leadership roles within religious institutions to be open to women. Initially, they focused on synagogue schools. Female presence in these was regarded as a 'natural' extension of child-rearing responsibilities in the home. From the 1960s onwards, Reform Judaism embraced feminism; campaigns for access to full ritual participation (understood as the opening up to women of previously male roles and responsibilities) accelerated. Sally J. Priesand became the first American woman ordained a Reform rabbi in 1972; Jacqueline Tabick followed her in Britain, in 1975. Also in 1972, an American group rooted in the *havurah* movement and taking its name, *Ezrat Nashim* ('women's gallery'), from the women's section of a segregated synagogue, presented its manifesto for change to the Rabbinical Assembly of Conservative rabbis.

Conservative Jewish approaches stress the idea that changing social conditions may warrant reconsideration of the religious status quo. At the same time, individual Conservative congregations are free to make their own decisions regarding practice. For example, the Talmud indicates that women are *halakhically* qualified to read the Torah in public, but should not do so on the grounds of *kavod ha-tzibbur* – congregational honour or reputation (*Megillah* 23a). This is often interpreted as implying that to allow a woman to read in public would cast doubt on the piety or intellectual abilities of the men in the community (reflecting an assumption that women's place in public ritual life is secondary, and underscoring the relational character of gender as a category). The same texts are now mobilized in support of women's Torah reading, by those who argue that practicing exclusion injures a synagogue's reputation in the present-day. Following such a line, the first Conservative woman rabbi was ordained in America in 1985, and most American congregations have adopted egalitarian worship practices. Indeed, some observers have suggested Jewish communities in America now face a new kind of 'gender crisis'. Outside Orthodoxy, Jewish public life is becoming increasingly feminized, as a majority of rabbinical and cantorial students (a cantor or *hazzan* is someone trained to lead synagogue worship), synagogue congregants and participants in religious education are now women.[25] In other countries, the situation differs. Britain has no women Masorti rabbis. Jaclyn Chernett is the movement's only female ordained *hazzan*.

Life cycle rituals: birth and religious majority

While some twentieth and twenty-first century developments facilitate female access to previously male-only roles, others provide alternatives to rituals like *berit milah*, male circumcision (which marks membership of the Jewish people) and *bar mitzvah* ceremonies (which recognize a young man's assumption of responsibility for observance of the *mitzvot*).

Over the centuries numerous rituals developed to mark the attainment of religious majority or maturity by Jewish males. Some of these were festive (celebratory meals date from medieval Europe) and others were public displays of the ability to fulfil particular religious functions (reading the Torah scroll in the synagogue service; delivery of a sermon or talk on a religious topic). The first *bat mitzvah* ceremony took place in 1922. Judith, daughter of Mordecai Kaplan, standing in 'a place below the *bimah* [reading desk] at a very respectable distance from the Scroll of the *Torah*' pronounced the blessings and read from her *Humash* (a bound copy of the Pentateuch) in Hebrew and English.[26] The practice became more widespread – and began to involve reading from actual Torah scrolls – in the second half of the twentieth century amongst Conservative and Reconstructionist Jews, and within American Reform Judaism, which had previously followed the nineteenth-century German reformers' practice of holding boys' and girls' Confirmation ceremonies modelled on Protestant Christian practice. (Nowadays, preparation for a Confirmation a few years after *bar/bat mitzvah* is regarded by some Reform Jews as an opportunity to encourage young adults to develop and extend their religious literacy and commitment.) The details of the ceremonies vary. In Reform Judaism, boys' and girls' ceremonies are identical and follow a pattern that has been customary for Ashkenazi boys since the late medieval period. On reaching the age of religious responsibility (maturity) at the age of 13, the young person is called to recite the blessings over and read from the Torah in the synagogue, and often to make a small speech about the text. After the service, a meal or party celebrates the occasion. Amongst Orthodox Jews it is now the norm for the attainment of religious responsibility to be marked by girls as well as boys, but not by doing anything that could be interpreted as leading worship. Rituals are often held in the home, after a service or in a synagogue side-room. Reflecting a wider trend in modern Orthodoxy and within some Haredi groups, the United Synagogue in Britain introduced a *bat mitzvah* test (at age 12) parallel to its *bar mitzvah* test (at 13) for boys in 2007. The girls' ceremony does not include a Torah reading. In some Orthodox settings, *bat chayil* ceremonies, in which groups of girls who have turned 12 during the previous year present religious readings in Hebrew or the vernacular, continue alongside or instead of *bat mitzvah*. This reflects a tension amongst those Orthodox Jews who wish to balance traditional gender distinctions with the desire for a greater public recognition of women's religious lives. It also underscores the modern character of Orthodox, including Haredi, Judaism.

Providing a female counterpoint to *berit milah*, the circumcision of male babies on the eighth day after birth (Gen. 17.12; Lev. 12.3) has proven more elusive. *Halakhically*, circumcision marks membership of the Abrahamic covenant but does not confer Jewish identity – a boy whose circumcision is not possible for health reasons is still a Jew – but socially, it functions as such. For example, circumcision is the point at which a Jewish boy is given his Hebrew name.[27] Thus while only 38% of Israeli Jews surveyed for the Guttman Report identified as 'strictly observant' or 'observant to a great extent', 92% felt it was important to circumcise a baby boy.[28] For some, the lack of an equivalent girls' practice implies that males are normative Jews, and females are of marginal, secondary importance in relation to the covenant between God and Israel. Attempts have been made to devise new ceremonies that celebrate a girl's birth. These typically include elements such as naming over a cup of wine, wrapping the baby in a *tallit* (prayer shawl), dipping her fingers in the *mikvah* (ritual bath) or foot-washing.[29] Amongst Sefardim, there is also a longer established tradition, *zeved habat* ('gift of a daughter') in which a girl is named and her mother recites *birkat ha-gomel*, a blessing to give thanks for deliverance from the dangers associated with childbirth. Arguably, however, none of these rituals possesses the dramatic power of circumcision. Mary Gendler's 1974 proposal for a ritual rupturing of the hymen using a sterilized instrument was never implemented.[30] As explored in Chapter 4, the popularity of particular rituals is linked in part to the plasticity or flexibility of their meaning. The novelty and the deliberateness of new life cycle rituals for girls mean that, while for some they will be intensely personal and meaningful, their longevity remains uncertain.

Language socialization and gender

Cross-cultural evidence shows that families, schools and other agencies relate to and raise boys and girls differently. One recent study of a Californian Hasidic community focuses on how children are socialized to use language. Susan Bunin Benor found that boys present themselves as learned students of religious texts through, amongst other things, frequent use of Hebrew, Aramaic and Yiddish loanwords when speaking in English, and intonation styles (variations of pitch) resembling those used when chanting sacred texts. Girls are less familiar with Yiddish. They know many of the Hebrew terms used by boys, but using them frequently might cause them to be regarded as too learned, or even masculine. Benor concludes that in such communities males are, and are expected to be, more distinct from outsiders than females are:

> Orthodox Jews are expected to be more learned and use more learned language than outsiders ... Orthodox males are expected to be more learned and use more learned language than Orthodox females. The same recursivity applies in other domains ... Although both men and women in this community are expected to dress according to the laws and customs of *tsnies* [modesty], Hasidic men are expected to wear the traditional garb of Eastern Europe, including black hats and long black coats. Women's dress, though quite distinct from that of non-Orthodox and non-Jews, is more influenced by contemporary fashion.[31]

Other research highlights how children are socialized *through* language. By answering, praising, ignoring or ridiculing appropriate and inappropriate questions, Hasidic women in Brooklyn, New York, encourage their children to adopt communal norms relating to age, gender and religious practice:

> Requests for knowledge that crosses gender boundaries spark either teasing or caregivers' evocation of immutable and divinely sanctioned gender differences which require reminding but no explanation. For example, when Mrs. Weiss, the first-grade teacher, was asked by Chana about a sacred text, the Mishna, Mrs.Weiss shrugged off her question by telling her, 'When you're a boy, you'll understand.' Everyone laughed, including Chana and Mrs. Weiss.[32]

Ritual purity

Reflecting the general rabbinic principle of making a 'fence around the Torah' so as to guard against its accidental infringement, one of Meiselman's arguments against women's prayer groups was that they might lead to the desecration of Torah scrolls. According to the Torah, any Jew is prohibited from entering the Jerusalem Temple and eating from the sacrifices offered there if they are in a state of ritual impurity, which may be caused by (amongst other things) touching a corpse (Num. 19.11) or the carcass of a non-*kosher* animal (Lev. 11.26–39), ejaculation (Lev. 15.15), menstruation (Lev. 15.19) and childbirth (Lev. 12.4). Ashkenazi *minhag* (custom) holds that women in *niddah* – menstrual impurity – should avoid touching a scroll, although codes like the *Shulhan Arukh* say that 'all those who are impure, even *niddot*, are permitted to hold a Torah scroll and to read from it as long as their hands are not filthy or dirty' (*Yoreh De'ah* 282.9).

The laws and customs of *niddah* are mainly upheld amongst observant Orthodox Jews, especially Haredim. In order to avoid defiling contacts with people and objects, a woman separates from her husband 12 hours before her period is due, during the period, and for seven 'clear' days afterwards. Careful checking of garments, sanitary products and cloths is required to determine correct timings. Afterwards, she presents herself at a *mikvah* for thorough immersion and inspection by the attendant. She is then no longer *niddah*.

In modernity, the discourse of 'family purity' has increasingly displaced that of 'ritual impurity'. This shift arose in the wake of changing gender roles and criticisms of *niddah*. Early reformers held that conceptions of women's biology as somehow polluting or unclean were primitive and inappropriate in an age in which the purpose of menstruation was understood and there was ready access to bathing facilities. In return, Orthodox apologists have advanced notions of Jewish femininity that emphasize a woman's role in keeping her family and home 'pure', and the potential benefits of temporary periods of sexual abstinence:

> The discipline of *taharat hamishpachah* [family purity] usually eases the tensions that may permeate a marriage and ... injects the spark of excitement and magic which is often absent. As husband and wife must abstain from all physical contact, even the merest touch, during the *niddah* period, they will experience a feeling of renewal and romance when they are reunited each month. This leads to a deeper and more satisfying relationship ... based on love, understanding and respect.[33]

As Jewish feminists (Orthodox and non-Orthodox) note, *niddah* affords women opportunities to exercise power. In some instances, groups of women have refused to visit the *mikvah* (thereby remaining unavailable sexually to their husbands) until a particular injustice against one of them has been rectified.[34] A woman determines the end of the period of clear days, and decides when to seek guidance in cases of doubt. She also has a degree of freedom in deciding whom to consult on such matters. Communal recognition always plays a part in rabbinical authority (see Chapter 3), but the private nature of *niddah* confers even greater scope for discretion. The decision to approach one *posek* rather than another may, for example, reflect a woman's estimation as to whether he will give the answer she wants. The past decade has also seen the emergence of internet forums in which Orthodox women can anonymously discuss issues relating to ritual purity and sexual and emotional relationships,[35] and *halakhic* consultants, women trained in the laws of *niddah*, psychology and reproductive health. Effectively, this is a professionalization of an advisory function performed by the *rebbetzin* (rabbi's wife) or a family member. Some *halakhic* consultants give advice themselves. Others serve as intermediaries between women and *posekim*, protecting their clients' embarrassment and ensuring that legal queries are raised in a pertinent manner.[36]

At the same time, there are objections to aspects of *niddah*, even amongst those women who keep them. Sered's respondents recalled how,

> in the Old Country [Yemen or Kurdistan] the women had to dip in a freezing cold river at the end of the period of menstrual impurity. Others remember that even ... in Israel they would sleep on the floor while menstruating (so as not to touch their husbands).[37]

This last practice that underscores both the variations in religious practice between different Jewish communities and the degree of material deprivation experienced by many Mizrahi migrants to Israel in the mid-twentieth century.

The prevention of all physical contact is felt by some women (and some men) to elide intimacy into sex, or to leave them feeling isolated. This is true during *niddah* and childbirth, another source of impurity. Numerous responsa have been generated by the tension between the *halakhic* prohibition on a man assisting his wife during labour (unless her life is endangered) and contemporary cultural constructions of childbirth as a familial bonding experience, during which fathers are present and provide active emotional and physical support.

As noted in Chapter 3, in Israel Jews must marry according to Orthodox *halakhah*, so all brides must visit a *mikvah* and have the attendant verify their purity before the wedding. In addition, some groups (especially Mizrahim) hold *mikvah* parties at which the bride immerses in front of her future mother-in-law and female relatives. These events can be experienced as important moments of female solidarity and celebration, or as humiliating and stressful. 'It is not uncommon ... to find that the mother-in-law competes with the *mikvah* attendant for the right to inspect, supervise, and control the bride's body,' observes Sered, for whom such rituals create and reinforce relationships of authority and subordination, grounded in assumptions that women's bodies are legitimate sites of social control.[38]

Modesty

Tzniut – modesty, or humility – is little dealt with in Judaism textbooks.[39] But arguably it constitutes an increasingly significant feature of contemporary Orthodox Jewish religious life.

Women … who do not have the *mitzva* of learning Torah, were given the special *mitzva* of veering their hair in public – a *mitzvah* which symbolizes the *tznius* of the Jewish woman. This constant religious mode of dress … enables them to unmask and expel the *yetzer horah* [the 'evil inclination'].

The person most directly responsible for ensuring that a woman dresses correctly is her husband.

Not only do these [modest] women encourage their husbands and sons to drink from the lifesprings of Torah and *daven* [pray] as a person should … they infuse them with a desire and a yearning to learn more and more Torah and to come closer to *Hashem* [God] through *tefilla* [prayer].[40]

These quotations from Pesach Falk, a Gateshead *posek*, illustrate how although the regulations on *tzniut* relate overwhelmingly to female dress and behaviour, they articulate ideas about both masculinity and femininity. Women's activities and attitudes are linked to the spiritual wellbeing of men and male children, which licences their scrutiny within the home and by the wider community.

Haredi women are expected to dress and behave in ways that reflect norms of modesty. Adult women are subject to a greater number of regulations than young girls and men (whose dress is discussed in Chapter 8). Typically, a married woman will cover her hair (with a wig, hat or scarf), arms, legs (but not with trousers) and torso from the collarbone downwards; her clothing will not be tightly fitted or eye-catching. She should avoid physical contact with any man who is not her husband or a close blood relative, and eschew talk or conduct that might be considered showy or flirtatious.

Although *tzniut* is positively valued in the *Tanakh* (Micah 6.8) and discussed in many subsequent law codes and responsa, it is commonly perceived to be assuming renewed prominence within Orthodoxy. For its advocates, this shift is a necessary response to the erosion of moral standards in wider society. From a religious studies' perspective, *tzniut* can be interpreted as functioning as a boundary-marker between different Jewish religious movements and between Jews and non-Jews. Women who dress modestly will appear different to their Jewish and non-Jewish neighbours, although the precise character of that 'difference' varies according to context. They may also purchase garments from specialist religious retailers who cater for their needs.

Just as rituals like the *seder* have complex, varying meanings, so women who dress in similarly modest ways do so for different reasons. For some, dressing in a particular way is not a reasoned response to the arguments offered by Falk and others, it is simply an expression of norms internalized in childhood, or perhaps during conversion or encounter with a *ba'al teshuvah* movement. Dressing modestly may also be done for strategic reasons (in order to attend a particular religious school or college, for example) or under duress. Orthodox women (and men) are not passive, unquestioning dupes who lack individual agency. Criticisms of writers like Falk appear on internet forums, some from women who dispute his fitness, as a man, to advise on female dress. For some women, *tzniut* is a quasi-political assertion of religious values in the face of secular and/or non-Jewish ones, or an opportunity to exercise control over their bodies and display their piety. In the early twenty-first century, a very small number of Haredi women have begun to practice so-called 'hyper-*tzniut*'. Exceeding *halakhic* requirements, they dress in many layers of clothing and veil their faces. While most religious Jews are critical of this practice, for others it exemplifies a growing trend towards female initiative in the religious arena:

> the modesty issue, and obsessive discussion about the body, was all in the hands of the rabbis ... the women took it over and brought it to the edge ... It's as if they say, 'If that's my expertise — I'll excel at it'. Thus, they move the power to their own hands.[41]

Marriage and divorce

In early Judaism, a man 'acquired' a wife with money, or a ring, which she accepted in the presence of witnesses, with a legal contract or through sexual intercourse performed with the intention of creating a marriage (*m.Kiddushim* 1.1). Orthodox weddings incorporate elements based on these criteria: the giving and acceptance of a ring; the reading and signing of a *ketubah*, a contract in which the husband agrees to provide his wife with food, clothing and sexual intercourse, and to pay her a sum of money if he divorces her; and *yihud*, a period in which the couple are secluded in a room by themselves.

Figure 6.1: A Ketubah from Bombay [Mumbai], India

To view the image of this *ketubah*, please visit http://beinecke.library.yale. edu/dl_crosscollex/brbldl/oneITEM.asp?pid=2040851&iid=1162028&srchtype

This is the *ketubah* of Shalom bar (son of) Aharon and his bride Rivka bar (i.e. bat, daughter of) Binyamin who married on 14 August 1911 in Bombay, India. It is hand written in Aramaic and Hebrew. The rectangular panel in the lower part of the document contains the terms of the contract; the texts in the upper (oval) part and the border are blessings for the couple and biblical verses. Many *ketubot* are similarly decorated with floral and geometrical designs. The peacock is more distinctively Indian: the bird is native to South Asia, and is a common motif in the art, folklore and religion of the region. The crown may be a reference to the British monarchy, which ruled India at this time or to divine kingship and the 'crown' of the Torah.

Reflecting Jewish and non-Jewish norms of modesty and propriety, in previous generations couples had comparatively little contact before the wedding day itself. In Haredi circles, casual dating is discouraged, and a rabbi or professional matchmaker may arrange meetings between people with similar levels of learning, religious observance, social standing and character.

> The days leading up to the *chasunah* [wedding] were days of *yirah* [awe]. ... The day of the *chasunah* itself was one of great solemnity, both the *choson* [groom] and *kallah* [bride] felt this way. They would cry under the *huppah* [wedding canopy]. The day of my *chasunah* I fasted and *knew* it was *Yom Kippur*, that I could make everything in my life better that day ... I could become much closer to *Hashem* [literally 'the Name', i.e. God].[42]

These memories of Zlota Ginsburg, who married in Mir, Belarus, before World War Two, reflect a traditional idea that one's wedding day is a personal *Yom Kippur*, a new starting point in one's relationship with God and others, preceded by a period in which one seeks forgiveness from those previously wronged, visits the *mikvah* and fasts. During the ceremony, her groom would have worn a *kittel*, the white robe also worn at *Yom Kippur*, and in which he would eventually be buried.

Many rituals and customs have developed around the *halakhah* of marriage. Many weddings take place beneath a *huppah* or canopy (see Chapter 4). This is often explained as symbolizing the new couple's home, or God's oversight of their relationship. Breaking a glass, a custom attributed to the fourth century Rav Ashi (*Berakhot* 31a), is often held to be a reminder that, amidst celebration, Jews should mourn the destruction of the Jerusalem Temple. The *ketubah* is not only a functioning contract, it is often a highly decorative document. Some couples, particularly Reform and Conservative Jews, display it in their homes.

Just as in Orthodox Jewish practice men alone may initiate marriage, so only they may initiate a divorce. In strict *halakhic* terms a man can give his wife a *get* or bill of divorce arbitrarily, but in reality, the process is overseen by a *bet din* or religious court and cannot be undertaken without reason. For example, a husband might argue that his wife's adoption of hyper-*tzniut* against his wishes is destructive of *shalom bayit* (domestic harmony). Other regulations are designed to ensure that divorced women are not left destitute. Although reflecting a view in which men alone are active agents, the *ketubah* confers rights on wives and former wives, as discussed above. But the inability of women to initiate and terminate marriages creates a situation where some women find themselves becoming *agunot*, 'chained' or 'anchored' to their previous husbands. A woman becomes an *agunah* when the husband:

- deserts his wife and disappears;

- is believed, but not proven, to have died;

- is legally incompetent, perhaps as a result of mental illness;

- is careless, or ignorant of the need for a *get* (bill of religious divorce);

- is vindictive, and refuses to issue a *get*. There are a number of situations in which a *bet din* may instruct a man to divorce his wife (these include adultery, apostasy, male impotency, and refusal of sex) but the sanctions that the court may apply to a man who ignores its rulings are limited, particularly in the diaspora.

An *agunah* may not marry another man, and any children she has with a new partner would be *mamzerim*, bastards who may only marry converts to Judaism or other *mamzerim*. Conversely, if a woman disappears or groundlessly refuses to accept a *get*, or if she is mentally incapable of doing so, a *bet din* can permit a man to contract a second marriage. This possibility exists because polygamy is banned by rabbinical edict (from 1000 CE for Ashkenazi Jews, more recently for others)[43] and not by the Torah. Gen. 29.25–28 describes Jacob marrying two sisters, while David inherits wives from Saul, his predecessor as King of Israel and Judah (2 Sam. 12.7–8).

There is a popular perception that the issue has reached crisis point. Recent cases involving women whose husbands are missing in military action, or whose bodies were unrecoverable after the September 11th, 2001, terror attacks in the US, have generated many responsa. The number of *agunot* is also believed to be increasing, partly because many couples who undergo traditional marriage ceremonies do not appreciate the *halakhic* consequences. The situation is most acute in Israel, where there is no possibility for civil marriage and divorce and the number of women estimated to be affected varies from a few dozen to several thousand.

The *agunah* problem differs qualitatively from the other issues discussed in this chapter. Expectations concerning dress and behaviour are defended by their proponents on the grounds that Judaism regards the genders as 'separate but equal'. But this reasoning breaks down when a separated woman who wishes to obey the *halakhah* becomes an *agunah*, and must remain single or enter into a legally prohibited relationship, while a careless or malicious husband who refuses to obey the rabbinical court and issue a *get*, is able to father legitimate children, and perhaps even to marry a second time.

Not least because such cases threaten to undermine the credibility of the *halakhah* itself, members of all modern religious movements agree that all possible measures must be taken to release *agunot*. The *halakhah* permits religious courts to take sanctions against husbands who refuse to release their wives, but in the present day these are less readily applied, and less effective, than was the case previously, when communal rabbis exercised significant authority over particular territories (see Chapter 3). For centuries, rabbinical courts relaxed the usual rules of evidence, accepting the testimony of women and secular Jews, and some kinds of circumstantial evidence, as sufficient to verify a husband's death. As a last resort, the ketubah was examined, in an attempt to identify errors that would nullify the contract and hence the marriage. Today, the most widely accepted solution amongst Orthodox and Conservative Jews is a prenuptial agreement. In 1954, Conservative Jews began adding the Lieberman Clause (named after Saul Lieberman, a professor at the Jewish Theological Seminary in New York) to ketubot. This commits the couple to implementing the decisions of the movement's Rabbinical Assembly – including a ruling that a husband must deliver a get – in the event of marital breakdown. In 2006, the Rabbinical Council of America ruled that no Orthodox rabbi operating under its auspices should officiate at a wedding unless an approved prenuptial agreement was in place, granting the Beth Din of the United States of America binding juris-diction over divorce matters. In Britain such agreements are recommended, but optional, before marriages in United (mainline Orthodox) Synagogues. This provision is reinforced by the Divorce (Religious Marriages) Act 2002, which allows a civil court in England or Wales to withhold a civil divorce from a Jewish couple unless a get is already in place. In keeping with their inter-nalization of modern Western values, Reform, Reconstructionist and Liberal Jewish groups in various countries either accept civil divorce as sufficient for the termination of a Jewish marriage, or have implemented egalitarian processes in which both men and women may initiate and terminate marriage.

EXERCISE

In 1973, Rachel Adler wrote an article, 'The Jew Who Wasn't There: Halacha and the Jewish Woman' in which she suggested that women were peripheral in Jewish law and practice, and demanded changes that would allow 'justice and growing room' to women within a halakhic framework. On the basis of your reading in this chapter, do you agree with her claim? Is gender equality compatible with the halakhah? Consider how a representative from each of the major modern religious movements might respond to this question.

7

Politics

Smart closed one of his later books on religions with a brief discussion of their 'political effects'.[1] The decision to use the language of 'effect' rather than 'dimension' seemingly implies that 'religion' and 'politics' are essentially discrete entities. Such an approach echoes an ambivalence towards politics amongst many contemporary religious adherents or practitioners, particularly (but not only) amongst those who identify as 'spiritual but not religious', and whose beliefs and practices are often eclectic and highly personal or individualistic. As described in Chapters 1 and 2, belief in a civil realm distinct from the religious one is arguably one of the hallmarks of *modern* thought. Particularly in the West, it informed the development of states characterized to some degree by secular constitutions and religious freedom. These contexts have helped structure the frameworks within which the critical study of religions, and much Jewish religious activity, takes place today. This is true of religious movements like Reform Judaism that have consciously internalized Enlightenment values. It is also true of others, such as Haredi groups, that seek to dethrone these in favour of some form of theocratic arrangement. However, the view that any religion is apolitical is difficult to sustain. This is true whether we understand 'politics' as being concerned with political sovereignty and statehood, or think of it in the more diffuse sense of a human effort to address physical needs, conflicts and natural disasters.[2] Examples in this chapter and book show how these kinds of questions are very much part of Jewish religious tradition, not apart from it.

One factor underlying Smart's difficulties in relation to the politics–religion nexus may has been his awareness of changes in the ways in which religions function and manifested themselves in the late twentieth century. Almost a decade on from Smart's death, and as he had suggested it would do, the relationship between religions and politics and the political dimension or character of religion occupies a more significant place on the agendas of religious adherents, political policy makers and those engaged in religious studies.[3] This reflects the newly increased visibility of religion in the public sphere in a variety of different national contexts, a phenomenon David Herbert has called religious 'publicisation' or, in instances where religion is reoccupying public spaces and discourses which have previously undergone secularization, 're-publicisation'.[4] Amongst other things, this chapter will suggest that the Israel–Palestine conflict is one example of a situation in which religion became publicized in the late twentieth century.

The politics of statelessness

Jewish identity and religion has a strong political dimension in the *Tanakh*. The Torah's accounts of the development of the covenant relationship between God and the Jewish people stress an inseparable link between the former Hebrew slaves' observance of the commandments and the promise of a land of their own. *Nevi'im*, the books of the prophets, describe the military conquest of that land, its division amongst the various Hebrew tribes or families, the founding of a monarchy and national capital in Jerusalem and a series of military and political defeats that are interpreted as resulting from failures to remain faithful to the covenant.[5]

In the wake of the destruction of the Second Jerusalem Temple by the Romans in 70 CE, early rabbinic texts developed models of ideal relations between Jewish and non-Jewish authorities that reflected both biblical sources and changing social conditions. Officially expelled from Jerusalem after the Bar Kokhba revolt of 135 CE, the Jews ceased to exist as a nation in conventional geopolitical terms. Jewish life in the land of Israel did not end, but became much less significant in terms of its size and influence. Jewish statelessness became the norm. Throughout the medieval, and into the modern, post-emancipation period, the *kahal* or *kehillah* ('congregation') was the basic communal unit. These extracts describe a *kehillah* in Abaújszántó, northern Hungary, and give a sense of its character as a self-governing entity within the state during the eighteenth century:

> The rabbi shared the organizational and self-governing power of the kehilla. He was usually selected from a number of candidates at a meeting of the home-owners or by a representative body of [male] electors. ... The rabbi's responsibility for keeping vital records gave him the status of a government officer. ... The synagogue was the center of Jewish communal life. ... The kehilla administered its own judicial system ... in addition to its ritual aspect, the rabbinical court resolved business disputes and sometimes criminal cases. ... The president represented the kehilla before government authorities. ... [Some presidents] were professionals with

advanced educational backgrounds; others were merchants with excellent religious training and a general academic education; still others were affluent merchants who had neither a religious nor a secular education. ... Elections for kehilla representatives were held by secret ballot on the third day of Passover, when the rich as well as the poor members were home.[6]

Above and beyond the boundaries of an individual *kehillah* were regional and national organizations. For example, between 1580 and 1764, when they were ordered by the Polish parliament to cease activity, delegates from *kehillot* in the regions of Poznan and Kraków (Poland), Lvov and Ostrog (now in Ukraine) met at a Council of the Four Lands to consider issues of general concern, including taxation. A similar Lithuanian council drew representatives from Brisk (now Ukraine), Grodno and Pinsk (now Belarus), Vilna (Lithuania) and surrounding areas.

Recalling biblical models, which present a variety of forms of authority[7] and power being exercised within an overall religious framework, functions were generally divided between rabbis and teachers, responsible for the interpretation and application of *halakhah*; *hazzanim* and other officials responsible for communal worship; and elders who, like Abaújszántó's president, managed civil affairs and relations with non-Jewish bodies. Without explicitly rejecting their ideas about the divine sufficiency of the Torah, then, rabbis cooperated with leaders selected on the grounds of secular experience and resources. At times, they also competed with them for authority.

In the context of semi-autonomous statelessness, aspects of *halakhah* that applied only in the land of Israel were neglected, or occasionally pursued as topics of theoretical interest. At the same time, others were developed to facilitate Jewish existence within non-Jewish states. This resulted in a system of checks and balances that preserved the *kehillah*'s stability such as the principle of *dina de-malkhuta dina*. Translated as 'the law of the [non-Jewish] government is the law' – that is, the law of the land in which a Jew lives is binding and must be followed – *dina de-malkhuta dina* is first articulated in the Talmud (*Nedarim* 28a; *Gittin* 10b). There are exceptions to the rule, particularly in life-threatening situations and areas of ritual and personal status. As discussed in Chapter 6, for example, Orthodox Jews do not accept civil divorce as sufficient to end a marriage. In general, however, *dina de-malkhuta dina* has functioned to provide 'a *halakhic* reason for obeying non-*halakhic* laws – and for acknowledging the legitimacy, not only the power, of non-Jewish rulers'.[8] In the ritual dimension, a similarly pragmatic stance towards non-Jewish authorities is reflected in the long established custom of praying on *Shabbat* for the welfare of the government, a practice based on a biblical command to 'Seek the welfare of the city to which I have exiled you and pray to the LORD in its behalf; for in its prosperity you shall prosper' (Jer. 29.7).

Enlightenment, emancipation and Jewish statehood each prompted reappraisals of *dina de-malkhuta dina*. Samuel Holdheim (1806–1860) attempted unsuccessfully to invoke the concept as a justification for observing *Shabbat* on Sunday, a move that would assimilate German Jews to the religious norms of their Christian neighbours. Since 1948, questions have been raised as to whether *dina de-malkhuta dina* applies to the laws of the Israeli state, which is a Jewish state but not legally a religious one. In 2005, when the Israeli government adopted a policy of disengagement from the Gaza strip, some rabbis argued that the policy violated a fundamental aspect of Jewish law and self-understanding, the goal of *yishuv eretz Yisrael* ('living in the land of Israel'), and that the state did not therefore have authority of *dina de-malkhuta dina* over religiously-motivated settlers[9] who wished to remain in the area. Others concluded that, given the dangers that might be faced by settlers, the principle of *pikuah nefesh*, the idea that saving or preserving human life takes precedence over other areas of *halakhah* (*Ketubbot* 19a), applied.[10]

Judaism and Socialism

Karl Marx's (1818–1883) parents were Jewish converts to Lutheran Christianity. Some of his earliest political writings addressed the question of Jewish emancipation. Marx rejected the arguments of those who wished to make enfranchisement conditional on a willingness to abandon Judaism. However, in referring to the political and social dominance of financial interests as 'civil society's Judaism', he reiterated what were then common stereotypes of Jews as money-obsessed.[11] Marx generally regarded religious institutions and organizations as sources of social control that legitimated the power of ruling elites and justified the exploitation of the proletariat (working class), therefore inhibiting change.

Marxism and other forms of socialism (political philosophies advocating public or state ownership of the means by which goods are produced and distributed, as a means to creating a fair, egalitarian society) appealed to many European Jews in the late nineteenth and twentieth centuries. Many early Zionists believed that their goals would be realized through the creation of large urban and rural proletariats able to redeem the land of Israel. 1897, the year of the First Zionist Congress, also saw the founding of the Bund, a secular Jewish socialist party that aimed to achieve Jewish civil and political rights within the Russian Empire.

Pre-1948, left-wing Zionism was particularly associated with the *kibbutz* movement. *Kibbutzim* were (and are) collective settlements in which private property was largely or partially abolished. Ostensibly secular, they often developed customs and rituals that were grounded in Judaism. Most contemporary *kibbutzim* observe a day of rest on *Shabbat* and celebrate festivals, particularly those with agricultural and national overtones. In the late 1940s, a small religious *kibbutz* movement emerged. For example, Kibbutz Lavi in northern Israel was founded in 1949. It supports itself through agriculture, the manufacture of synagogue furniture and a *glatt* (strictly) *kosher* hotel.

Today, Israel has the world's largest Jewish population (approximately 5,393,400 people in 2007), but the majority of Jews (approximately 7,761, 800 people) live in the diaspora.[12] While Israel's existence has had a worldwide impact, it remains the case, then, that for most religious Jews day-to-day politics is about striking a balance between communal ('stateless') Jewish politics and the politics of a non-Jewish nation-state. Finally, it is important to return to a theme introduced in Chapter 4. Features of globalization – the rise of multinational corporations, instantaneous communications, conventional and online international media and unprecedented levels of international travel – have profound social and political consequences that cut across the state/stateless dichotomy. In some instances globalization has fostered a sense of interdependency – there is seemingly an emerging consensus that ecological challenges like global warming require action that transcends national and religious boundaries – but it is also a factor in the rise of conservative religious and political forms that seek to restore an idealized past in the face of fast-changing, uncertain conditions.

Judaism, Zionism, and the State of Israel

The LORD appeared to Abram and said, 'I will assign this land to your offspring' (Gen. 12.7).

But the land must not be sold beyond reclaim, for the land is Mine (Lev. 25.23).

You must keep My laws and My rules, and you must not do any of those abhorrent things [prohibited sexual relationships] ... for all those abhorrent things were done by the people who were in the land before you, and the land became defiled. So let not the land spew you out for defiling it, as it spewed out the nation that came before you (Lev. 18.24–28).

As these quotations show, the authors and redactors of the Torah regard the land of Israel as having been promised to Abraham and his descendents. But they, and it, are ultimately God's possessiosn. As part of the covenant, God permits Jews to live in the land, but a failure to keep God's laws will result in their expulsion from it.

Reflecting and reinforcing a belief in the sanctity or holiness of the land, numerous *mitzvot* may only be observed there. These include the sacrificial forms of worship associated with the Temple, and the laws relating to sabbatical and jubilee years defined in Lev. 25, in which land lies fallow (or nowadays, is sold temporarily to a non-Jew) and the produce that happens to grow on it may be harvested by anyone.

The theme of exilic longing for a return to the land begins in the *Tanakh*. Ps. 137.1 speaks of a community, ostensibly that exiled after the First Temple's destruction in the sixth century BCE, weeping 'by the rivers of Babylon' as it remembers 'Zion'. Zion was an ancient name for the mount on which the Temple stood. Over time, it has also come to describe Jerusalem and the land of Israel as a whole. After the unsuccessful conflicts with Rome, most early rabbis appear to have opposed military conquest, teaching that the loss of the land resulted from Jewish sinfulness, and resettlement and redemption would only be brought about by an eschatological Messiah, who would re-build the Temple and gather all nations into God's plan (see Chapter 5). The rabbis did, however, continue to stress the land's sanctity. The *Mishnah* (*m.Kelim* 1.6) states that 'the land of Israel is holier than any other land', fostering the view that Israel remained the preferred place of residence for living Jews, and the ideal resting-place for the dead. In a practice that continues today, many diaspora Jews undertook pilgrimages to Israel – in particular, to the Temple's surviving Western Wall, and to the locations near Hebron and Bethlehem which were believed to be the sites of the tombs of important biblical figures such as Abraham and Sarah, Isaac and Rebecca, Jacob and Leah and Rachel.[13] Others sought to die or be buried in Israel, or had a bag of soil from the land placed in their grave. While such undertakings were often difficult and dangerous, in the twelfth and thirteenth centuries, there were significant migrations of Western European Jews into the region, which was variously controlled by local Muslims and Crusader Christians. At the same time, Maimonides (who lived briefly in Israel) ruled that refusal to emigrate to Israel was sufficient grounds for divorce (*Hilkot Ishut* 13) – a decision that illustrates both the readiness of some Jews to practically implement their belief in the land's unique character, and others' ideological or pragmatic resistance to the practice.

Until the late nineteenth century, the population of the *yishuv* (Jewish 'settlement'), in what was then part of the Ottoman Empire, was small and mostly Sefardi and Mizrahi. New forms of communication and transport then enabled more Jews, particularly Ashkenazim, to go to the land of Israel. Many of the migrants were old and poor. The *yishuv*'s *kollelim* (institutions that provide money and accommodation for married men so that they can pursue advanced religious studies) instituted charity collection schemes to encourage diaspora Jews to support their former compatriots.

Around the same time, nationalism and the persistence of antisemitism in post-emancipation Europe helped trigger the emergence of modern Zionism. Dismissing the hope of minority Jewish equality as unrealizable, advocates of Jewish 'auto-emancipation' like Leon Pinsker (1821–1891) argued that only a national homeland or Jewish nation-state would solve the 'Jewish problem'. Such views gained wide credibility during the Dreyfus Affair (1894–1906), in which a French Jewish army captain, Alfred Dreyfus, was wrongfully convicted and imprisoned for treason. The case divided French society – or revealed divisions that were previously latent. It indicated that anti-Jewish prejudice persisted, even in the country popularly regarded as the cradle of the Enlightenment. Having reported on the story, journalist Theodor Herzl (1860–1904) formulated his programme for political Zionism, a campaign for a Jewish state outside Europe:

> The Jewish Question still exists ... This is the case in every country, and will remain so, even in those highly civilized – for instance, France, until the Jewish question finds a solution on a political basis ...
>
> We are a people – One People.
>
> We have honestly endeavored everywhere to merge ourselves in the social life of surrounding communities, and to preserve the faith of our fathers. We are not permitted to do so ... In countries where we have lived for centuries we are still cried down as strangers, and often by those whose ancestors were not yet domiciled in the land where Jews had already had experience of suffering ...
>
> We are one people – our enemies have made us one without our consent, as repeatedly happens in history. Distress binds us together ... Yes, we are strong enough to form a State, and, indeed, a model State.[14]

Some, but not all, early Zionists were religious. Herzl himself received a secular education in Vienna, and hoped for a state in which male and female Jews and non-Jews enjoyed equal rights and an extensive social welfare programme supported by a mixed economy that combined private enterprise, cooperatives and state ownership of utilities. Zionist assertions that Jewish identity was about more than 'the faith of our fathers' and that Jews were a 'nation', raised problems for many of Herzl's contemporaries. Orthodox opponents criticized Zionists on the grounds that, in campaigning for a return to the land of Israel, they ignored traditional teachings that stressed the importance of waiting for God to redeem the people through a messiah. For them, Zionism was tantamount to idolatry: it sought to displace God and set the nation at the heart of Jewish thought and action. This concern was one factor underlying the formation of the Ashkenazi Haredi movement, *Agudath Israel*, in Poland in 1912. Progressive religious criticisms of Zionism bore some similarities to Orthodox ones. 'Zionistic activities ... depress Judaism by putting nationality first and religion second,' wrote Claude Montefiore, one of the founders of Liberal Judaism in Britain.[15] Reform and Liberal Jews, whose movements had removed prayers for a return to Zion from their liturgies earlier in the nineteenth century, also offered distinctive arguments against Zionism, regarding it as contradicting their emphasis on Judaism as a *universal* religion, with an ethical-moral message for the whole world. Conservative Jewish leaders took a different view, identifying similarities between Zionism and their emphasis on Jewish peoplehood. Reconstructionism emerged at the height of Zionist aspirations, and aimed to foster Jewish peoplehood in antici-pation of the creation of a state. Judaism, Kaplan believed, was ultimately 'unlikely to survive either as an ancillary or as a co-ordinate civilization [in diaspora], unless it thrives as a primary civilization in Palestine'.[16]

Since the Holocaust, the founding of the State and the Six Day War of 1967, during which Israel captured East Jerusalem, the site of the Temple Mount (and of the Al-Aqsa Mosque and Church of the Holy Sepulchre), there has been far less opposition to Zionism amongst religious Jews. Many Jewish communities in Europe were destroyed during the Holocaust. The survivors regarded the establishment of the State of Israel in newly pragmatic terms, as did Jews in many parts of the Muslim world, which had been sympathetic to the Axis powers (Germany, Japan, Italy and their allies) and witnessed the growth of new nationalist movements after the war. While many contem-porary Haredim are not ideologically committed to the State, they may live there and participate in its political and economic life because they see it as an instrument that permits Jewish living on the *land* of Israel. A few thousand, notably members of *Neturei Karta* (Guardians of the City), founded in 1935, continue to oppose Zionism and the State itself, on the grounds that any human attempt to end the exile of Jews is an affront to divine authority. Many more religious Jews, particularly modern or mainline Orthodox Jews, follow the views of either Abraham Isaac Kook (1865–1935) or his son, Zvi Yehuda Kook (1891–1982).

Abraham Isaac Kook was born in Latvia and, following the partition of the Ottoman Empire at the end of the First World War, was amongst the several thousand Jews who emigrated from around the world to what became known as the British Mandate of Palestine. Appointed first Ashkenazi Chief Rabbi of Palestine by the British, he founded a *yeshiva* in which the renewed study of Temple ritual, agricultural and other *halakhot* relating to the land of Israel was pursued. While he regarded Zionism as secular, Abraham Isaac Kook believed that Zionists were, albeit unwittingly, engaged in a religious task. He anticipated a revival of Judaism, and the advent of redemption, once more Jews returned to the land.

Zvi Yehuda Kook developed his father's ideas, teaching that the State's institutions, including its army, had a religious character. After the Six Day and Yom Kippur (1974) wars, he founded *Gush Emunim* ('Block of the Faithful'; known more recently as *Ne'emanei Eretz Yisrael*, 'Those Who are Faithful to the Land of Israel') which opposes the exchange of land for peace with the Palestinians. *Gush* has been influential in organizing religious (and some secular) settlement of the West Bank, to which it refers using the biblical names, Judea and Samaria.

The Kooks believed that Israel should be a Jewish state in religious terms, and not simply in the sense of having a predominantly Jewish population. However, the State of Israel is secular, in that it is constitutionally a democratic republic in which justice is administered in municipal courts, by judges who are appointed by a President, who is in turn elected by a majority in the Knesset (parliament). Despite the efforts of some campaigners, *halakhah* has relatively little direct role in the legal system. Judaism's official place in the Israeli polity, first articulated by David Ben-Gurion, who became the state's first Prime Minster, in a 1947 letter to the Orthodox *Agudath Israel* party, is overseen by the Ministry of Religious Affairs and largely restricted to four areas:

- Sabbaths and Jewish religious festivals are public holidays;

- Government institutions serve *kosher* food;

- The state school system operates both a National Secular and a National Religious stream;

- The Sefardi and Ashkenazi Chief Rabbis are legally recognized as having supreme authority over Israeli Jews in religious matters, including issues of personal status.

Some implications of Orthodox hegemony in Israel were discussed in relation to *agunot* in Chapter 6. Other consequences include ongoing conflicts over the interpretation of the Law of Return. Adopted in 1950, this gives 'every Jew the right to immigrate to the State of Israel', but did not initially specify who was and was not a Jew. While the Minister of the Interior ruled in 1958 that any immigrant who sincerely expressed a commitment to Judaism would be regarded as a Jew for the purposes of the Law, Orthodox authorities argued that the right to determine personal status matters was theirs, and that the *halakhic* definition of a Jew as 'a person born of a Jewish mother or who has become converted to Judaism and is not a member of another religion' must apply. In 1970, the Law was amended further, and gave rights to the children and grandchildren of Jews and their spouses; many immigrants from the former Soviet Union entered Israel on this basis at the end of the twentieth century. This move had strong emotional and historical resonances, as it extended provision to the categories of people who were the targets of Nazi antisemitism during the Holocaust. But it was also criticized as a- or anti-*halakhic*. Further controversies concern the status of people who have undergone Reform or Conservative conversions to Judaism, which Orthodoxy does not recognize. In 2005, the Supreme Court ruled that people who completed non-Orthodox conversions *outside* Israel are recognized as Jews for the purposes of the Law of Return, but this decision continues to be vigorously opposed by Orthodox leaders.

Members of the Israeli Knesset are elected by a system of proportional representation with a low election threshold of 2%. This has tended to result in coalition governments that rely on the support of minority religious parties for their survival. In this context, participation in the secular Israeli political system has enabled Haredi Jews to shape debates over the Law of Return and win concessions such as legislation on food laws and financial support for religious students. Despite widespread secularity, then, Judaism – particularly in its Orthodox forms – is likely to remain a significant feature of Israeli political culture. In turn, Jewish religious expression has been profoundly shaped by the experience of statehood.

Religion was a, or the, crucial element of Jewish identity in the pre-modern era, and continues to function as such in many diaspora settings. In Israel, new Jewish identities have emerged, in which religion occupies a different role.[17] In sociological terms, a new Israeli civil religion has developed, which has incorporated aspects of the religious traditions of Judaism into broader, more diffuse expressions of national identity and unity. As described by Liebman and Don Yehiya, this civil religion is a set of norms, values and symbols embedded in political and social discourse and institutions. Speeches and policies, for example, regularly express the belief that Israel is the guarantor of Jewish security, and/or that the Jewish people's destiny is *moral* statehood. The country has its own quasi-religious symbols (a flag, which features a star of David on a blue and white design evoking the *tallit* or prayer-shawl traditionally worn by men during prayer). It also has its sacred sites, some of which are ancient religious ones like the Western Wall in Jerusalem or Masada,[18] and others which are newer, like the site of Yitzhak

STUDYING JUDAISM

Rabin's assassination in Tel Aviv or *Yad Vashem*, the Holocaust Memorial complex in Jerusalem. There are also special festival days, such as *Yom ha-Atzma'ut*, the anniversary of the proclamation of Israel's independence. Arguably, the practice of Israeli civil religion evidences a shift in Israel from substantive to more openly functional forms of religion; a move away from traditional Jewish forms of meaning to newer ones which are more readily suited to meet the needs of a young, highly diverse nation.[19]

The Eighteenth Knesset (Israeli parliament)

Summary of the results of elections for the Eighteenth Knesset (Israeli parliament) held on 10th February 2009, listed by political party and country of birth.

Party	MKs	Country/ies of Birth
Kadima (centrist party with some secularist policies)	28	Ethiopia (1) Former Soviet Union (3) Great Britain (1) Israel (17) Iran (1) Iraq (1) Morocco (3) Syria (1)
Likud (centre-right party)	27	Belgium (1) Former Soviet Union (2) Germany (1) Israel (21) Morocco (1) Tunisia (1)
Yisrael Beitenu (right-wing nationalist, secularist party)	15	Former Soviet Union (8) Israel (7, of which one Druze)
Labor (centre-left party)	13	Iraq (1) Israel (10) Morocco (2)

Shas (Sefardi and Mizrahi Haredi party)	11	Algeria (1) Former Soviet Union (2) Israel (6) Morocco (2)
United Torah Judaism (Ashkenazi Haredi party)	5	Germany (1) Israel (4)
Ra'am-Ta'al (Arab religious and nationalist party)	4	Israel
Ichad Leumi (right-wing religious nationalist party)	4	Israel
Hadash (socialist party)	4	Israel
New Movement-Meretz (left-green party)	3	Israel (2) Romania (1)
HaBayit HaYehudi (right-wing national religious party)	3	Israel
National Democratic Assembly (Arab nationalist party)	3	Israel

(source: *Knesset Members of the Eighteenth Knesset*, www.knesset.gov. il, accessed April 2009).

These figures are not representative of the Israeli population as a whole, but illustrate something of its 'newness' (nearly a third of members were born elsewhere, as were the parents of many Israel-born MKs) and its diversity.

A distinctive 'Russian-Jewish' political identity has emerged in recent years. 1,100,000 mostly secular people born in the former Soviet Union[20] currently make up around 20% of the Israeli Jewish population and dominate Yisrael Beitenu (YB), founded in 1999. The party has campaigned for civil marriage and divorce, as Orthodox regulation of personal status creates problems for its voters, many of whom are not *halakhically* Jewish, although they consider themselves Jews and may have been the victims of anti-Jewish discrimination in their previous countries of residence. In March 2010, the Knesset passed a YB-initiated bill permitting civil marriages between two partners of 'unclear' religious identity. The party also advocates a hard line approach to negotiations with Palestinians. This policy challenges any assumption that secular Israelis are likely to be 'Dovish' in their attitudes to the Israel–Palestine conflict, while those with 'Hawkish' attitudes are likely to be motivated by religion.

Less visible politically than Russian Jews are 'Ethiopian Jews' (80,000 people, of whom 30% are children, mostly enrolled in religious schools) who also migrated to Israel in the 1980s and 1990s. Low levels of economic and social capital, racism and tensions with Russian Jews have inhibited their participation in mainstream cultural and political life.

Classical civil religion theory is influenced by the approach of Talcott Parsons (1902–1979), who translated Weber's writings into English. Drawing on Weber and the consensus-oriented approaches of Emil Durkheim, Parsons advanced the idea that as societies modernize, particular religious values are increasingly generalized and subsumed within a broader culture.[21] Despite conflicts and tensions, societies have a shared underlying value-system. Such approaches have a degree of explanatory appeal in relation to the early post-1948 years, when Israeli Jews privately and publicly expressed a desire to be, and to define themselves as, an integrated nation, even as there were significant variations in the experiences and life chances of different ethnic groups.[22] They are less compelling when applied to the period since 1995, when Prime Minister Yitzhak Rabin was assassinated by Yigal Amir, a right-wing religious Zionist. During the past decade, religious, ethnic and political divisions within Israel have become wider and more widely acknowledged. It is far from clear that Israelis share common attitudes and goals, particularly in relation to Judaism.

Israel as a democracy versus Israel as Jewish state

When asked whether they would prefer Israel to be 'a democracy' or 'a Jewish state', Ashkenazi ultra-Orthodox and non-religious Israeli Jews answered as follows:

	Ultra Orthodox	Non-religious
Jewish state	84%	9%
Both equally important	10%	29%
Democratic state	6%	63%
Total	100%	100%

Between these two poles, Jews who identify as 'religious' or 'traditional', including modern Orthodox and non-Orthodox religious Jews, tend to endorse some kind of balance between Jewish religious and democratic values.[23]

In addition to the real differences between Israeli Jews, there are of course also significant ethnic and religious minorities in Israel who do not relate to Jewish religious symbols and concepts in the same manner as their neighbours.

EXERCISE

In what ways does Judaism function as a source of a) cohesion, and b) division in the State of Israel?

The Israel–Palestine conflict

It is perhaps unsurprising that the Israel–Palestine conflict is often regarded as a struggle between Judaism and Islam. As noted earlier, in many Western contexts, particularly in the United States, 'Jewish' is overwhelmingly regarded as a religious label rather than an ethnic one.[24] At the same time, in an increasingly mediatized world, distinctively dressed, passionately committed, religiously motivated Israeli settlers and Palestinian imams are attractive resources for journalists in search of material to use in their coverage of current affairs. Undeniably, both Judaism and Islam do have strong geo-political dimensions: while the *Tanakh* links the land and the people Israel, Muslims call Jerusalem *al-Quds* ('the Holy'), according it with a status surpassed only by that of Makkah and Madinah. It is believed to be the destination of Muhammad's 'night journey' and, from the perspective of many Muslims, conquest of the land in the seventh century means that Palestine is divinely ordained as Islamic territory.

In this book, the emphasis is necessarily on Judaism's position in the conflict, but it is relevant to note that, like Zionism, Arab political expression in the late nineteenth century, and for much of the twentieth century, was influenced by Western European nationalism, encountered in the context of colonialism. Since its inception in 1964, for example, the Palestine Liberation

Organization (PLO) has attempted to coordinate numerous, largely secular left-wing nationalist groups. Similarly, while various factors discussed in this chapter have contributed to the increasing assertiveness of Orthodox Jewish nationalists, in the past three decades particular interpretations of Islam have become more prominent within Palestinian society. The Shi'a Islamic political and paramilitary organization *Hezbollah* ('Party of God') began as a militia that opposed the Israeli army during the 1982 Lebanon War, and the Sunni organization *Hamas* ('Islamic Resistance Movement'), which has governed the Gaza portion of the Palestinian Territories since 2007, was founded as an offshoot of the Islamist Muslim Brotherhood in the late twentieth century. Like Israeli Jews then, Palestinians disagree as to whether a future Palestinian state should be a constitutional democracy, or an Islamic one, in which the Qur'an and Sunnah are the primary reference points.

Even given the growth of religious political parties, many of the specific tensions between Israeli Jews and Palestinians are not exclusively, or even primarily, religious in character. These include the fate of Palestinian refugees and Israeli settlers, and disagreements over rights to water and other natural resources. It is too simplistic, therefore, to describe the recent trends in Israeli politics as the political 'exploitation' or 'effects' of religion. But equally, in the light of such evidence, it is not possible to regard the Israel–Palestine conflict as a simple struggle between Judaism and the Palestinians, or Islam.

Finally, the trend towards increasing activism amongst religious Jews in Israel needs to be set alongside the kind of recent developments discussed in the text box on the Eighteenth Knesset. Some of the more hard-line nationalist views in contemporary Israel are articulated by secular Jews. Writing before the 2009 electoral success of the nationalist party Yisrael Beteinu, Ben-Rafael and Peres observed:

> Russian-Jewish political elites are at the forefront of the fight over the retention of the West Bank and Gaza Strip in the frame of the Israeli sovereignty, a posture that corresponds both to the power-oriented political culture that Russian Jews brought with them from the USSR [Union of Soviet Socialist Republics]/FSU [Former Soviet Union] and to the elite's aspiration to insert itself in the all-Israeli leading stratum.[25]

In other words, new groups may emerge within the Israeli political scene, and may express themselves in ways that draw on traditional political and religious categories, even as they are also estranged from the premises that have historically underpinned these positions. Russian-Israeli interventions in the Israel–Palestine conflict may be understood at least partly as a matter of their attempts to position themselves as a significant force in Israeli society.

Judaism in the public square: public *menorahs* in the United States

In the Talmud, the practice of lighting a *menorah* at *Hanukah* is linked to a commandment to 'publicize the miracle'. On this basis, in the late 1980s the Chabad-Lubavitch movement began erecting giant *menorahs* in public locations in cities worldwide.

The First Amendment to the United States Constitution, passed in 1789, states that, 'Congress shall make no law respecting an establishment of religion, or prohibiting the free exercise thereof'. Since the time of Thomas Jefferson (1743–1826), this has been interpreted as erecting a 'wall of separation' between religion and the state, so that government may not privilege one religion over another, or interfere with religious observance unless there are compelling reasons for doing so. In *County of Allegheny v. ACLU* in 1989, the US Supreme Court considered the legality of the erection of a public *menorah* and a nativity scene in Pittsburgh, Pennsylvania. The American Civil Liberties Union argued that because both items were on public property, their presence amounted to illegal endorsements of religion. The Court decided 'for' the *menorah* and 'against' the legality of the nativity. Although the *menorah* was erected by Chabad for religious reasons, the court ruled that, partly because of its specific location next to a brightly-lit municipal Christmas tree, it functioned as a symbol of a secularized 'winter holiday season'.

Some Jewish groups oppose public *menorahs*. Most notably, the American Jewish Congress, an organization that seeks to defend Jewish civil rights in the US and overseas, filed a brief *against* the *menorah* in *County of Allegheny*. While the Congress opposes restrictions on the display of religious symbols on private property, it regards the rigorous application of the First Amendment as an important guarantor of Jews' civil rights in the United States.

8

Culture

The suggestions that studying Judaism and other religions entails the study of culture, and that religious studies' contemporary willingness to study everyday artefacts and activities reflects the influence of cultural studies, are threads running through this book. At the very least, culture is part of religion, and religion is in turn an important aspect of culture.

Like that of 'religion', the definition of 'culture' is contested. In the 1970s, it was the 'difficult word' that prompted Raymond Williams to write *Keywords*, an influential guide to the evolution of the critical vocabulary used to discuss everyday experiences and events.[1] A decade later, reflecting on the use of the term in the humanities and social sciences, James Clifford wrote, 'Culture is a deeply compromised idea I cannot yet do without'.[2] Despite ambivalence over its application in particular instances, 'culture' continues to enjoy widespread use in academic and other discourses, as does the related adjective 'cultural' (as in 'cultural diversity', or 'cross-cultural dialogue'). Following Williams' initial scheme, 'culture' may be seen to be commonly used in three sometimes discrete, sometimes overlapping ways, to refer to:

- 'high' or elite culture; that is, to forms of expression that are considered by those with economic and political power to be of intellectual or aesthetic excellence. Within Judaism, examples of high culture might include texts like the *Tanakh*, which can be appreciated as a world literature classic as well as for its religious qualities; the performance of a celebrated *hazzan*; or ritual objects displayed in museums because they are considered to be of noteworthy quality or beauty.

- 'popular' culture, including cultural products with mass appeal, and the culture (artefacts, activities and attitudes) of ordinary people. Examples might include the music of reggae artiste Matisyahu and hip hopper Eprhyme, whose work is influenced by their Orthodox

Judaism; or items like the 'Say-A-Blessing' Keychain, which plays eight commonly used blessings for food and drink (and two 'bonus prayers') in Hebrew and English translation (see Fig. 8.1).

- the entire way of life of a society or group of people: 'what people do, what they *say* about what they do, and ... how they understand both of these activities'.[3] Almost everything discussed in this, or any, Judaism textbook might fall under the heading 'culture' as defined by this final, broad rubric.

As explored in previous chapters, some nineteenth-century Jewish historians, partly motivated by a desire to bolster the reputation of newly enfranchised European Jewish communities, produced studies that provided accounts of great men and achievements, or that emphasized Jewish suffering and persecution. By the century's end, later writers like B. Lionel Abrahams called for a re-centring of academic attentions on the everyday; 'Jews,' he said, 'were not always being persecuted or writing books or reading them'.[4] Even so, the study of religions has tended to focus on elite artefacts and activities, only comparatively recently turning to culture in the latter senses described by Williams. (Smart, for example, added the material dimension, under which heading high and popular art and architecture are typically located, to his

Figure 8.1: 'Say-A-Blessing' Keychain, © K. Hannah Holtschneider

account of religion's salient features in the 1980s.) To suggest how things might be done differently, this chapter addresses 'culture' as broadly defined by looking at food, aspects of the synagogue and clothing. It also discusses Judaism in relation to some cultural products or aspects of 'culture' more narrowly understood, especially film.

Synagogues

At their simplest, synagogues are functional spaces to house worship and other activities. For Smart, they, like other religious buildings, can be understood as 'congealed ritual and conceptual hardware': their design and decoration reflect their use in religious practices, and this in turn reinforces religious ideas about the universe and humanity's place within it.[5] But synagogues also reflect the tastes of, and resources available to, those who construct, adapt and use them. Just as there are many Jewish cultures, so there is no single Jewish building. Most synagogues reflect the architectural idiom of the broader surrounding culture, either because of a conscious desire to employ/challenge current styles, or because the building was previously used for another purpose. Civil law influences synagogue construction, too, as illustrated in Fig. 8.2.

Most synagogues share a few common internal features. A cupboard or curtained recess, known in Ashkenazi synagogues as the ark (*aron kodesh*), and in Sefardi ones as the sanctuary (*heikhal*), houses the Torah scroll or scrolls, usually on the Jerusalem-facing wall. It is often highly ornate, as are the fabric and silver cover and decorations used to protect and beautify the scrolls themselves. Other common prominent elements include the *bimah* (or *tevah*), a raised platform or desk from which the Torah is read, the *ner tamid* ('eternal light') that burns above the ark (symbolizing the divine presence) and seating. Usually, interiors are decorated in some way. Exod. 20.4–5 prohibits the making of representational art for worship purposes, but not art *per se*, so geometrical designs and calligraphy are commonly used. Figurative art is rare and avoids human faces.

The activities that take place in synagogues, and the meanings attached to them – synagogue cultures – vary. Alternative names for such buildings, including *bet ha-knesset* ('house of meeting'), *bet ha-midrash* ('house of study'), *shtibl* ('room') and *shul* or *shool* ('school') attest to the diversity of functions that 'synagogues' (the English word is derived from a Greek term meaning simply, '[place of] assembly') may serve. As noted in Chapter 2, American Reform Jews often refer to their houses of worship as Temples.

The synagogue is a gendered space. In buildings used for Orthodox services, women typically occupy a separate gallery or area behind a *mehitzah* (partition). In some Haredi synagogues and very old buildings, women occupy

Figure 8.2: Bevis Marks synagogue, London. © Daniel Zylbersztajn

Bevis Marks, opened in 1701, was constructed in a courtyard because Jews were forbidden from erecting synagogues on public roads. The building resembles the Spanish and Portuguese Synagogue in Amsterdam, where Jews practiced Judaism freely in the early modern period. Most Jews who settled in England after the formal re-admittance of Jews (1655) were Sefardim with links to the Amsterdam community, which had campaigned on their behalf. The Amsterdam building in turn resembles dissenting Christian chapels and meeting-houses – and the builder of Bevis Marks was a Quaker.

a side room from which they can observe what is happening in the main body of the synagogue through a window or grill in the wall. While such features are striking to many outside observers, the organization of space within *any* synagogue is *always* political, in that it reflects authority structures and values within a community, not just those between the genders. For example, in many Orthodox synagogues, as in Rhodes, the reading desk occupies a central position. Those who are called to read the Torah and the leader of the service (any suitably skilled adult males) are placed amongst and within the congregation. In contrast, many Reform communities site the *bimah* on a stage in front of a congregation whose seats are arranged auditorium-style. The leader stands apart from and faces the congregation, and guides their worship. He or she is often the rabbi, reflecting prevalent understandings of rabbinic authority within the movement.

Visiting a synagogue

Your study of Judaism may include a visit to a synagogue. Examining a building's physical features, and observing or interviewing its users *in situ* are useful counterweights to text-based understandings of religion. In relation to Smart-type models of religion, visits provide opportunities to encounter the experiential and emotional, ritual and practical, and social and institutional dimensions.

To make effective use of the experience it is important to plan beforehand and consider:

- What do you hope to learn?
- How will you collect data (e.g. observation, interviews, participant observation)?
- When will you visit? Many synagogues are only open during services or by appointment. If necessary, establish the start-times and length of services, and the effect that your hosts' religious observance will have on the information you can gather. For example, most religious Jews regard taking photographs and writing notes as forms of work prohibited on *Shabbat*;
- What dress codes apply? In Orthodox synagogues, women should generally wear a skirt or dress, and married women should cover their heads. Practically all synagogues require men to cover their heads. As a guest, follow these norms, like the ones on prohibited work, to avoid offending your hosts;
- Do men and women sit together or separately? Consider how this will affect the kind of data you can obtain.

Establish contact with the synagogue beforehand, as a matter of courtesy and to ensure access. Some congregations have members who are experienced in explaining the building and aspects of Judaism. This is useful if you have never visited a synagogue before, and your interests are broad. Bear in mind, however, the limitations as well as the strengths of the data that this will yield. What your guide wishes to communicate may not answer your own questions, and the views of an individual, however enthusiastic or learned, are not a reliable guide to the diversity of Jewish religious experience that exists even within a single congregation.

Finally, consider ethical issues. Seek permission to take photographs, record or quote someone. Consider whether or not to participate in worship, or to share in *kiddush*, blessings over food and drink that often take place after *Shabbat* services. If participation would be detrimental to your study-goals or make you feel uncomfortable, explain this to your contact beforehand.

Dress

Most textbook treatments of Judaism mention a small number of ritual garments and worn objects, chiefly the 'prayer shawl' (*tallit*) and 'phylacteries' (*tefillin*).[6] These items evolved as responses to specific biblical commandments. Deut. 22.12 prescribes the placing of fringes, *tzitzit*, on the four corners of garments as a reminder of God's laws. In medieval Europe, wearing a *tallit*, a rectangular, fringed garment, developed as a means of fulfilling this requirement. Nowadays, Jews who wear the *tallit* (both genders in Reform and some Conservative communities, men only in Orthodox ones) usually do so only during prayers, although some wear a kind of four-cornered vest beneath their outer clothes throughout the day. *Tefillin* are small leather boxes containing parchments on which passages from biblical texts are written (Exod. 13.1–10 and 11–16; Deut. 6.4–9 and 11.13–21) and attached to the head and 'weaker' (non-writing) arm using leather straps. Like the *tallit*, they are most widely worn by Orthodox and Conservative men during morning prayers. Reform and Liberal Jews are more likely to interpret the scriptural injunctions to place the words of Torah on one's hand and head figuratively, as calls to let scripture continually influence one's thoughts and deeds.

Tefillin and *tallit*-wearing invite attention because they are visible, consciously ritual practices, but other phenomena might also be considered under the rubric of 'Judaism and dress'. For much of its history, the study of religions largely neglected dress, reflecting, perhaps, a gender bias that regarded a preoccupation with clothing as a trivial, female preserve. Recent scholarship has begun to address this gap, drawing on developments in other disciplines. Sensory historians, for example, suggest that we read clothes from the inside out in order to understand wearers' tactile experiences and the meanings they attach to them.[7] Online retailers of modest clothing for Haredi women frequently emphasize the *feel* of garments ('no more sweltering, no more itching'[8]) as well as the coverage provided by higher necklines, below-the-knee skirts and lengthier sleeves. Drawing on cultural studies approaches, dress can also be read 'from outside in'; that is, in terms of how it performs various social functions relating to identity and status, as well as the more narrowly 'religious' purposes described in conventional accounts of specific ritual garments. Chapter 6 suggested that modest dress defines and identifies Haredi women against other Jews and non-Jews. Skirt length and fabric, type of head covering and make-up (or lack of it) all locate a woman in terms of her position on the Orthodox spectrum.[9]

Male religious identities are also communicated by dress:

> If you are a Chasid, on weekdays this will mean an elongated version of a standard suit jacket … There will be no outside pocket, it will always be double-breasted, and for reasons of Kabbalistic symbolism (denoting kindness over strength) it will … [button] from left to right. Chasidim of Hungarian origin go for the same designs, but with short jackets.
>
> On Shabbat, Chasidic men will wear a long satin or polyester jacket called a *bekishe* for prayers, and then change in to a less expensive version with a belt … for meals and synagogue on Saturday afternoon. … Mitnagdim … wear a normal short suit, and traditionally have a preference for double-breasted. If you [are] … a rabbi, yeshivah teacher or dayan [judge] you are likely to wear a frock coat.[10]

Each of the sub-categories of dress described here could be elaborated, and to the list of garments we might add the *gartel*, a string belt or sash worn particularly by Hasidim during prayer to symbolically separate the upper ('pure') part of the body from the lower ('impure') part. Figure 2.1, a photograph of pilgrims to Elimelech of Lizhensk's grave, illustrates some of the garments described here. The men who stand to the right of the foreground are wearing a black felt fedora, made popular amongst Lubavitch Hasidim by Menachem Mendel Schneerson, and a *bekishe*, a long black coat made of silk or polyester. Others may also wear a *streimel*, a fur hat worn mainly by married men from Hasidic groups originating in Galicia (parts of present day Poland and Ukraine).

Even those who adhere to such codes are not isolated from fashions or cycles of changing patterns, cuts and colours. Haredi men's clothing fabrics have traditionally been plain, but patterned black fabrics, and navy and grey ones, have recently become popular amongst younger men. Distinctive cufflinks, belts, and spectacle frames are also increasingly sought-after, and the crowns and brims of hats are increasing in size. Such trends illustrate the need to avoid simplistic definitions of religious dress, the possibility and desire for individualistic expression within religiously and socially conformist and traditionalist settings, and the impact of rising living standards and consumerism, even within communities that espouse alternative value-systems.

The importance of nuance in dress does not only apply in the case of Haredim. A man or woman may decide to wear a *kippah* (small skull cap) out of a desire to adhere to the traditional acknowledgement that 'the *Shekhinah* [Divine Presence] is above my head' (*Kiddushim* 31a). Alternatively he or she may wish to assert a Jewish identity in a predominantly non-Jewish society, perhaps to appear exotic, subversive or just different. Still other factors may influence the decision about when to wear the *kippah* – in the synagogue, when studying the Torah, or at all times? Finally, distinctive meanings attach to the kind of *kippah* that is worn. In Israel, for example, *kippot serugot*, 'knitted kippot' has become a nickname for religious Zionists, after the crocheted head covering commonly favoured by men in such groups. Similarly, traditionalist Orthodox males are sometimes known as *kippot shehorot*, 'black kippot'. Lighter colours and fabrics are favoured by children and adults in non-Orthodox movements.

Food

In Judaism, the relationship between cuisine and culture is rooted in *halakhah*.[11] Lev. 11 and Deut. 14.3–21 categorize certain foods as *kosher*, 'right' or 'fit' to be eaten, and other ones as *treifah*, 'torn' or prohibited. Permitted foods include animals which have cloven hooves and chew the cud (including cattle, sheep and deer), and fish with scales and fins – no shellfish or other sea creatures. Specific insects and birds are permitted, but as it is not always clear which creature is being referred to in the scriptural passages, communities have evolved different traditions concerning their consumption.

Kosher foods must be prepared appropriately, as described and codified in rabbinic literature, particularly the *Shulhan Arukh*. Animals and birds are ritually slaughtered by the swift cutting of their windpipes, so that the blood drains away. The carcass is inspected to ensure that it is defect-free, and a rinsing and salting process removes the remaining blood (Lev. 7.26–27; 17.10–14). Finally, the cooking process is also circumscribed by numerous *halakhot*. Rabbinic protocols have understood the prohibition on 'boiling a kid in its mother's milk' (Exod. 23.19; 34.26; Deut. 14.21) to ban the cooking or eating together of meat and milk, and the derivation of any benefit from such a mixture – for example, by selling it.

Ritual slaughter, *shehita*, uses a blade which must be sharpened and checked daily for imperfections that would prevent a clean cut being made. In the modern period, it has become a subject of controversy and the target of campaigns by Jewish and non-Jewish animal welfare advocates. As of 2010, *shehita* is illegal in several of the Nordic and Baltic states and in New Zealand, where pre-stunning of animals and birds for slaughter is required; members of the European Parliament have also voted in favour of proposals to require the labelling of 'meat from slaughter without stunning' throughout the European Union.[12]

Some religious Jews, especially those identifying as Reform or Liberal, follow a vegetarian diet for reasons of convenience or ethics. From an Orthodox standpoint, however, vegetarianism is non-*halakhic*; meat consumption is given to humans in Gen. 9.3. Arguably, *shehitah* is also relatively humane: since it cannot be fully automated or industrialized, the slaughterer is required to adopt a respectful attitude, and blood loss causes animals to lose consciousness almost immediately, before registering pain.

EXERCISE

Based on your knowledge of the different modern Jewish religious movements, what do you expect to be the main contours of first-order/insiderly approaches to dietary laws articulated by Orthodox and Reform Jews? Are other ways of understanding *kashrut* suggested by second-order, analytical concepts that have been introduced so far in this book?

The Torah links *kashrut* with the holiness or separation of the Jews:

I am the LORD your God who has set you apart from other peoples. So you shall set apart the clean beast from the unclean, the unclean bird from the clean. You shall not draw abomination upon yourselves through beast or bird or anything with which the ground is alive, which I have set apart for you to treat as unclean. You shall be holy to Me, for I the LORD am holy, and I have set you apart from other peoples to be Mine (Lev. 20.24–6).

Of course, the kind of separation fostered by dietary laws varies according to time and place. In historically Muslim countries where grains, vegetables and oils are food staples, not eating pork, and not mixing meat and dairy, is less distinctive than in many Christian cultures.

Medieval writers described numerous advantages that they believed were associated with a *kosher* diet – perhaps reflecting a desire to encourage reasoned observance, or to counter anti-Jewish polemics. Maimonides argued that animals and dishes prohibited in *halakhah* were frequently unhealthy and indigestible. Biblical commentator and *kabbalist* Nachmanides (1194–1270) suggested that prohibited animals and birds were predators, whose violent characteristics affected those who ate them, while permitted species were calmer, promoting human refinement. Theoretically, Nachmanides' linkage of food consumption patterns and spiritual development only provides ancillary support for *kashrut* – laws warrant allegiance because of their divine nature – but it is regularly invoked in Orthodox apologetics today.

Contemporary approaches to the dietary laws vary widely. Haredim and Orthodox communities attach considerable value to their observance, and in the developed world, aspects of *kashrut* have become less taxing for those who wish to maintain a *kosher* kitchen. Whereas previously much of the work of meat preparation was carried out in the home, it is now possible to buy a wide range of pre-prepared products that carry seals or stamps indicating that they have been certified *kosher* by a *bet din*. The average American supermarket stocks 13,000 such items; around 75,000 products are available nationally.[13] *Kosher* butchers, bakers and restaurants are similarly licensed. At the same time, it is possible to observe a tendency towards increased stringency regarding food, which places new burdens on *kosher* consumers. In 2004, numerous New York institutions and families installed filtration equipment to remove zooplankton from the water supply, even though the microscopic creatures were invisible to the naked eye, and so were not, in Talmudic or public health terms, significant enough to render the water impure. Some Haredi rabbis urge their followers to patronize only 'Torah-true' businesses, linking the acceptability of foodstuffs to the morals and ethics of their manufacturer, rather than compliance with *kashrut* alone. While, like the renewed preoccupation with dress, such moves may reflect a broader concern to establish markers of observant Orthodox identity, it is also the case that within Jewish cultures in which gender roles are highly differentiated, the kitchen remains an important place for women to express and exhibit their piety. Stringent observance of the food laws becomes a means to women's acquisition of cultural or religious capital.[14]

The history of the Reform movement illustrates quite different approaches to *kashrut*. Today, some Reform Jews choose to keep some of the food laws, particularly biblical ones, such as the list of forbidden and permitted animals. Others may observe laws at home but not elsewhere, or vice versa. (The same is true of some Conservative and non-Haredi Orthodox Jews.) In many respects, this is representative of the wider returning to ritual in Reform Judaism. For German reformer Samuel Holdheim, they had 'lost altogether their religious truth and significance for us now ... we ... consider and love all men as his [God's] children and our brethren'.[15] The authors of the Pittsburgh Platform followed suit 40 years later when they, too, openly rejected the dietary laws (see Chapter 2, Fig. 2.1). *Kashrut's* sociological function as a means of creating and maintaining a distinctive Jewish identity was considered an obstacle to the universalistic ideals that reformers espoused. A rejection of *kashrut* in the past (or present) was (or is) not, then, necessarily a hallmark of secularism and declining religious commitment. As Kraemer notes, 'these rabbis [Holdheim and others] ... are acting in what they believe to be a genuine Jewish spirit. For them, the identity of the modern Jew is best reflected in a thoroughly open dietary regime. *Though they are now eating as others, they are still eating as Jews*' (my italics).[16]

In short, contemporary attitudes towards the dietary laws reveal the extent to which ritual practice or performance is often not a matter of absolutes – yes or no; *kosher* or *treifah* – but of *occasional distinctions*, of observances which for many Jews today are subject to repeated, ongoing re-negotiation. They also illustrate that any study of food and food consumption in Judaism that refers to *halakhah* alone cannot be exhaustive. Further underscoring this point, anthropologist Jack Kugelmass has described the emergence of 'ethnic theme park restaurants' in New York's Lower East Side, whose patrons can listen to piped recordings of Yiddish songs and look at sepia photographs and curios while consuming non-rabbinically supervised, and in some cases non-*kosher*, but stereotypically 'Jewish foods' like bagels, chicken soup and fried fish.[17] The foods, and the context in which they are eaten, differ from those envisaged in the classical legal accounts of *kashrut*, as do the diners' nostalgic or comfort-seeking motivations. Nevertheless, such phenomena illustrate the extent to which food continues to play a significant role in the construction of Jewish identity and experience. Studying Jewish food remains, then, a critical issue for those studying Judaism.

Cultural products

The categories of elite and popular culture as described by Williams both refer in large measure to *cultural products*, or as Nye puts it, 'what people do in literature, art, music and so on'.[18] Such products, and their potential to shed light on culture in Williams' third sense ('way of life') are of increasing interest to scholars of religion. Given the dizzying range of phenomena that such work might embrace, this section can only be suggestive of the potential of such work for a critical understanding of Judaism.[19]

EXERCISE

Look at the brief notes on the *mezuzah* in Chapter 1, and the examples of *mezuzah* cases depicted in Fig. 1.1. From a cultural studies perspective, artefacts, embed beliefs, concepts and relationships, and everyday objects like the *mezuzah* case provide fertile ground for critical analysis because 'the ordinary often signals what people believe, what they take for granted, what they do unselfconsciously.'[20] How would you interpret the decision to use one of these cases rather than another?

The *halakhah* contains no detailed guidelines concerning *mezuzah* cases. Strictly speaking, a *mezuzah* can be fixed directly to a doorpost, and the case is simply a practical way of preventing damage, which would invalidate the scroll. Figure 1.1 indicates the range of contemporary possibilities. As is the case with other objects linked to domestic piety (for example, *tzedakah* or charity boxes), the decision to opt for one rather than another is partly a matter of personal preference and taste; an opportunity to express or represent one's piety and identity to oneself and others. For example, a relatively plain case might reflect a general preference for simplicity or functionality, or perhaps a religious commitment to the norms of *tzniut* outlined in Chapter 6. Still different meanings attach to a conscious decision to use a box made in Israel (in which case we might interpret a particular consumption practice as an act of Zionism) or by a child in a local synagogue youth group. The Spiderman case in Fig. 1.1 is marketed particularly for children; its featuring of a masked (semi-)human form is unlikely to make it an attractive choice for many observant Orthodox parents.

Things that matter – the Torah scroll

Shalom Sabar's recent study of Torah scrolls illustrates the importance of the material dimension of religion.[21] Many Talmudic and later regulations govern the production and use of Torah scrolls. There are rules concerning the type and preparation of the parchment that is used and the style and spacing of the letters written upon it. A special covering and decorative finials or *rimmonim* (literally, 'pomegranates') protect and adorn the scroll when it is not being used. Referring to the ark, in which the scroll is stored, 'It is,' said Maimonides, 'praiseworthy to ... respect that place, and make it very beautiful.'[22]

It is forbidden to touch a scroll with a bare hand, or move it without reason. It is also a *mitzvah* to stand, as a sign of respect, when the scroll is removed from the ark, and a scroll that is damaged beyond repair cannot be thrown away but should be stored in a *genizah* prior to burial.[23]

These rules illustrate how the status of Torah scrolls as physical objects far exceeds their function in the synagogue. Beyond this, Sabar describes how Jews, particularly those living in Islamic countries, developed popular beliefs in the miraculous powers of Torah scrolls, some of which persist today. For example, Libyan Jews kept new scrolls for a week in rooms specially decorated for the purpose, and during this time women seeking husbands, or experiencing difficulties during pregnancy and childbirth, would sleep there. Belief in the power of scrolls also finds expression in the various objects that decorate them. In Kurdistan and Afghanistan, Torah finials were constructed to allow them to contain water. Because of its proximity to the scroll, the water was regarded as holy and given to women during childbirth. The image of a small fish, thought to protect against the evil eye (a look believed to be able to invoke injury or bad luck on the person at whom it is directed) decorates Torah finials from Yemen while the *hamsa* (palm-shaped amulet) is found on finials from many regions including present-day Georgia, Iraq, Iran and Israel.

While cultural products like *mezuzah* cases or Torah scrolls are distinctive to Judaism, others, like novels, film or music are not, but their examination is increasingly recognized as forming a legitimate part of the study of Judaism, as evidenced by university and college curricula, if not yet by most textbooks.[24] This development is partly motivated by pragmatism: many teachers recognize that their courses operate in a 'marketplace' and need to appeal to learners with diverse educational and cultural backgrounds, many of whom are increasingly visually literate but do not have much prior knowledge of religion. It also reflects the fact that many films portray religious people, activities and values, providing viewers with opportunities to engage religious cultures that they could not otherwise readily access and experience, and thereby playing an important role in shaping perceptions of those cultures. However, screen images of religion are always partial, in both senses of the word. Consequently, the use of film presents its own challenges for the study of Judaism.

Each aspect of a film's *mise-en-scène* (setting, subjects and how they are composed or arranged), cinematography, editing and sound is the result of a choice and is intended to construct viewers' experiences of and relation to its subject-matter. No film, therefore, can provide a straightforward 'window' on to Judaism. Many early screen depictions of Judaism (and some later ones, too) are overtly negative. For example, in *The Jazz Singer* (directed by Alan Crosland, 1927), religious practices (specifically the observance of *Yom Kippur*) and roles (that of the *hazzan* or synagogue cantor) are things that the lead character Jakie must leave behind in order to pursue a career as a popular entertainer. In other words, Judaism is presented as a primitive, outmoded tradition that must be cast off as a precursor to achieving one's 'happy ending'. On other occasions, images may be more neutral or positive, but function primarily as visual shorthands to establish a character's Jewishness, not to tell us about Judaism *per se*. The brief depictions of Sabbath observance (the lighting of candles and recitation of *kiddush* over wine) work this way in *Schindler's List* (Steven Spielberg, 1993). Films like *The Quarrel* (Eli Cohen, 1990) in which two Holocaust survivors debate issues of theodicy and survivor-guilt on *Rosh ha-Shanah* are rare, partly because such dialogue-heavy approaches do not readily lend themselves to the medium of cinema. In crime thrillers and romances, Jewish identity, often signalled in religious terms, similarly serves as a variation on a stock dramatic device: religious differences are obstacles that the detective, or the would-be couple, must negotiate in order to solve the mystery or achieve romantic happiness. *A Stranger Among Us* (Sidney Lumet, 1992) shows some aspects of observant Orthodox culture, touching on prayer and study, and regulations surrounding food and sexual modesty. But this milieu is ultimately a picturesque backdrop to undercover detective Emily Eden's hunt for the murderer of a Hasidic diamond-cutter. Documentaries, too, cannot be regarded as providing uncomplicated depictions of Judaism. Like fictional features they are selective, edited (and often) staged representations of events. While a sense of accuracy and balance are often crucial to securing audience attentions, documentary filmmakers are also motivated by various goals – to communicate information and foster understanding, and/or perhaps to campaign for particular political or social changes – that affect the ways in which they handle their subjects. For example, Sandi Simcha DuBowski's *Trembling Before G-d* (2001) combines cinéma vérité sequences (naturalistic footage shot on location using unobtrusive equipment) with interviews and overtly staged performances of religious rituals by actors who appear in silhouette, behind a screen. DuBowski has described how his motivations shifted during the six-year production period from initial curiosity (he is gay and a Conservative Jew) to a sense of responsibility for his subjects, Haredi and other Orthodox Jews who are gay and lesbian. The film is widely regarded as establishing homosexuality as a subject of public debate within Orthodox and Conservative Jewish circles, partly through the campaigning work of DuBowski and Steven Greenberg[25], who hosted several hundred film screenings and related discussion events around the world.

Bearing in mind these factors, film can, if treated with the same critical caution that is applied to other sources in religious studies, be a useful tool in the study of Judaism. As a medium, film can be suggestive of aspects of contemporary Jewish religious experience that are hard to describe on paper. One of these is the postmodern character of much contemporary Jewish religious practice. *Dieu est grand, je suis petite* ([God is Great, I'm Not] Pascale Bailly, 2001) is a comedy about a relationship between Michèle, a Parisian model who adopts Catholicism, Buddhism and then Judaism in her quest for 'meaning', and François, a secular Jew. Contrary to normal genre conventions, it is the non-Jew's fascination with Judaism that eventually drives the couple apart. The film explores both the observance of Judaism by non-Jews (despite François' concerns, Michèle fixes a *mezuzah* to their door, attends Judaism classes and begins to observe *Shabbat*) and by Jews who are largely removed from the religious symbols and traditions they enact in order to satisfy the appetites of a predominantly non-Jewish 'audience' (at Michèle's insistence, François dons a *kippah*, keeps *kosher* and learns how to pray). As such, it is not a factually accurate or representative account of Judaism in France, but does engage an emergent trend that anthropologist Ruth Ellen Gruber has identified in many parts of Europe, and which she has described as a 'virtual Judaism' performed by 'virtual Jews'.[26]

In a different vein, shifting trends in Israeli films reflect and contribute to the publicization of Judaism in the modern state. Like Orthodox observant Jews elsewhere, religious Jews in Israel have typically regarded the early cinema in highly negative terms. Screen images of bodies and faces are viewed as potentially idolatrous violations of the commandment against the creation of graven images in Exod. 20.3, while darkened film theatres are potential sites of inappropriate contact between the sexes. Made by and for non-Orthodox and secular audiences, most early Israeli films downplayed the significance of Judaism in the construction of Israeli and Jewish identities, or portrayed it in negative terms, as something largely irrelevant to, or downright obstructive of, the Zionist project of nation-building. Some recent productions reflect a recent weakening of confidence in the Zionist master narrative and a greater and more public awareness of the ethnic and religious diversity – divisions, even – in Israeli society, resulting in more varied treatments of Judaism. *Kadosh* ([Sacred] Amos Gitai, 1999) centres on the lives of Meir and Rivka, an Hasidic couple who are infertile, and Rivka's sister Malka, who is forced into a violent arranged marriage. It is unusual in its attention to the spaces and rhythms of Orthodox observance. Extended sequences show Meir's daily prayers, the two women's painstaking preparation of *kosher* foods, the crowded atmosphere in a traditional *shtibl* (prayer room) and Meir and Rivka's dependence on their *rebbe* for advice as to the correct course of action in even the most intimate of matters, namely their failure to conceive a child. Ultimately, however, Hasidic Judaism serves as a negatively valued figure for the differences that exist in Israeli society. In particular, Gitai suggests that it is a patriarchal system which women must overcome or be crushed by in their struggle for self-realization. At the film's end, Malka has left the community in order to pursue a relationship with a non-observant man and Rivka (whom Meir, at his *rebbe*'s direction, reluctantly divorces, so that he may remarry and fulfil the commandment to procreate with another woman) dies, broken-hearted.

A quite different perspective is represented by and in *Ushpizin* ([Guests] Giddi Dar, 2004), whose title alludes to a kabbalistic ritual in which participants invite seven biblical characters (Abraham, Isaac, Jacob, Moses, Aaron, Joseph and David) to become 'guests' in their *sukkah* or shelter during the festival of *Sukkot*. The principal characters, Moshe and Malle, are a *ba'alei teshuvah* (newly observant) couple who find themselves playing host to visitors from Moshe's criminal past. After attempting to rid themselves of the embar-rassment, the couple eventually recognize the experience as a test of their faith. Unusually, the film was conceived partly as a bridge-building exercise between secular (like Giddi Dar) and religious (like Shuli and Michal Rand, who play Malle and Moshe) Israelis. Before its release, the film was shown to a Hasidic audience, and by agreement in Israel it is not exhibited on *Shabbat*. *Ushpizin* is distinguished, then, from the other films discussed in this chapter, not only because of its interest in Judaism as a total, lived culture, but also because its production rests on assumptions about the ability of film as a medium to communicate a particular form of Judaism to a broad and largely secular audience.[27]

9

Memory

Memory is central to Judaism. In the *Tanakh*, 'remember[ing] the days of old' (Deut. 32.7) is presented as a vehicle through which Jews can understand God's nature and relationship with the world. When Moses first encounters God it is as the God of his ancestors, 'the God of your father, the God of Abraham, the God of Isaac, and the God of Jacob' (Exod. 3.6), and later God is presented as prefacing the giving of the covenant at Sinai with a reminder of historical events: 'I the LORD am our God who brought you out of the land of Egypt, the house of bondage' (Exod. 20.2). This idea, that God is revealed in the biblical past, persisted during the pre-modern, rabbinic era. Liturgies and other sacred texts transmitted accounts of moments of deliverance and judgement to educative ends, using them to shape and express the meanings of subsequent experiences. The tradition of proclaiming a *Purim sheni* (Second Purim), complete with its own *megillah* or scroll, to celebrate a local community's escape from a fate that is likened to that faced by Jews in the time of Esther is one example of this phenomenon. Another is the Passover *seder*, in which participants are encouraged, through the performance of a series of rituals including bodily gestures and food consumption, as well as through their reading of the *haggadah*, to feel as if they themselves have experienced slavery and exodus from Egypt. This tendency to collapse the distance between present and past, and more specifically, to turn to ritualized memory in order to express and shape the meanings attributed to contemporary events, existed alongside a comparative lack of interest in the details of those later events. Maimonides' apparent disdain for historical works (*Commentary to m.Sanhedrin* 10.1) is consistent with a tradition which derives the meaning of contemporary events from their assimilation to biblical patterns of explanation. Thus, rather than generating historical narratives, experiences of persecution and suffering were linked to the condition of exile, finding their expression in poetry and martyrologies, compiled in *Memorbücher* (Memorial Books), and also included in memorial services for the dead.

With the advent of modernity, attitudes to historical experiences changed along with changing conceptions of Judaism. Historical criticism applied to ancient source texts queried the historicity or facticity of events described in the Torah and led to the historicization of Judaism, a tradition subject to development and change. Along with historical change – new events and contexts – conceptual changes develop which enable various perspectives on Jewish scripture and tradition, giving expression to the idea that Judaism may not be seen as an immutable body of truth transmitted through the generations. More recently it is possible to observe a rise in the theorization of memory as a critical concept, an interest in the ways in which past events are brought into present consciousness, and the ways in which that memory may be used and abused.

This chapter focuses on several examples and aspects of memory in Judaism. It considers rituals surrounding the treatment and memorializing of the dead, before discussing pilgrimages, Holocaust remembrance and museums. Being mindful of Smart's 'ritual and practical dimension' of practices surrounding death, pilgrimages and Holocaust remembrance allows us to observe the various ways in which individuals may invest traditional rituals, adapt these to contemporary needs and express concern for *klal Yisrael*, the whole of the Jewish people.

Remembering the dead

As Marcus notes, death is a personal event *and* a social and cultural moment.[1] Rituals surrounding the treatment of a dead body, and the behaviour of those who remember the deceased person, express and give rise to values and beliefs.

In many communities, especially Orthodox ones, a *hevra kadisha* or 'holy fellowship' of respected volunteers is responsible for the washing and dressing of a corpse, which is wrapped in white garments and (in the case of men only in Orthodox Judaism) a *kittel* and a *tallit*, from which one of the fringes is cut, marking the fact that the dead are no longer subject to the *mitzvot*. In Israel, the *hevra* also publicize the death, and the funeral – which may be on the same day as the death – by pasting notices on walls near to the deceased's home. The Talmud (*Mo'ed Katan* 27b) requires that shroud and coffin be simple, 'out of deference for the poor'.[2] Orthodoxy also requires burial in consecrated ground; cremation is eschewed on the grounds that it constitutes a mutilation of the body, and is seemingly an affront to belief in bodily resurrection. Progressive Jews, however, may practice cremation because they believe in the immortality of the human spirit or soul, or because they reject or are broadly speaking indifferent about belief in any kind of post-mortem existence.

Mourning rites in Judaism offer close relatives (parents, siblings, spouse, children) of the dead person a structure of brief retreat from, and gradual return to, the routines of everyday life. In this sense, they are a ready illustration of the 'rite of passage' or life crisis rite as described by Arnold van Gennep. According to van Gennep, rites of passage help manage changes in an individual's status by means of a three-part structure:

- removal from the immediate social group;

- isolation in a temporary or liminal state;

- incorporation into the social group, with a new status.

When first hearing of a parent's death, Orthodox Jews may carry out *keri'ah*, or rending of garments, a traditional sign of grief (Gen. 37.34, Job 1.20, 2 Sam. 1.11). Nowadays, this is often symbolic (the cutting of a tie or lapel.) *Halakhically*, their status is that of an *onen* and they are exempt from many *mitzvot* including the obligation to pray. But the desired swiftness of burial means that most rituals occur after interment, at which point the mourner or *avel* is subject to a different set of expectations and regulations. During a period of seven days (*shiva*) after the funeral, family members remain at home, sitting on low stools or pillows, and avoiding a range of activities such as bathing, shaving, sexual intercourse and religious study. The mourning family is effectively isolated from the everyday world, save for visits from friends and others who come to console and pray with them. Although one is a mourner by obligation for parents, siblings, children and spouse only, it is a *mitzvah* or good deed to visit mourners at this time.[3]

After *shiva* is ended, less intense periods of 30 days and 12 months (in the case of one's parents only) begin (see Deut. 34.8). To a large extent 'normal' life is resumed, but Orthodox observant mourners do not attend most religious celebrations, such as weddings or circumcisions.[4] Bereaved sons traditionally say the mourner's *kaddish* in synagogues on weekday mornings for 11 months. This prayer does not refer to death, but emphasizes God's power over the universe and asks for peace. (In Reform and Liberal movements, in Conservative Judaism and now also some Orthodox congregations, women can also perform the ritual.) At the end of one year, the death anniversary (in Yiddish, *yahrzeit*) is marked by prayer and the lighting of a candle in the synagogue. This custom is ostensibly based on the Proverb, 'the lifebreath [soul] of man is the lamp of the LORD' (20.27) although the Ashkenazi prayer *El male rachamim* ('God full of compassion ...') originated in seventeenth-century Europe (Sefardim recite prayers known as *Hashkaba*, 'laying to rest'). Like *shiva*, *yahrzeit* is more widely observed than the restrictions relating to secondary mourning periods. It is repeated each year and today many synagogues and charities offer *yahrzeit* reminder services, as well as facilities to create their own online memorials.[5]

Various religious reasons are offered for these practices. At a basic level, they are a way of observing the biblical injunction to honour one's parents (Exod. 20.12). In medieval Ashkenaz, where the *yahrzeit* was first developed, there was a belief in an ongoing relationship between the living and the dead. Rabbinic sources from the time suggest that one can atone for the dead by remembering them and giving charity on their behalf.[6] In this context, the *Yizkor* ('May He remember the soul of ...') prayer, recited on the final day of *Pesach*, *Shavuot*, *Sukkot* and *Yom Kippur* was also developed as a means of remembering departed parents. From a secular psychological or sociological perspective, however, close family and friends of the deceased are clearly the prime 'beneficiaries' of rites surrounding death and burial. As outlined earlier, the structured mourning period facilitates the gradual return of the mourner to normal life, enabling them to reintegrate within religious and secular society. More specifically, in a study of a modern Orthodox synagogue in Canada, Simcha Fishbane found that mourning rites were a means of re-socialization for middle-aged men who had previously been estranged from organized religious life. Saying *kaddish* for their parents provided a route to the maintenance or rebuilding of contacts with a synagogue community. After the first *yahrzeit*, a proportion of the men would remain active members of the congregation. The incorporation of the *kaddish* sayers into the synagogue also attracted their immediate family members, further augmenting membership.[7]

Fishbane's findings illustrate the extent to which even very personal acts of memory and remembrance are not the functions of disembodied, individual consciousness. Rather, they are bound up with physical acts (like cutting one's clothing, travelling daily to a synagogue, or reciting a prayer) and they link the individual to the collective. If individuals remember, they do so as members of groups that provide them with contextualizing frameworks into which their memories are woven.

Pilgrimage

Whether undertaken individually or as part of a larger group, pilgrimages to religiously and nationally significant places, or to the graves of important figures can be understood as another way of connecting Jews to each other, and to particular interpretations of Jewish history. The emphasis in Jewish pilgrimage is less on the journey than on the destination; it is important to *be* in a particular place, how one gets there is of lesser significance. In contrast to Christian and Muslim pilgrimages, there is no expectation for the Jewish pilgrim to be changed fundamentally by having been in a particular place, though more recently the notion of some kind of spiritual transformation begins to be emphasized by individual pilgrims.

Since biblical times, journeys to Jerusalem at set times of the year formed an important part of the religious calendar. Three times a year, during the so-called 'pilgrim festivals' (*shloshah regalim*) of *Pesach*, *Shavuot* and *Sukkot* which coincide with harvests, Israelite men would travel to Jerusalem to make offerings in the Temple (Exod. 34.18–23 and Deut. 16). Such collective pilgrimages were ways of cementing a common narrative of origin – the exodus (recalled at *Pesach*), the reception of the Torah (*Shavuot*) after wanderings in the wilderness (*Sukkot*). With the loss of sovereignty and dispersion of the majority of Jews in the Diaspora, the practice of collective pilgrimages to Jerusalem ceased, though the significance attached to being in the sacred land of Israel continues to prompt Jews to travel there.

In traditional understanding, the land of Israel is inherently sacred, and the act of visiting or living there conveys particular religious benefits. In addition to the desire to observe the *mitzvot* relating to the pilgrim festivals, some medieval Jewish travellers to the land of Israel were motivated by a belief that they should die or at least be buried there. This would help them be among the first to be resurrected, a process believed to begin on the Mount of Olives in Jerusalem, or that prayers made there would be more likely to secure a favourable response due to the proximity of holy sites.

Critical studies of religion, however, adopt a different approach to pilgrimage, focusing on such issues as the perceptions and meanings that pilgrims bring to the sacred places they visit. Issues which the study of pilgrimage may bring to the scholar's attention can be illustrated with reference to pilgrimages associated with holy figures. In addition to biblically mandated pilgrimage to particular places, we can observe the development of pilgrimage to sites associated with particular figures, in the land of Israel (tombs of the Patriarchs and Matriarchs), and especially in Morocco, Israel and continental Europe. These sites often have to do with *tzaddikim* ('righteous persons', a term applied in particular to spiritual leaders of Hasidic sects).

Visiting the grave of a Hasidic *rebbe*, a *tzaddik*, is associated with the pilgrim seeking a closer connection to the divine facilitated through the power of the deceased holy person. Pilgrims may seek assistance through petitioning the *rebbe* to intercede with God on their behalf, a practice which rests on the understanding that the charisma of the *rebbe* is able to effect a direct communication with God. Hasidism stresses the personal emotional communication of the individual with God, and visiting the graves of particularly revered rabbis is supposed to become a conduit for such intense encounters with the divine.

These practices are not only significant for the individual. They also communicate particular ideas about identity and the memory of previous generations. The Holocaust devastated the Haredi communities of Eastern Europe, many of which were Hasidim. Contemporary Hasidic communities understand themselves as their successors, but also as their spiritually inferior descendants (*yeridat ha-dorot*, see Chapter 3). At the graves of the *rebbes* of Eastern Europe from Lishensk (the grave of Elimelekh of Lishensk, see Chapter 2) to Uman (the grave of Nachman of Bratslav) Jews – Haredim, Hasidim and those of other movements, as well as secular Jews – may not only seek individual religious experiences. Among other motivations to visit these sites may be the desire to connect with the history of their ancestors, literally as well as spiritually and physically.

Not all motivations for pilgrimage need be religious. Many touristic explorations of Eastern Europe marketed to Jews in the Western world and Israel can be understood as pilgrimages which commemorate particular aspects of Jewish history and seek to create, strengthen and affirm the Jewish identifications of the travellers. 'Roots tourism', a movement of increasing popularity among Jews since the opening of the countries of the former Eastern bloc in the early 1990s, offers Jewish travellers from Western countries the opportunity to visit places significant to Jewish history in countries associated with large Jewish settlements in the pre-war era, such as Poland, the Ukraine, Belorussia and Lithuania. Other aspects of such tours are visits to sites of the Holocaust, notably the former death camp at Auschwitz-Birkenau, and the cities of Kraków and Warsaw, where large ghettos were situated. Kraków in particular has seen increased 'Jewish tourism' through the restoration of its former Jewish quarter of Kazimierz, associated for many with Spielberg's *Schindler's List* (1993), and associated 'Schindler tourism': tours visiting the sites of the film set (which differ considerably from the original historical locations of the story narrated in the film).

A particular target of this kind of tourism, which may be described as pilgrimage, are young people in their formative years. Since the late 1980s, tours such as *March of the Living* take Jewish teenagers and young adults on a tour of Holocaust sites in Poland and finish by observing the spring memorial days of the Holocaust and founding of the State of Israel in Israel, literally taking participants on a journey from death to life.[8] *Birthright Israel* offers young people in the diaspora a tour of Israel with the aim of strengthening their Jewish identity through attachment to Israel.[9] Here, pilgrimage in the sense of life-changing journey is instrumentalized to teach particular lessons about Jewishness which are to be experienced as a part of a group. Whether participants' experiences match the aims of the organizers of such tours is difficult to measure. Participants may concur, challenge, subvert or otherwise relate to the offerings of an organized travel tour, or have various motivations for participating, such as being young and looking for romance.[10]

Sefardi Jews also have a tradition of pilgrimage to the tombs of *tzaddikim* or *tzadikot* ('holy women'). A *tzaddik*'s *brakhah*, a blessing or aura which is believed to be inherent in everything that had physical contact with the person and their tomb, is invested with powers to heal, guide and protect, and the aim of pilgrims is to partake of it. Today it is possible to observe a different dimension to the pilgrimages to the graves of *tzaddikim*, or to newer sites of pilgrimage substituting for inaccessible tombs. The identity of the pilgrim is invested in the pilgrimage which can serve as a confirmation, for example, of their Moroccanness; their connection to the culture of their ancestors in ways similar to the identity formation and affirmation of Ashkenazi pilgrimage and tourism to Eastern Europe. *Hillulot* ('celebrations'), usually held on *Lag ba-Omer*, commemorate not only the *tzaddik*, but also offer the possibility to reconnect with Sefardi heritage, be this through travel to the village in Morocco in which a family and community originated, or through the enactment of traditional rituals at *hillulot* in Israel. Both serve to recall the history of a community and reinforce a distinctive Moroccan Sefardi identity in the present. Another aspect of such pilgrimages and festivals is the public demonstration of Sefardi difference in Israel, a country still dominated by Ashkenazi cultural heritage.[11]

For both Ashkenazim and Sefardim, pilgrimages can be understood not only as expressions of religiosity of individuals seeking particular experiences, but also as events which seek to strengthen religious, ethnic, national and cultural identifications and allegiances. While the journeys to some sites are designed to emphasize the common heritage and ancestry of all Jews, thereby seeking to enhance the notion of 'one nation', other pilgrimages are about the assertion of difference and Jewish plurality, the connection with very particular ancestral heritage, culture and customs not shared with Jews of a different provenance. Memory plays an important part in all aspects of pilgrimage and it seems fair to characterize pilgrimage as an example of Jewish memory work.

Holocaust memory

The Holocaust, the systematic genocide of Jews in Europe by Nazi Germany 1939–1945, occupies an important place in the study of Judaism. At the same time, it has also had a profound impact on the field of memory studies. Maurice Halbwachs, whose work is part of the foundational texts of 'memory studies' in the humanities, contributing significantly to the distinction between the writing of history and the workings of social and collective memory, was arrested when protesting against the deaths of his Jewish parents-in-law, and died in Buchenwald. Of his own childhood wartime experiences, Pierre Nora, a historian whose work on memory develops the work of Halbwachs, has written, 'since I was Jewish, I experienced exclusion, pursuit

... solidarities as unforeseen as the betrayals ... It was an adventure inscribed in the flesh of memory, sufficient to make you different from all other French children of your age.'[12] More generally, theories of memory raise questions about the possibility of remembering and representing historical events in a variety of media.

The biblical imperative *zakhor*!, (remember!) not only applies to religious festivals and observances which recall God's workings in history. Subsequent historical events have been added to the experiences Jews collectively recall through evolving rituals and interpret their Jewishness with. Some events have been interpreted through biblical categories while others, such as the Holocaust and the creation of the State of Israel, have not been readily integrated into the existing calendar of memorial practices. Some communities, mostly situated on the traditionalist end of the religious spectrum, seek to commemorate the Holocaust as part of the mourning mandated for other catastrophes in Jewish history, such as the destruction of the two Jerusalem Temples on *9 Av*. For others, new liturgies of remembrance had to be created, and the desire to mark the magnitude and singularity of the Holocaust has found its expression in the creation of *Yom ha-Shoah*, Holocaust Remembrance Day. This day is situated in the calendar in spring just before Israel Independence Day, *Yom ha-Atzma'ut* and *Yom ha-Zikkaron*, the Memorial Day for those who died in the War of Independence and subsequent wars. Sirens are sounded and the country comes to a virtual standstill as the population is called to remember the victims of the genocide. The date for *Yom ha-Shoah* was chosen in memory of the Warsaw Ghetto Uprising which begun on 19 April 1943, and coincided with *Pesach*. Now 27 *Nissan* removes the memorial day from the religious observance of *Pesach*. However, its occurrence in the *Omer* period angers and disappoints some Jews. Not only does the recalling of the Warsaw Ghetto Uprising privilege military resistance against the Nazis in line with the self-image of modern Israel as a state able to defend itself and its citizens from harm, it also interrupts the period of mourning for the destruction of the Temple in Jerusalem for which the days of the *Omer* between *Pesach* and *Shavuot* are reserved. Hence not all Jews are able to embrace this new addition to the civil religious calendar of the State of Israel. *Yom ha-Shoah*, *Yom ha-Atzma'ut* and *Yom ha-Zikkaron* are also problematic observances for the non-Jewish population of Israel who cannot connect in the same way to the history of the country, some associating suffering and persecution with the creation of the state.

In *Zakhor: Jewish History and Jewish Memory*, historian Yosef Yerushalmi argues that Jews are latecomers to the writing of history, having preferred until the *Wissenschaft* movement to interpret historical events through biblical and rabbinic categories which assign little significance to historical particularity, looking instead for 'types' of experiences and events which illustrate aspects of the Jewish relationship with God. Segments of the Jewish community did and do follow such a pattern of interpretation in relation to the recent experience of genocide, the Holocaust or *Shoah* ('destruction') as some Jews prefer to call it, seeking to avoid the sacrificial overtones associated with Holocaust (Greek for the Hebrew *olah*: 'burnt offering'). The Holocaust is then described with the Hebrew/Yiddish word *Hurban*, which aligns Jewish suffering during the genocide with previous episodes of persecution and murder. In these interpretations the Holocaust is quantitatively, but not qualitatively different from Jewish experiences of persecution in other times and other places. Such understandings of the Holocaust tend to be the provenance of Haredi communities whose perception of historiography is closest to that of the rabbinical tradition.

Scholars of memory, while not uninterested in the place and function of particular religious forms of remembrance and historiography, tend to focus their attention on collective or social aspects of memory, namely those observable in the public sphere through an analysis of Holocaust representation in a variety of genres. These range from literature to the building of museums and curating of exhibitions, from the architecture of monuments to the rituals of commemoration and political discourses. What kind of shape the Holocaust takes in these forms of public commemoration, and how this contributes to a public historiography of the Holocaust are at the forefront of scholarly concerns.

The building of museums dedicated to the Holocaust such as *Yad Vashem* in Israel and the United States Holocaust Memorial Museum in Washington, DC (USHMM), communicate the significance of the memory of the genocide of European Jews to the societies in which they are situated as well as to the wider world. In particular, the establishment of Holocaust exhibitions at locations not connected with the historical events has led some commentators to suggest that Jewish historical memory is usurped by Holocaust memory. Pilgrimages to sites of the Holocaust or substitutes such as the USHMM appear to invert the original purpose of Jewish religious pilgrimage: to be in a particularly holy place and experience an enhanced sense of communication with the divine. Rather, pilgrimages to Holocaust sites invoke the absence of the divine and the depravity of humanity, rendering these places 'unholy'. For some Jews, the Holocaust supplies a sense of identity, being Jewish *davka*, in spite of the persecution. Holocaust memory is invoked in order to imprint the necessity of being Jewish – not to grant Hitler a posthumous victory[13] – on the consciousness of young people in particular. In a way, however, this places the Nazis in charge of giving reasons for Jewish continuity and links Jewish identity inextricably to the attempt to annihilate it. The proliferation of Holocaust remembrance in the public sphere through films, television series, documentaries, Holocaust memorial days and other commemorative events have led scholars like Norman Finkelstein to draw the conclusion that there is a 'Holocaust industry', i.e. large parts of society interested in 'marketing' the Holocaust to enhance their own public profile rather than honouring the memory of the deceased.[14]

Holocaust representation and Holocaust memory

Exhibitions in Holocaust museums and at sites connected to the Holocaust necessarily have to curtail the amount of detail and diversity of the historical events. At the same time, they also have to find ways of making their exhibitions attractive to an audience who may need to be persuaded to expose themselves to a narrative of discrimination, persecution and murder narrated from the perspective of the victimizers. Often this is done via attempts to 'personalize' the 'story' of the Holocaust through seemingly direct access to its victims. For example, the USHMM works with 'identity cards' which detail the fate of an individual during the Holocaust, thus allowing the visitor to zoom in on the effect of Nazi persecution on one person and their family. The Imperial War Museum Holocaust Exhibition uses video testimony at crucial points to give visitors access to the way in which the experience of persecution impacted individuals. In other contexts, prominent personalities are used to open up the complex history of the Holocaust, such as through the diary and life of Anne Frank – an untypical story, but one which seemingly lends itself to Holocaust education in secondary schools due to the assumed proximity of the protagonist, Anne, and youngsters today. Most exhibitions offer a way for the visitor to 'return' to their own reality through providing some kind of 'closure'. This may be done through a meditative space or a link to contemporary forms of discrimination on which the visitor is asked to take a stand, thus suggesting that each individual is empowered to influence society and its politics.

Such forms of Holocaust representation have been met with sharp criticism. Critics take issue with the personalization of the historical narrative, something which is also prevalent in other popular genres of Holocaust representation such as film. Reducing historical complexity to the life of an individual is seen as akin to falsifying the reality of the Holocaust by suggesting that it can be contained in familiar narrative structures, and by creating analogies to today's social situations. This rebels against the notion of the 'uniqueness' of the Holocaust which places it beyond comparison into a category of its own. While critics are aware of the limitations such an approach puts on the communicability of historical experiences – recognizing the emphasis placed on 'experience' in much of today's historical learning – they maintain that it is necessary to preserve the radical otherness of the Holocaust in order to honour the memory of its victims.

Alongside the critics, however, stand the realities of Holocaust remembrance which thrive on the adaptation of experiential learning to an extraordinary topic, traditional liturgical forms and the assumption of the communicability of experiences, lessons and truths through visual media.

Holocaust memorialization, as it is currently practiced in both Jewish and non-Jewish circles, assumes a self-evident Jewishness of the victims of the Holocaust. Yet for a number of reasons this is too simplistic. Firstly, it may inscribe Jewishness through biology, which continues aspects of the Nazi ideology of Jews in the 'biologization' of Jewishness. Secondly, it assumes that all victims of the Nazis understood themselves to be Jewish, even though that is highly problematic, in particular with regard to Germany where many people with Jewish ancestry no longer wanted or were able to articulate a meaningful relation to Jewishness or Judaism, religious or cultural, and in effect were 'made Jewish' by the Nazis' biological notion of 'who is a Jew'. Finally, tying Jewish identity to Holocaust memory carries the danger of remembering Jews in the ways in which the Nazis would have liked to have them remembered, and firmly inscribing Jewish victimhood into contemporary Jewish identity.[15]

Holocaust testimony and Holocaust education

Projects recording the testimony of Holocaust survivors began in the 1980s with initiatives such as the Fortunoff Video Archive for Holocaust Testimonies at Yale University,[16] and are designed to preserve and study testimony of the genocide. Testimony of Holocaust survivors has since been given wider publicity. In the wake of his successful film *Schindler's List* (1993), Steven Spielberg established an archive of video testimonies with the Shoah Foundation which seeks to promote the educational and public use of Holocaust testimony. The emphasis on the collection of testimony occurs parallel to the decline of Holocaust survivors and the very real knowledge of the last survivor dying in the foreseeable future. Testimony, however, remains an integral part of Holocaust education as it is promoted in the Western world. Among its aims are the prevention of xenophobia, sectarianism and further genocide – or, positively put, the aim of establishing and enhancing a multicultural, tolerant society. By upholding the negative example of a civilized country adopting segregation and genocide as state policies, Holocaust education seeks to mobilize younger generations in particular to swap prejudice for understanding and inclusiveness. The methods of Holocaust education are increasingly criticized by scholars who argue that genocide cannot be taught in order to promote its prevention. Other problematic aspects of Holocaust education and public Holocaust commemoration concern the links with Jewish identity and history which are inadvertently established by its prevalence in Jewish and non-Jewish social circles.

On closer inspection, there is considerable diversity in Jewish Holocaust memory, a fact that is obscured by global attempts to establish and communicate a unified and thereby simplified Holocaust memory mainly for the purpose of civil education. For example, the Holocaust is usually narrated as an Eastern and Central European, Ashkenazi experience. However, Sefardi and Mizrahi communities were also affected, such as communities in Greece, Serbia, Croatia and North Africa. Serbian Sefardim were the first Jews to be gassed to death in experimental vans used in early 1942.[17] While the experience of Greek Jews, mainly Sefardim and Romaniotes, Greek-speaking Jews who traditionally trace their roots to Jews exiled from the land of Israel following the destruction of the First and Second Jerusalem Temples, echoed that elsewhere in Europe – ghettoization, deportation and murder – the same is not true elsewhere. For example, anti-Jewish measures, the *Statut des Juifs* applied in Algeria, extended beyond those adopted elsewhere in Vichy France and its colonies, and not all of these were removed when the American and British allies defeated the German forces there. Many Jews continued to be interned until late 1944.[18] In Tunisia, the *Statut* was less rigorously applied. The same was true in Morocco, where the impact of its legal measures to isolate Jews from political and social life was further lessened by the already isolationist character of the community.[19] Such local diversity tends to be eroded when 'the memory of the Holocaust' is evoked politically to underline lessons of citizenship and multiculturalism.

A consequence of the public proliferation of Holocaust memory may be the distortion of Judaism by tying it into a restrictive conceptualization of Jewishness and an inscription of victimhood into what it means to be Jewish. These limitations on the perception of what is Jewish can work externally, narrowing what non-Jews are willing to regard as Jewish. They can just as well work internally, suggesting limited options to conceive of Jewish history and identity in the present by linking Jewish identity solely with the threat of its extinction in the Holocaust.

EXERCISE

Although Haredi society concerns itself intensively with the Holocaust, the use of the word *Shoah*, Hebrew for "Holocaust," cannot be taken for granted in Haredi writings even though these sources have used it for decades. From the Haredi point of view, the term Shoah is problematic because of the notion that it denotes a unique event, in contrast to *hurban* (destruction) or *gezerot* (decrees), and consequently entails a theological explanation.[20]

Write down different names for the Holocaust, and consider how this reflects on the way in which the Holocaust is conceptualized and remembered.

Museums

The first Jewish museums opened in Europe and North America in the late nineteenth century. Like Graetz's multi-volume *History of the Jews* (1856–1870), which was discussed in Chapter 1, their emergence was linked to Jewish emancipation: their creators sought to develop Jewish historical consciousness even as they also assimilated culturally to the norms of non-Jewish societies.

Early collections typically had two foci. They emphasized Jews' historic presence in and connectedness to a particular place, while *Judaica* (objects associated with religious rituals), chosen because they were deemed to be of aesthetic excellence, dominated the artefact displays. The stress on Jewish belongingness, coupled with the effective elision of 'Jewish' into 'Judaism' reflected and reinforced the exhibitors' desire to reposition Jews politically and socially in the modern world.

In the late twentieth century, new trends emerged within Jewish museums and museological discourses. *Judaica*-oriented collections have been widely criticized as presenting one-dimensional, elitist accounts of Jewish life. At the same time, it can be argued that, by presenting ritual objects in cases, they suggest that Jewish religious observance is itself a 'museum piece', something belonging only to the past. Accordingly, many museums have re-evaluated their objectives and scope. A large *Judaica* collection continues to form the basis of London's Jewish Museum, which was first founded in 1932 and reopened in Spring 2010. However, much of this is now displayed in a gallery retitled 'Judaism: a *Living* Faith' (my italics), with visitors to the Museum passing through a Welcome Gallery (admission to which is free; charges apply elsewhere) with a multimedia display emphasizing 'the many ways there are of being Jewish' in 'modern, multicultural Britain'.[21] Similar impulses – the desire to resist a tendency to equate Jewish cultural life with specific religious practices, and the attempt to convey a sense of what it means to be Jewish today as well as in the past – underpin other Jewish exhibition projects, not least those which address the Holocaust. The desire to educate about what was lost, as well as how it was destroyed, come together in the desire to exhibit the history of the Holocaust alongside the exhibition of Jewish cultures and religion.

Dedicated Holocaust museums opened from 1970s onwards, and nearly if not all Jewish art and culture museums have something on Holocaust. Here, as in earlier Jewish museums, religion is firmly implicated. While Jewish museums which include an exhibition on the Holocaust – such as in London's Holocaust gallery – generally emphasize the positive cultural contribution of distinctive Jewish religious practices, objects and cultural production, embedding the Holocaust in a longer historical trajectory which focuses on Jewish life, this is not necessarily the case in museums solely dedicated to the Holocaust. In museums such as the USHMM, the emphasis is on the destruction of Jewish life, and generally little attention is given to the cultures that vanished as a result. Here religion is implicated, though more often as a negative which is distorted in antisemitic representations of Jews displayed as part of the explanation for the Holocaust. A slightly different case in point is *Yad Vashem* in Jerusalem, the institution formally charged with the preservation of the memory of the murdered Jews of Europe. While the destruction of Jewish life and cultures is in the foreground of the exhibitions at *Yad Vashem*, these are embedded in the wider public historiography of the establishment of the State of Israel, the surrounding Jewish culture(s) and the celebration of Jewish life in the diaspora in *Bet Hatefutsoth*, the Museum of the Diaspora, in Tel Aviv. However, not all Israelis agree on the representation of the Holocaust in *Yad Vashem*. Haredi Jews have long established counter-memorials which celebrate a distinctly Haredi narrative of the *Shoah*, emphasizing spiritual rather than military resistance and include a reflection on the 'Torah-true' life of the 'martyrs' of the Holocaust. Institutions such as the Chamber of the Holocaust in Jerusalem[22], meanwhile, presuppose the active connection of the visitor not only to the communities commemorated there, but in particular to Haredi Jewish practices and cultures which mediate or establish a shared ground between the world of the murdered and that of the visitor.

By contrast, New York's Museum of Jewish Heritage is subtitled 'A *Living Memorial* to the Holocaust'[23] (my italics), indicating the emphasis the institution places on the commemoration of pre-war Jewish life in the 'old world'. Contemporary Jewish life in the diaspora and the State of Israel is understood in important ways to be discontinuous with Jewish life in the 'old world' of which the museum can remind, but which it cannot restore. Similarly, the Museum of the History of Polish Jews,[24] due to open in Warsaw in 2013, is supporting the 'Virtual Shtetl' project, which invites members of the public to contribute with their recollections and materials to the historiography of Jews in small Polish towns, designating the site a 'museum without barriers'.[25]

More recently, it is possible to observe moves to diversify the display of objects relating to Jewish history and religious ritual by moving these out of the confines of dedicated Jewish museums. *Judaica* is beginning to find its way into mainstream art museums displayed as examples of artistic production rather than objects of ritual significance. This allows curators to show items which originate in different religious, cultural and ethnic groups – for example Jewish, Christian and Muslim – in the same geographical context in a particular time period, thus highlighting artistic cross-fertilization.[26]

EXERCISE

'In large measure Jewish identity is forged through acts of remembering shared experiences.'[27] Consider how you position yourself to this statement in light of this chapter.

10

Jews and Others

EXERCISE

There can be no systematic study of religion ... without cross-cultural perspective. Lacking this, studies of religion would amount either to separate collections of unrelated historical data, or to speculative generalizations based only on the perspective of one culture.[1]

How far do you agree or disagree with this view? What, potentially, are the advantages and pitfalls of a comparative approach to the study of Judaism?

Studying Judaism, studying religions

There is considerable academic debate as to whether a religious tradition is best studied separately or 'comparatively', either by deliberately comparing and contrasting aspects of religions, or by adopting a synoptic approach that examines a particular phenomenon across a number of traditions.[2] While studying one religion arguably allows greater possibility for in-depth work, it also risks ignoring the often complex realities of people's actual lives and internalizing essentialist constructions of a particular tradition, such as those that regard it as *sui generis*. Conversely, the comparative approach championed by early leaders of the *Religionswissenschaft* movement, and by figures such as Smart and William Paden (the author quoted above), recognizes that similarities may exist across traditions: some forms of Judaism, for example, have much in common with forms of Christianity that have strongly internalized Enlightenment values, and may help scholars to foster the critical distance necessary for rigorous analytical work. But it may result in the imposition of distorting analytical categories upon religions, and in dehistoricized, decontextualized understanding. Ideologically speaking, comparative approaches may reflect a desire to present one tradition more favourably than another, or a universalist view that all religions are ultimately paths to the same goal, in which case differences may be inappropriately suppressed. In other words, comparativism, if it fails to take seriously the distinctive concepts and language of a religion, effectively deprives adherents of their own voices, and risks becoming a kind of 'conceptual imperialism' exercised by one culture over others.[3]

This chapter occupies an unstable position in relation to such debates. On the one hand, it appears in a book that focuses on a single tradition and the chapter heading, 'Jews and Others', implies that the boundaries between 'Jew' and 'Other' are clearly defined. On the other hand, this book deploys concepts like 'religion' and 'ritual', and it engages Smart's dimensions – all products of comparative attempts to make sense of the ways in which people act in and interpret the world. It also describes many instances in which Judaism has shaped and been shaped by contacts with Others; that is, with individuals or groups that its adherents have understood to be in some way different from themselves.

As noted in Chapter 2, interreligious boundaries are not always as clear cut as many textbooks and religious insiders suggest. They are often blurred or porous:

Yes, I was a good Moslem. I was the smartest boy in class, and the teacher always asked me to lead the prayers to Mecca. But after school I went home to study Hebrew and read the Torah.[4]

They are all baptized, and none is circumcised. They marry in church ... and are buried in a Catholic cemetery, a cross usually marking their grave. Yet they hardly go to church on Sundays or other Christian holidays. Every Friday night they light candles to honor the Jewish Sabbath, and hide them inside a closet or fire-place. Their most sacred events of the year are Passover and Yom Kippur.[5]

The words in the first passage are those of a Mashhadi man. The Jews in Mashhad, Iran, were forcibly converted to Islam in 1839, but continued to live privately as Jews, forming their own distinctive religious identity that was transmitted between generations. Today, most Mashhadis live in America and Israel, places where they can practice Judaism openly. However, many are critical of Israeli and diaspora Judaism, contrasting the divided Ashkenazi community unfavourably with what they regard as their own unique emphasis on 'the true meaning of modesty, honesty, fear of G-d' and 'love of one another'.[6] The second extract describes a group of *Marranos* or *Conversos*[7], living in Belmonte, Portugal, in the 1930s. *Conversos*, converts (often forced) from Judaism to Christianity, who continued to observe Jewish rituals in secret, emerged in the wake of anti-Jewish violence and expulsions in fourteenth- and fifteenth-century Spain and Portugal. There is considerable debate as to the nature of their religious lives. When the opportunity arose to do so, some fled to more tolerant locations (Britain, the Netherlands, parts of the Ottoman Empire and emerging settlements in the New World such as Curaçao, Jamaica, Suriname and New Amsterdam [now New York]) and resumed the open practice of Judaism, but most rabbinic sources, while lenient towards former *Conversos*, do not regard those who continue to live as *Conversos* as Jews. Data suggests that the numbers of *Conversos* were small, and that within a generation or two they were largely indistinguishable from other Christians. Visiting Belmonte in the 1980s, Yovel found that some *Conversos* had become absorbed either into Catholic society or into Orthodox Judaism, others wished to maintain their inherited traditions: they had come to regard secrecy and duality not as expediencies fashioned in the wake of persecution, but as religious values in themselves.[8]

Beyond such striking examples, borrowings from, amalgamations of and interactions between religions are widespread.[9] Chapter 5 described how Maimonides' (whose own family were secret Jews in Islamic Spain) account of belief was shaped by his contact with religious Others; Chapter 4 discussed the impact of Christmas on *Hanukah* celebrations. For insiders, examples of the influence of one tradition on another, or of syncretic processes like those in Mashhad and Belmonte, may present challenges to exclusive truth-claims that need to be fought against as corruptions of the 'authentic' tradition, or that demand a rethinking of the notion of truth itself. For those engaged in the critical study of religion, they may serve as reminders of the potential limitations of static conceptual models in the face of the dynamic character of religious identification and activity. They also underline the importance of a study of interreligious contacts and exchanges for a critical understanding of any religion.

Rabbinic attitudes to religious others

Because of their role in shaping normative belief and practice, the *Tanakh* and subsequent rabbinic tradition provide one possible starting point for an account of Jewish religious attitudes to Others.[10] Many biblical passages differentiate people as male or female (see, for example, Deut. 22.5), able-bodied or disabled (Lev. 21.:16–23; compare Lev. 19.14 and Jer. 31.7–8) and Jews or *goyim* – gentiles or non-Jews. The text's primary implied reader is male, Jewish and able-bodied.

Developing these emphases, rabbinic literature is comparatively disinterested in *goyim* or gentiles, except insofar as Jewish interaction with them gives rise to questions of religious law. Many passages in the *Tanakh* define worship of Israel's God against polytheism (belief in multiple deities) and 'idolatry', the worship of gods in physical forms, be they human constructions (like statues) or naturally occurring formations (such as streams or mountains). The condemnation of idols (for example, Ps. 135.15–18) is strongest in passages criticizing Jews who, by worshipping other deities, have contravened Exod. 20.3. Provided that Jews do not take part in such rituals, the worship of other deities by *goyim* is presented as acceptable, evenly divinely instituted: 'the sun and the moon and the stars ... you must not be lured into bowing down to them or serving them. These the LORD your God allotted to other peoples' (Deut. 4.19).

The *Mishnaic*/Talmudic tractate *Avodah Zarah* explores how Jews may have contact with religious others while avoiding idolatry. Chapter 3 of this book discussed *Avodah Zarah* 47a-b, which debates how a Jew whose property adjoins a pagan shrine may avoid benefiting from or supporting idolatrous worship. Other texts are more permissive in tone:

> Proclus the philosopher asked Rabban Gamliel[11], who was in Acco[12] bathing in the bathhouse of Aphrodite: 'It is written in your Torah "let nothing that has been doomed [associated with idolatry] stick to your hand" (Deut. 13.18), why then do you bathe in Aphrodite's bath-house?' He replied: 'One does not respond in the bath-house.' When he had come out he said to him ... 'One does not say, "Let us make the bath-house an ornament to the bath-house" rather it is Aphrodite who is an ornament to the bath-house' ... [Scripture] only states [cut down the images of] their gods (Deut. 12.3) so that which is treated as a deity is prohibited while that which is not treated as a deity is permitted (*m.Avodah Zarah* 3.4).

Aphrodite, represented as a naked or partially clothed woman, was the Greek goddess of beauty and love, hence Proclus queries the propriety of Gamliel's behaviour. Gamliel's response defines the statue's function in the bathhouse as decorative, and not idolatrously religious.[13] (Leaving the bathhouse before discussing Torah reinforces the notion that it is an a-religious space.) This type of reasoning permitted Jews to participate in a public realm – bathhouses were important venues for political, social and economic activity[14] – saturated with images, places and objects associated with Gods, without considering themselves to have committed idolatry.

Tractate *Sanhedrin*, an important source of rabbinic theology, discusses gentiles' place in *olam ha-ba*, the World-to-Come. It suggests that God began the human race with only one man, Adam, 'so that no one of his descendants should be able to say: my father is better than your father' (*Sanhedrin* 37a). However, it also says that, in order to merit a share in the World-to-Come, gentiles must observe seven commandments. According to the Talmud, these were given to Noah, whose family re-founded the human race following a great flood (Gen. 6.9–10.32). The Noahide Laws prohibit idolatry, blasphemy, incest, murder, robbery and eating meat from an animal that is still alive, and require the setting up of a fair legal system (*Sanhedrin* 59a).

According to Maimonides, Jews were commanded at Sinai to promote the Noahide Laws, and in order to have a share in the World-to-Come gentiles must observe the laws *and* acknowledge their divine origin.[15] For much of Jewish history, as in Maimonides' time, however, the Laws' significance has been symbolic. This is partly because Jews have rarely been in positions of power or security that might enable them to enforce or promote observance, and partly because, at least so far as the authors of many rabbinic texts were concerned, despite the theoretical possibility of gentile righteousness, most non-Jews were assumed to be morally suspect. The *Mishnah* states that Jewish women should avoid being alone with gentile men and Jewish men should avoid patronizing gentile barbers in private, proscriptions reflecting an assumption that non-Jews are unable to control their physical desires.[16] More recently a different, proactive approach has been taken by the Lubavitch Hasidim, who run a campaign to promote universal observance of the Noahide laws, which they regard as a necessary precursor to messianic redemption.[17] The United States Congress referred to the campaign and described the Noahide Laws as 'ethical values and principles [that] have been the bedrock of society from the dawn of civilization' in the preamble to a bill designating Lubavitch *rebbe* Menachem Mendel Schneerson's ninetieth birthday (26 March 1991) 'Education Day, U.S.A.'.[18]

Judaism, Christianity, and Islam

For many centuries, Jews lived in societies dominated by Christianity and Islam, religions with historical and theological roots in Judaism. The history and historiography of relations between Jews, Muslims and Christians are highly complex. Subsequent relations between Jews, Christians and Muslims have frequently impacted the ways in which the past is constructed and inter-preted. For example, scholars of the *Wissenschaft des Judentums* movement devoted much attention to medieval Spain, when Jews were relatively accepted by their Muslim rulers and neighbours. According to Graetz, 'The cultured Jews of Andalusia spoke and wrote the language of the country as fluently as their Arab fellow-citizens, who were as proud of the Jewish poets as the Jews were themselves.'[19] In other words, Graetz believed that medieval Sefardim had achieved the kind of integration and acceptance that he and his contemporaries sought in nineteenth-century Germany. More recently, the term *convivencia* or co-existence, coined in 1948 by literary and cultural historian Américo Castro to describe medieval Spanish society has become increasingly popular, often in the context of discussions of a so-called 'Golden Age' of medieval Jewry, as a concept that could provide inspiration for present day amity between Muslims and Jews, or encourage Jewish tourism to the Iberian peninsula.[20] Meanwhile, as Wolfram Kinzig has recently observed, anti-Judaism or antisemitism is widely assumed to be the 'hermeneutical key' to understanding the history of Jewish-Christian relations.[21] This view emerged in the nineteenth century, in the wake of the rise of modern antisemitism[22], and received further impetus after the Holocaust, the enormity of which, it was thought, 'could only be explained by assuming a long and gradually strengthening tradition of anti-Jewish hatred'.[23]

It is important for critical scholarship to be aware of the impact of contemporary factors and fashions on the reconstruction of the past. This chapter does not, however, attempt to provide detailed coverage of Jewish experiences under Islam and Christianity, except insofar as they have shaped Jewish religious attitudes towards those traditions and their adherents.

Jesus and almost all of his early followers were Jews. It was only after a period of several centuries, during which the movement gained increasing numbers of gentile converts and articulated exclusivist[24] and supersessionist[25] theologies that Christianity fully separated from Judaism, which was itself undergoing significant change in the wake of the destruction of the Jerusalem Temple (see Chapter 3). It is impossible to provide a full account of Jewish attitudes to and relations with early Christianity, because the Christian sources are often highly polemical in character and the main rabbinic sources, the *Mishnah* and Talmud, contain little discussion of the subject. The following outlines some positions prominent among Jews from the rabbinic period onwards and the changes to these since Enlightenment and emancipation.

Jews did not regard Christianity as idolatry in the biblical sense, but did believe that it relied on idolatrous forms of worship (see *Hullin* 13b). So medieval Ashkenaz used and adapted the case law developed in response to paganism. Other rabbis disagreed, and did not hold it to be idolatry for gentiles (see *Tosafot* on *Avodah Zarah* 2a).

As [the Venetian rabbi] Leon da Modena [1574–1648] noted, it was not the doctrine of the Trinity in itself that was objectionable (after all, in the kabbalistic doctrine of the Sefirot there is much talk of three, and more, aspects of [the] Deity) but its elaboration, in which the Trinity is composed of three divine Persons, one of which became incarnate in a human being. The medieval thinkers who held Christianity but not Islam to be an idolatrous faith did so particularly because of the worship of the Cross; to bow before an icon or a crucifix was held to be akin to bowing to idols.[26]

Maimonides – generally more sympathetic to Islam because it was uncompro-misingly monotheistic than Christian trinitarianism – however, also believed that Christianity was better insofar as it accepted the text of the *Tanakh* as scripture while the Qur'an incorporates it in a less direct and more selective way.

> Jesus was instrumental [or, 'was an instrument'] in changing the Torah and causing the world to err and serve another beside God. But it is beyond the human mind to fathom the designs of our Creator, for our ways are not God's ways, neither are our thoughts His. All these matters relating to Jesus of Nazareth, and the Ishmaelite [i.e. Muhammad] who came after him, only served to clear the way for the Jewish Messiah to prepare the whole world to worship God with one accord, as it is written 'For then will I turn to the peoples a pure language, that they all call upon the name of the Lord to serve Him with one consent.' (Zeph. 3.9). Thus the Jewish hope, and the Torah, and the commandments have become familiar topics of conversation among those even on far isles, and among many people, uncircumcised of flesh and heart. (*Mishneh Torah*, XI.4.)

The above paragraph was often excluded from many printed versions where Christian censorship was felt.

Judah ha-Levi (1075–1141), the Spanish poet and philosopher, also gave an account of his understanding of the relations between Judaism, Christianity and Islam. In the *Kuzari*, the king of the Khazars, contemplating conversion of himself, his family and people, engages a rabbi in a dialogue on the teachings of Judaism. The ensuing imaginary conversation has the rabbi outline the tenets of Judaism and defend these towards objections brought by Christianity, Islam and Platonism. Ha-Levi was not interested in rationalizing Judaism. Rather, he suggested that Judaism originates with revelation communicated through Israel's prophets. Revelation is posited as a truth higher than that which can be arrived at through reason alone. Ha-Levi's interpretation argued for the superi-ority of Judaism over her 'daughter religions' Christianity and Islam, prophecy being the source (the Torah) and foundation of Israel's divinely ordained role in the world as an intermediary between God and humanity.

With regard to Islam, as to Christianity then, the texts do not evidence a position of religious pluralism. Maimonides' positive statements were intended simply to clarify the nature of the Islamic religion, statements which, in turn, will have numerous *halakhic* consequences and as discussed earlier, the favoured – albeit largely theoretical – alternatives for Muslims were conversion to Judaism or adherence to the Noahide Laws.

It is only in the modern period that one can observe significant shifts in the attitudes to Christianity. In the intellectually more open climate of the Enlightenment, Moses Mendelssohn valued Christianity's embodiment of universal religious truths while staking out ground for the particularity of Jewish life which mandates a particular way of life based on a unique revelation given only to Jews. This 'revealed legislation' is not in conflict with the rational truths accessible to all humankind, but requires their manifestation in particular ritual practices. However, Mendelssohn is wary of Christianity's imperialistic tendencies which go beyond the Jewish claim to a specific revelation placing certain demands on a specific people and require the conversion of the world to Christianity.

Another shift in Jewish interpretations of Christianity took place in the nineteenth century and with the burgeoning of historical-critical scholarship. Jewish academics such as Abraham Geiger turned their attention to New Testament texts and contributed significantly to the quest for the 'historical Jesus', not least through in-depth knowledge of rabbinical materials of the first century. Such efforts at historical scholarship were not appreciated by their Christian contemporaries, and it is difficult to speak of a 'Jewish-Christian dialogue' before the twentieth century. Jewish scholars such as Martin Buber and Franz Rosenzweig initiated formal encounters and dialogues between Jews and Christians in the early twentieth century – with mixed resonance from Christian counterparts who often were not interested or indifferent. Only after the Second World War have Christians shown a rising interest in dialogue with Jews, not least due to a desire to understand the failures of Christians and Christianity in the face of Nazism and the Holocaust. Hence it is only possible to speak of a Jewish–Christian dialogue from the second half of the twentieth century onwards, a dialogue in which Christians have largely taken the lead and Jews have articulated various reasons for participation or lack thereof. Jewish—Muslim dialogue is growing, but Jewish–Christian dialogue has been formally organized almost since its inception as an activity which can enhance the understanding of one's own faith and that of the Other, and it has a longer (not always commendable) history. Therefore most Jewish positions discussed here are in relation to Christianity, but can also apply to Islam.

Since 1945 religious, mainly non-Orthodox Jews have become involved in religious dialogue with non-Jews. Abraham Joshua Heschel took an active interest in Vatican II and the Roman Catholic Church's re-evaluation of its teachings on Judaism and the Jewish people. He suggested that Jews have a religious responsibility to be interested in such matters: 'Should a mother [Judaism] ignore her child (Isaiah 49:15) even a wayward ... one?'.[27] At least initially, these developments took place primarily in Europe and North America, often in response to overtures by Christians seeking to re-evaluate Church teachings that they believe helped to create a context in which the Holocaust was able to happen. Amongst non-Orthodox Jews, engaging in dialogue, reflects belief in ideals shared with gentiles through the universal and liberal elements of Judaism. For Mark Washofsky, the emphasis on the universal elements in Judaism reaches a peak in wishing to affirm holiness in the practices chosen by Jews and others as equally valid. This enables Washofsky to appreciate Jewish participation in interfaith worship as well as Jews participating in the worship of other religious communities, endeavours prohibited by or at least regarded with suspicion and hostility by other Jewish movements.[28]

Dabru Emet ('Speak the Truth'),[29] a document concerning the relationship between Judaism and Christianity, was published by a group of Jewish scholars with a specialization in the study of Christianity in September 2000. It is seen as a landmark indication by its signatories of religious attitudes to Christians and Christianity, and the following discussion will illustrate the variety of positions articulated by contemporary commentators on this issue. Conceived as a response to Christian efforts at reinterpreting Christian theology and history in the light of dialogue with and learning from Jews, *Dabru Emet* affirms in eight theses that

1   Jews and Christians worship the same God.

2   Jews and Christians seek authority from the same book – the Bible (what Jews call 'Tanakh' and Christians call the 'Old Testament').

3   Christians can respect the claim of the Jewish people upon the land of Israel.

4   Jews and Christians accept the moral principles of the Torah.

5   Nazism was not a Christian phenomenon.

6   The humanly irreconcilable difference between Jews and Christians will not be settled until God redeems the entire world as promised in Scripture.

7   A new relationship between Jews and Christians will not weaken Jewish practice.

8   Jews and Christians must work together for justice and peace.[30]

The statement has received a mixed response in the Jewish community. The majority of signatories to the document – like its authors – do not align with Orthodoxy, and indeed, the main objections have been voiced by Orthodox Jews. Jon Levenson's critique of *Dabru Emet* is a robust defence of the Orthodox position towards some forms of dialogue with members of other religious traditions, in particular Christianity. While Levenson is willing to concede that there may be a need for a Jewish statement on Christianity, he is at odds with what he perceives as the underlying ethos of Jewish dialogue with Christians:

> Dabru Emet suffers from one of the great pitfalls of interfaith dialogue ... it is inevitably tempting in such exercises to avoid any candid discussion of fundamental beliefs and to adopt instead the model of conflict resolution or diplomatic negotiation... . Commonalities are stressed, and differences ... are minimized, neglected, or denied altogether. Once this model is adopted, the ultimate objective becomes not just agreement but mutual affirmation; the critical judgements that the religious traditions have historically made upon each other are increasingly presented merely as the tragic fruit of prejudice and misunderstanding.[31]

The standard Orthodox position on dialogue with Christians is based on Rabbi Joseph Soloveitchik's reasoning that matters of faith are private and incommunicable between religions:

> The great encounter between God and man is a wholly personal private affair incomprehensible to the outsider – even to a brother of the same faith community. The divine message is incommunicable since it defies all standardized media of information and all objective categories. If the powerful community of the many feels like remedying an embarrassing human situation or redressing an historic wrong, it should do so at the human ethical level. However, if the debate should revolve around matters of faith, then one of the confronters will be impelled to avail himself of the language of his opponent. This in itself would mean surrender of individuality and distinctiveness.[32]

Hence, theological dialogue is prohibited and encounters should encompass the social and political sphere. At its most dangerous, Christian theological witness to Jews may not be able to refrain from trying to convert Jews to Christianity. Similarly, Rabbi Eliezer Berkovits expressed scepticism towards the desirability of a theological encounter with Christians, not least due to the history of Christian hostility towards Jews. He argued long before *Dabru Emet* was conceived that theological dialogue with Christians is neither desirable nor possible:

> the idea of interreligious understanding is ethically objectionable because it makes respect for the other man [sic] dependent on whether I am able to appreciate his religion or his theology ... I am duty bound to respect the dignity of every human being no matter what I may think of his religion.[33]

However, non-Orthodox Jews cite the revolutionary and positive changes in Christian theological engagement with Jews and Judaism, and suggest that this justifies a statement such as *Dabru Emet* – as an acknowledgement of Christian change and trust in future co-operation which goes beyond the merely practical and includes a positive valuation of the other's theology. In a sense, positive experiences with Christians should find their way into Jewish theology (itself a red herring in Jewish thought and debate).

For some Jews, then, dialogue with Christians has gone beyond an 'insurance policy' against persecution and murder, and become an enterprise which affects their own understanding as religious Jews. For others, this is not possible for historical as well as religious reasons.

'Idolatry' revisited?: Judaism, Hinduism

In relation to religions with their roots in India, particularly Hinduism and Buddhism, the picture is more complex.[34] For much of rabbinic history, India was on the edge of the world as imagined by religious Jews[35] and the academic field of Indo–Jewish studies is a fairly new one.[36] Classic rabbinic texts regard Hindu religion negatively, dismissing the freedom that it affords to individuals to choose their own deity and interpreting *mūrti-pūjā*, or image-worship, as idolatry. More recently, there has been some reassessment of such positions with scholars arguing that Hinduism differs significantly from the idolatrous worship practices described in the *Tanakh*, because many Hindus understand themselves as worshipping not the image itself, but the deity it personifies, and regard the various deities or gods as different manifestations of one ultimate divine reality.

Not withstanding such re-evaluations, the majority Orthodox position is to regard Hindu religion with considerable caution, and to treat it with the same kind of circumspection that the Talmud advocates towards ancient paganism. For example, in 2004, it was discovered that many of the wigs worn by Orthodox women included hair from southern India, which had been ritually offered to Hindu deities and then sold on by temple administrators for commercial purposes. Several rabbinic authorities banned the wigs, on the grounds that their use would constitute the obtaining of a benefit from idolatry, and prompting a rise in demand for synthetic wigs, headscarves, and real hair wigs that could be reliably certified as *kosher*.

However, the experience of several Indian Jewish communities departs from this majority Orthodox view. These include the Malabar or Cochin Jews in Southern India, the Bene Israel (now mainly in Mumbai) and the Baghdadis (Jews who moved from the Middle East to Mumbai and Kolkatta in the eighteenth century). Numbers today are small – 85% of Jews in India left following Indian independence and the founding of the State of Israel[37] – but during centuries of co-existence uniquely Indian Jewish rituals have evolved. One of these is the *Malida* ('ritual offering' in Marathi, a language spoken in western and central India) in which prayers invoking the presence of the prophet Elijah accompany an offering of an elaborate plate containing a variety of fruits, nuts, spices and rice. After the *Malida*, the food is distributed among those present, echoing the practice of Hindu *puja*, in which food is displayed, offered to the deity and, after the deity has enjoyed (and therefore trans-formed) the food, distributed amongst worshippers.[38] Such practices indicate that despite official queries over Hinduism's valuation as monotheism, the incorporation of Hindu practices into the observance of Judaism was part of the Indian Jews' hybrid identities.[39] Studying Jewish migrants from India to Israel Egorova reports that some of her Bene Israel respondents suggested that their religious lives were richer in India 'because India was a much more "spiritual country, while Israel was "too secular"'.[40]

Intermarriage and assimilation

The terms 'intermarriage' (marriage between a Jewish and a non-Jewish partner) and 'assimilation' (the diminishing of a group's distinctive cultural norms, and its absorption of the norms of another, often politically or socially dominant group) appear, often in close proximity to each other, on the agendas of many modern Jewish religious movements. This reflects actual historical experiences such as, for example, those of German Jews, whose high rates of intermarriage and assimilation in the nineteenth century can account for the shrinking of the community as well as a willingness to dispense with distinctively Jewish practices, and passages in the Torah, which link a prohi-bition on intermarriage to a fear that it will lead to religious apostasy:

> The Torah's prohibition of intermarriage with the seven Canaanite nations ... is based on the fear that intimate contact with Canaanites will lead Israelites to imitate their idolatrous and immoral ways. This claim is supported by the explicit moral-religious rationale provided by various biblical texts ... (Dt 20:18, or 7:16; cf. Ex 34:15–16; Lev 18:27–28; Num 33:50–56).[41]

The modern era has in many respects been one of Jewish assimilation. Sometimes, Jews attempted to become like their non-Jewish neighbours in the hope that this would demonstrate their readiness for legal emancipation, or because of legal measures requiring, for example, education in the national language. Advocates of emancipation often argued their case on the basis that, as Jews took advantage of increased possibilities for political and social integration, it would be possible to, 'make of the Jews what we want them to become.'[42] The different modern religious movements emerged as a result of debates about how Jews should respond to this 'offer' and internalize the values and norms of the Enlightenment and/or their non-Jewish neighbours. Widespread migration has also accelerated assimilation. Jews who relocated to the United States and Britain in the nineteenth and early twentieth centuries often changed their language, dress and outlook in a conscious effort to 'fit in' by becoming more 'American' or more ' British' in lifestyle. However, more recently it is possible to observe a lessening in importance of boundaries between Jews and non-Jews due to a civic incorporation of references to Jewishness in mainstream American culture.[43] Not only do Jews share more in common with non-Jews, lessening the significance of differences to the non-Jewish majority as a constant reference point in Jewish self-understanding, but non-Jews have also become more likely to share concepts and vocabulary previously identified as exclusively Jewish.

Assimilation in Israel: Ethiopian Jewish migrants

Reflecting Zionist conceptions of the Jews as a single people, and the political power of Jews of European heritage, Israeli political and social policies have tended to downplay cultural and ethnic differences between the country's Jewish citizens and to privilege Westernized lifestyles, implicitly treating these as the norm to which others should assimilate. Fenster's study of Ethiopian Jewish migrants to Israel shows how this kind of approach has impacted on women's religious lives.[44]

Ethiopian Judaism has its own tradition that has evolved largely independently of rabbinic Judaism. In Ethiopia, women lived in a *yamargam gogo* (menstruating hut) while menstruating and immediately after childbirth. The hut provided a space away from the family home and domestic routine during a period of ritual impurity; it also facilitated the sharing of knowledge and news between women. Migrants to Israel in the 1980s and 1990s were housed in hotels and small government-owned apartments, with no provision for these practices. A minority of women assimilated to Ashkenazi Orthodox norms surrounding *niddah* and began visiting the *mikvah*; others attempted to improvise solutions by temporarily occupying hotel corridors, balconies and even cupboards in their new homes. Many found all of these alternatives unsatisfactory. Women reported feelings of guilt and shame, and contrasted their new 'dirty' homes with life in Ethiopia, remembered as a 'clean' place. In short, 'a very important traditional social institution' was lost.[45]

Male migrants are also subject to pressures to conform to dominant religious norms. In the 1970s and early 1980s, some were forced to undergo symbolic re-circumcision in order to establish their Jewishness. Today, many younger Ethiopian migrants and their children are either secular or receive education in Orthodox, mainly Ashkenazi, *yeshivot*, built around the study of the Talmud. Ethiopian Jews in Israel are also likely to celebrate *Purim* and *Hanukah*, two post-biblical festivals not observed by their communities in Africa.

If a degree of assimilation was viewed positively by most Jews in nineteenth-century Europe, today it is more often viewed negatively as a threat to Jewish identity and continuity, with intermarriage regarded as a particular challenge. In the United States, the rate of marriages between Jews and non-Jews was approximately 2–3.2% before 1940; by the end of the twentieth century, had risen to around 47%.[46] In many other countries, rates are similarly high, or higher: in 1996, 82% of Jewish men and 74% of Jewish women in Ukraine married non-Jews, partly because of the impact of mass migration of Jews from the former Soviet Union to Israel.[47] Between a quarter and a half of Indian Jews are estimated to marry non-Jews.[48] In other countries, there are strong internal and external pressures against Jewish/non-Jewish marriage. For example, in 2010, Egyptian courts ruled that the government should consider stripping Egyptian men who marry Israeli women of their citizenship.[49] In contrast to other Anglophone nations, only around one quarter of Australian Jews marry non-Jews, a phenomenon which may be correlated with high rates of Jewish school education.

Is it accurate, however, to trace a causal relationship between marrying 'out of the faith' and 'consequent decline in Jewish population and observance', as a recent textbook puts it?[50] Many sociologists would see intermarriage as an index of assimilation not as a determining causal factor. It is only after members of a minority group have become to some degree assimilated that they are likely to meet and form relationships with members of the majority group. Recent research has queried the assumption that intermarriage necessarily leads to radical assimilation in other ways, too. Keren McGinity's historical study, *Still Jewish*, explores how broader cultural and political context alter the meanings and the practical consequences of intermarriage. It also suggests the need for a gendered approach to the topic. In the early and mid-twentieth century, Jewish women who married non-Jews merged into the dominant culture when they did so, *sometimes* out of a wish to abandon the ethno-religious identity of their childhoods. In many cases, they raised their children in the religion of their spouse or as Unitarian. In the late twentieth century, Jewish women who intermarried were in contrast more likely to retain their own names following marriage, to construct their own marriage ceremonies and, in some cases, to increase their levels of religious observance and affiliation.[51] Such shifts reflect a growth in individualism and ethnic revivalism in American society, as well as the impact of feminism, which has enabled many women to act as their own authorities and fashion their own Jewish identities. They have also been facilitated by the growth in secularism, which has affected men disproportionately. Many of McGinity's Jewish respondents married a-religious men and consequently argued that the term 'interfaith marriage' was no longer an accurate one.[52]

Conversion to Judaism

There have been rare instances of forced conversion to Judaism. When the Hasmonean John Hyrcanus conquered Idumea in the second century BCE, he made the indigenous population's continued presence there conditional on their adoption of the Jewish religion. However, conversion to Judaism has generally been an unusual and voluntary decision, perhaps because of the difficulties associated with it both for the individuals involved and for Jews as a minority community within sometimes hostile non-Jewish societies. According to the Babylonian Talmud, would-be converts should be discouraged at first, and conversion for motives other than religious ones, for example, for monetary gain or to marry a Jew, is not permitted.

Following the biblical precedent of Ruth (an ancestor of King David) converts are regarded as adopting a religion *and* acquiring membership of the Jewish people (Ruth 1.16). There is no single, universally accepted procedure but conversions typically take several years and are structured around three central components – *mitzvot* (studying and observing the commandments), *milah* (male circumcision) and *mikvah* (immersion in a ritual bath). A *bet din* or similar panel establishes that these elements have been sincerely and successfully completed. Crucially, the kind of ritual observance required or envisaged, and expectations concerning a convert's beliefs about the nature and origins of the commandments varies, reflecting the different modern movements' approaches to Torah and *halakhah*. Orthodox authorities generally do not recognize conversions overseen by Conservative, Reform or Reconstructionist bodies, just as they also reject the validity of these forms of Judaism.

Significant numbers of people who have entered Israel under the terms of the Law of Return (see Chapter 7) are not regarded as Jews by the Orthodox authorities. Those who wish to convert, to marry or to avoid the social stigma associated with 'uncertain' status, must adopt an observant Orthodox lifestyle. In 2010, Yisrael Beitenu, a nationalist political party which mainly represents immigrants from the former Soviet Union, tried unsuccessfully to have the power to conduct conversions extended to communal rabbis, whom it believed would adopt more flexible approaches to the matter.

11

Studying Judaism: the critical issues: the future

This book has introduced a range of topics that are important for a critical understanding of Judaism, and a number of different ways of studying Judaism. Chapter 1 outlined traditional approaches to the study of Judaism as practiced by some of its adherents. It also traced the emergence of the *Wissenschaft*, or 'Science' of Judaism movement, amongst early advocates of Jewish emancipation, and noted key aspects in the development of the field of Religious Studies, including dimensional or 'salient features' approaches advocated by Smart and others, and the recent engagement with other academic fields including cultural studies.

Research conducted in England and Wales suggests that A-level religious students (16- to 18-year-olds) interested in pursuing theology or religious studies at degree level express high levels of interest in religion and gender issues (71%), religion and the media (62%) and religion and politics (55%).[1] Latter chapters of this book have focused on these and related topical themes. This is partly because in an increasingly marketized higher education sector, within which departmental survival is often pegged to student recruitment, curricula in the study of Judaism and in religions generally, increasingly attempt to strike a balance between student expectations, broader intellectual and social trends and disciplinary tradition, which Cush summarises as 'historical perspective and the languages and literary skills to access religious texts.'[2]

At present, it also seems that an emphasis on diversity will continue within the study of religions, and with it the eschewal of attempts to offer an essentializing or unified account of Judaism. To take one recent example, *Religions in Focus*, edited by Graham Harvey, focuses primarily on 'the doing of religion ... the present day lived reality of religions as they are practiced not only by religious leaders but by a far larger population'.[3] The book, and more specifically Holtschneider's contribution, 'Jews' (which has at its core the imagined *Shabbat* preparations of four Jews in present-day Germany), exemplify both the broadening geographical focus of recent introductions to Judaism, and the increasing move away from discussions of elite and text-based accounts.[4] Again, this is a tendency that *Studying Judaism* has attempted to reflect and shape.

Setting aside the very real institutional, intellectual and practical constraints within which teaching and learning takes place, the future of the study of Judaism is of course in large measure dependent on the future of Judaism itself. To predict that future in any detail is unfeasible. Nevertheless, it is possible to see trends emerging in the present day, which are suggestive of future concerns.

Demographic trends

While not all Jews are adherents of Judaism, Judaism cannot survive without Jews. For this reason, the size and characteristics of the Jewish population is an important topic of study. This is true whether one's definition of 'Jew' reflects a particular 'insider'-position, such as that of an Orthodox Jew whose perspective is grounded in the *halakhah*, or deploys 'outsider' – or second-order – concepts. As described in Chapter 2, self-identification with the Jewish people is one of the three family resemblances Satlow lists as common to all forms of Judaism through the ages.

Recent estimates vary, but tend to place the total world Jewish population at somewhere between 13 and 14 million. It is, however, difficult to determine how many of these are adherents of Judaism, as recent attempts to count the number of ultra-Orthodox or Haredi Jews in Britain illustrate. In 2001, the United Kingdom Census, which informs national and local government planning and decision-making, asked a voluntary question inviting people to indicate their religion (the question was repeated in 2011). 266,740 respondents identified their religion as Jewish, but subsequent studies have suggested that this figure does not include significant numbers of Haredim.[5] Under-numeration may have happened for several reasons. People living in multiple occupancy buildings (like *yeshiva* halls of residence and old people's homes) are more likely not to be counted than are nuclear families. Recent immigrants and non-native speakers are also more likely to slip through the net, and analysis of recent marriage data for Haredi Jews in the UK suggests that in over two-thirds of cases, at least one spouse was a foreign national or was resident overseas before the ceremony.[6] More specifically, it is thought that memories of the Holocaust, when governments' data collection was a preamble to the persecution of Jews, deterred some people from completing the 2001 Census question, as did rabbinic instructions concerning 2 Sam. 24, a biblical text in which King David is described as being punished by God for taking a census of the Jewish people.[7]

Despite such difficulties, emerging population trends can be identified. Worldwide, Jewry is ageing. It is also either declining or, some recent figures suggest, may have stabilized. But as the preceding discussion suggests, there are other prominent aspects of Jewish demography, including migration.[8] Even more Jews left Central and Eastern Europe as migrants in the late-nineteenth and twentieth centuries than died in the Holocaust[9] and more recently, in addition to large-scale movements of populations like that of Jews from the former Soviet Union and Argentina to Israel, and the migration of individual marriage partners, there is widespread movement within nation states away from small population centres towards larger ones. The Jewish populations of Israel and the United States together constitute over 11 million – an overwhelming majority of the world Jewish population – and an increasing number of Jews are urban dwellers. Within the United States, for example, most Jews now live in major metropolitan districts on the East and West coasts and the Midwest.

Such developments have significant implications for diversity within Judaism. Some beliefs and practices are changed by encounter with new environments and even thrive in its wake. Chapters 4 and 9 discussed how in the late twentieth-century Moroccan immigrants developed *Mimouna* and *hillulot* in Israel, and how Jews with quite different religious and cultural roots participate in these rituals today. Similarly complex dynamics are at play in relation to *Saharane*, observed by Kurdish Jews, and *Sigd*, a festival traditionally observed by Ethiopian Jews, who mostly emigrated to Israel in the wake of civil war and famine in Ethiopia in 1984 and 1991 (see Fig. 11.1). Ethiopian Jews have faced significant barriers to participation in economic, political and cultural life in Israel, and their religious status has been queried by the Orthodox establishment, who required early migrants to undergo a modified form of conversion ceremony in order to establish their Jewish identities. In this context, the Israel Association for Ethiopian Jews launched a deliberate campaign for *Sigd*, which falls seven weeks after *Yom Kippur*, to be recognized as a national holiday (a status achieved in 2008) in recognition of the enhanced visibility that this would accord to Ethiopian Judaism as an important element in furtherance of its broader aim to raise awareness and advocate the rights of Ethiopian-born Jews and their descendants in Israel. Kurdish Jews[10], however, have been less successful in their attempts to negotiate a place for *Saharane*, a communal gathering with singing, dancing and other celebrations, on the Israeli festival calendar. Traditionally, *Saharane* was primarily observed at *Pesach*, but in Israel most Jews who identify as Kurds now celebrate the festival (which is not an official national holiday) at *Sukkot*, in the autumn – partly because its status as a distinctive Mizrahi springtime festival has been eclipsed by *Mimouna*.

Migration also impacts Judaism in other ways. While *Mimouna* has been successfully established in Israel, many small Moroccan towns and villages are largely empty of their former Jewish populations and some traditional pilgrimage sites abandoned. Likewise in India, a decline in Jewish population following mass migrations to Israel, the United States and Canada in the late twentieth century have forced the formerly distinct Bene Israel and Baghdadi Jewish communities to integrate their religious practices in order to ensure the viability of synagogue services.[11] In a different vein, David Lowenthal has suggested that interest in memory and heritage is particularly strong amongst migrants and diasporic populations.[12] Together with the need to deal with the legacy of the Holocaust, widespread experience of physical displacement forms part of the context both for the current preoccupation with memory discussed in Chapter 9 and for the current appeal of traditional – or more accurately, traditionalist – ritual observance.

Figure 11.1: *Sigd*, 2010 © Carol Shoval (of Tene-Briut Association)

Sigd means 'prostration' and recalls the renewal of the covenant by Ezra and Nehemiah when, according to Neh. 9.1–3, the people of Israel prostrated themselves before God.

Alongside migration, growth, both in absolute terms and as a proportion of the total worldwide Jewish population, in the number of Haredi Jews is another fact of contemporary Jewish demographics. In the UK, for example, the number of strictly Orthodox synagogue members has doubled in the period 1990–2010.[13] This trend illustrates well the difficulties associated with predicting religions' futures. For much of the nineteenth and twentieth centuries, it appeared to many commentators that, in order to survive, Judaism must acquiesce in the face of post-Enlightenment values. In retrospect, however, it seems that aspects of modern (and postmodern) cultures in fact provide a fertile context for the revitalization of Haredi Judaism. The toleration or celebration of difference has implicitly validated religious identities as 'lifestyle choices'. Moreover, isolationism or absolutism have seemed to some to offer more viable bulwarks against radical Jewish assimilation – the 'disappearance' of Jews *qua* Jews – than the various accommodationist strategies underpinning modern Orthodoxy, Conservativism and other progressive religious movements. Sociologist Samuel Heilman, writing about the rise of Haredi Judaism in the US, argues that,

> by the end of the 1970s, in the wake of racial turmoil, often violent anti–Vietnam War protests, growing radicalism on campus, polarization in the political process, the excesses of the sexual revolution, freethinking in lifestyle choices, and increasing signs of a decline in Jewish affiliation and involvement among young college graduates, the American dream seemed to growing numbers of Orthodox Jews to have become a nightmare.[14]

In the late twentieth and early twenty-first centuries, just when some religious Jews have been newly questioning post-Enlightenment values, and specifically, the appropriateness of the modernist enthusiasm for secular university and college education, Haredi Jews, who see themselves as surviving remnants of the 'Torah-true' European Jewish communities destroyed in the Holocaust, have become much better organized, particularly in relation to the teaching of young adults. While Heilman is primarily interested in American Judaism, similar conditions prevail in Britain and elsewhere. Instantaneous communications and the opening up of international travel opportunities mean that issues and pressures are no longer simply local or national, but global.

The growth of Haredi Judaism is linked with a hardening of boundaries between Jews and non-Jews, and between different kinds of religious Jews. Chapters 6 and 8 have discussed this dynamic in relation to clothing and diet. Similar processes may be observed in the recent rise in demand for *kosher* investment funds that offer financial products compliant with *halakhah*.[15] But diverse factors underpin such trends; even ideologically separatist groups are themselves subject to outside influences. For example, the financial services sector has in general seen an increase in the development of niche markets and funds that comply with the requirements of other religious communities – such as Muslims – are the subject of increasing media and political interest in the West.[16]

As the very recent rise of *kosher* investment products illustrates, Jewish and non-Jewish agencies and corporations are only just beginning to respond to the growth of Haredi Judaism, as are scholars and students of religion. In Israel, the matter is urgent and significant. School enrolments illustrate the extent to which Jerusalem Jews are increasingly likely to be Haredim. There are currently 120,000 pupils in the secular school system and 85,000 in the Orthodox religious stream, but at kindergarten (pre-school) level these figures are effectively reversed (33,000 and 59,000, respectively). Such trends may have a number of consequences, including a rise in tensions between Haredim and other Israelis. In 1991, 61% of respondents to the Guttman Institute study judged that relations between religious and non-religious Israelis were 'not so good' or 'not good at all'; by 1999, the figure had risen to 82%.[17] Other surveys suggest that while a majority of the Israeli Jewish population is willing to contemplate giving up Jerusalem's Arab neighbourhoods for peace with the Palestinians, only a minority of Jerusalem Jews would do so. At the same time, as the proportion of Haredim in Jerusalem increases, so does the number of young Jerusalemites who are exempted from military service in order to pursue advanced religious studies, or (in the case of women) on the basis of their religious lifestyle.[18] Some non-Haredim are highly critical of the exemption system, arguing that it is the responsibility of all to defend the nation, and that current arrangements are open to abuse: there is believed to be a growing number of women making false declarations of religious observance in order to avoid conscription. Exemption's Haredi advocates argue that God enables Israel to survive in large part because of the merits of those who engage in a carefully Orthodox lifestyle of Torah study and observance.

Gender and Homosexuality

As discussed in Chapter 6, the concept of gender and, more specifically, feminism have significantly influenced Judaism since the latter half of the twentieth century. In their attitudes towards these issues, the differences between Jewish religious movements are readily apparent. In Reform Judaism, men and women may lead worship and be ordained as rabbis; in the Conservative movement, the picture is more mixed, with female ordination and leadership in some countries and synagogues and not others; in modern and Haredi Orthodox forms of Judaism, women may not be ordained or serve as rabbis, and may not be called to read from the Torah or lead prayers.

Struggles over such matters will continue, between and within movements. In 2009, Yeshivat Maharat opened in Riverdale, New York State, to train Orthodox women for positions of legal authority and communal leadership. In 2010, the title of *rabba* – the feminine form of *rabbi* – was conferred on its Dean, Sara Hurwitz. The move was immediately condemned as 'radical and dangerous' by *Agudath Israel*,[19] while the modern Orthodox Rabbinical Council of America ruled that it could not accept 'either the ordination of women or the recognition of women as members of the Orthodox rabbinate, regardless of the title'.[20] These statements illustrate the extent to which the application of the title 'rabbi' to a woman is currently unthinkable to most Orthodox minds. Yet similar controversies seem more likely in coming years, not least because women's learning is one of the most rapidly growing areas within Orthodox religious education – in terms of both its seriousness and the numbers of participants.[21]

Issues regarding sexuality are also topics of growing debate. Lev. 18.22 ('Do not lie with a male as one lies with a woman: it is an abhorrence') and 20.3 ('If a man lies with a male as one lies with a woman, the two of them have done an abhorrent thing; they shall be put to death') have traditionally been regarded as prohibiting sexual relations between men. For centuries, execution has been very much a theoretical rather than an actual punishment for forbidden sexual contacts (including not just same sex intercourse between males, but also incest, adultery, bestiality and intercourse with a woman who is *niddah*).[22] But this provision, and its classification as one of just a few laws that one may not transgress in order to escape death, emphasize the ban's seriousness.[23] Lesbian sexual relations are not discussed directly in the *Tanakh*, but are deemed indecent in the Talmud (*Yevamot* 76a; *Shabbat* 65a) and in the *Mishneh Torah* and *Shulhan Arukh*, a woman who 'plays around' with another woman is regarded as having committed one of the 'Egyptian practices' prohibited in Lev. 18.3–4. Reflecting a broader willingness to re-evaluate religious law and tradition in the light of changing knowledge and values, many progressive Jews distinguish between the *halakhah*, which is primarily interested in the permissibility or otherwise of particular acts, and contemporary views of heterosexuality, homosexuality, bisexuality and transgenderedness as *identities* that deserve to be treated with respect, since all human beings are made *b'tzelem elohim*, in the divine image.[24] The Reconstructionist and Reform movements ordain openly homosexual women and men, and permit their rabbis to conduct same-sex commitment or marriage ceremonies. Within Conservative/Masorti Judaism, the picture is more mixed. In America, home to the largest and most influential Conservative movement, the Conservative Committee on Jewish Law and Standards (CJLS) adopted three differing responsa on homosexuality in 2006 – two maintaining the traditional prohibitions and one permitting the ordination of openly gay rabbis and cantors and officiation at same-sex ceremonies, and lifting many of the bans on homosexual acts (on the grounds that they are rabbinical, not biblical in character). Rabbis and institutions are free to choose which responsum they accept. The movement's seminary now admits openly homosexual students, and an association of gay, lesbian, bisexual and transgender-friendly Conservative rabbis and cantors, *Keshet Rabbis*, serves as a point of contact and coordination.[25] To date, a minority of rabbis and cantors belong to the organization. European, Israeli and South American Conservative movements tend to be more traditional in outlook and many have publicly rejected the more liberal responsa.

As Sylvia Barack Fishman and Randal Schnoor note, some gay and lesbian Jews feel ambivalent about their Jewish identity, in part because of the traditional religious emphasis on heterosexual marriage and parenthood.[26] Young Orthodox Jews may experience considerable pressure to marry early and fulfil the *mitzvah* of procreation, regardless of sexual attraction or orientation. A few Orthodox organizations, notably JONAH (Jews Offering New Alternatives to Homosexuals) offer counselling to Jews who are 'struggling with unwanted same-sex attractions [and wish] to journey out of homosexuality.'[27] Recent years have also witnessed the growth of rabbinic literature and public debate on homosexuality, stimulated in part by several films exploring the lives of Orthodox gay and lesbian Jews, including the documentary *Trembling Before G-d* (Sandi Simcha DuBowski, 2004) and *Eyes Wide Open* (Haim Tabakman, 2009) a fiction feature about a married Orthodox man who falls in love with a young male *yeshiva* student.

Lubavitch rabbi Chaim Rapoport's 2004 study, *Judaism and Homosexuality*, rejects the view that homosexuals should be encouraged or expected to pursue heterosexual marriage, on the grounds that a gay man is unlikely to be able to provide his wife with the emotional support stipulated in the marriage contract, and that living with a heterosexual partner may result in emotional or psychological injury to someone who is homosexual. Drawing on the *halakhah* and contemporary understandings of homosexuality as an orientation, he argues that a practicing homosexual should be regarded not as a *mumar le-hachis* – a rebellious or wilful sinner – but as a *mumar le-te'avon*, someone who sins in order to indulge him or herself. He or she should, therefore, be treated leniently. At the same time, Rapoport argues, people generally have the ability to control their desires and 'people of whatever sexual orientation must abstain from all sexual expression outside of marriage'.[28]

There are also more radical attempts to challenge the mainline Orthodox position. Steven Greenberg, an openly gay Orthodox Jew, points out that stances like Rapoport's discourage homosexual Jews from making their sexuality public: 'coming out may threaten to turn a *mumar le-te'avon* in to a *mumar le-hakhis*'.[29]

Greenberg links the quest for homosexual rights to the feminist debate, arguing that the Levitical codes regard same-sex relations between men as abhorent because such acts are seen as feminizing the male ('do not lie ... as one lies with a woman'). In the ancient world, women were regarded as weak and inferior, so 'it was wholly understood that to be like a woman in any way was degrading for a man.'[30] If, however, in the light of feminism, one rejects a hierarchical view of the genders, sex between men cannot be regarded as automatically degrading and abhorrent on the grounds that it in some way entails the kinds of acts that heterosexual men do with women. Greenberg proposes a re-reading of Lev. 18.22, which understands the verse as a prohibition against the sexual humiliation of anyone, male or female. Both Greenberg's arguments (the weight given to what his critics regard as non-Jewish concepts, including the practice of a hermeneutics of suspicion[31]) and his conclusions lack widespread acceptance among Orthodox Jews. What is more certain is that debates around sexuality will figure on the future agendas of the various religious Jewish movements, particularly Conservativism and Orthodoxy, as more people seek to challenge the view that it is impossible positively to accommodate homosexual relationships within a *halakhic* framework.

Just as gender and sexuality are important issues for future Judaism, so they may also more wholeheartedly influence how future scholars of religion study Judaism. If gender – albeit often elided into 'women' – now features in many textbooks and syllabi, it does so often as a discrete topic rather than as a lens through which the entirety of a tradition may be viewed. To an even greater extent, sexual orientation and expression typically receive little or no treatment.[32] To give these factors greater prominence would alter scholarship considerably. For example, dialogue and cooperation between different religious groups is often advocated and studied as a means of countering extremism and intolerance in society. However, opposition to social and legal recognition of diverse sexual identities is one of the notable sites of agreement between traditionalist members of different religions. In 2006, the leading Lubavitch rabbi in Russia joined Christian and Muslim leaders in condemning plans for Moscow's first Gay Pride parade,[33] and in the same year, some Haredi rabbis and Israeli Arab politicians called for a ceasefire in the Israeli–Arab conflict so that both sides could cooperate in order to campaign for a removal of gay rights in Israel.[34] Such data challenge existing assumptions and models and potentially open up fresh, genuinely pluralistic ways of approaching the study of religion.

Israel and diaspora

Present day Israel is the site of many questions concerning the relationships between religion and the state, religion's place in defining Jewish identity, and relations between Jews and non-Jews as well as between Orthodox and non-Orthodox or progressive movements. These issues show no signs of dissipating in the near future. The current *status quo*, whereby a dual Ashkenazi and Sefardi chief rabbinate has legal authority over personal status matters, is coming under increasing pressure from groups lobbying for the increased recognition of a diverse range of Mizrahi and progressive Judaisms, and from secular Jews, particularly those with roots in the former Soviet Union.

Internationally, Israel could for many years take for granted the political and financial support of many diaspora Jews. The 1967 Six Day War, in which Israel launched a series of air strikes on airfields in Egypt, Syria, Jordan and Iraq, and took control of the Sinai peninsula, the West Bank (including East Jerusalem), the Golan Heights and the Gaza strip, instilled feelings of pride in and affiliation with the state amongst many diaspora communities.[35] Around the same time, in 1968, the umbrella organization for the Zionist movement, the World Zionist Organization, revised its aims. Recognizing that not all Jews would make Israel their home, it developed ways of fostering support for the state amongst Jews worldwide. In particular, it promoted popular pilgrimage tours to Israel, which are marketed as means of strengthening Jewish cultural and spiritual values, and of guarding against assimilation and intermarriage. Since the 1990s, however, diaspora support for Zionism is no longer a given. Recent studies of Israeli attitudes reveal a growing sense that Israeli Jews and diaspora Jews are becoming 'different peoples', and the American National Jewish Population Survey found that just 20% of Jewish college students felt themselves to be emotionally very close to Israel, while only 31% strongly agreed that American and Israeli Jews shared a common destiny.[36] On a practical level, diaspora Jews today give less money to Israeli causes than was the case a generation ago.

The reasons for this shift are several-fold; many relate to the state's impact on Judaism. As touched on in Chapter 7, the birth of modern Israel led to the reinvigoration of religious laws relating to the exercising of Jewish political power, and more generally to Jewish life, in the land of Israel. The revival of a modern Hebrew language in Israel also influenced the return of Hebrew as a language of prayer in Reform and other progressive synagogues. More fundamentally, however, struggles as to the relationship between Jewishness and Judaism have proven to be a source of controversy not just in Israel, but globally.

Notwithstanding the rise of Haredi forms of Orthodoxy, the majority of Jews in America and other Western contexts understand Jewishness primarily as a matter of religious affiliation, an attachment to Judaism that is in turn viewed as a matter of individual choice and conscience. They live in national contexts characterized both by a separation of religion and state and by religious pluralism: there is no 'established' – uniquely privileged or authoritative – form of Judaism. In contrast, the majority of Israeli Jews primarily regard themselves as part of a Jewish nation, and view Judaism as an ancillary component of Jewish nationalism. While an individual's level of belief and observance is a personal matter, 'traditional' forms of Judaism are enshrined in and maintained by national institutions.[37] Thus when, as a result of a perceived lack of Judaism and Jewish values amongst younger Israelis, a decision was made to introduce compulsory Jewish studies in high schools, the new curriculum blended aspects of Orthodox and Zionist cultures.[38] And although there is growing support for calls for Reform and Masorti Judaism to be given equal status to Orthodoxy, and for civil marriage provision, most Israeli Jews do not wish to attend Reform or Conservative synagogues, or to opt for civil marriages themselves.[39]

A brief return to the subject of sexuality illustrates these differences. In America, gay and lesbian Jews organize primarily around synagogues and related communal organizations. The campaign for acceptance in American Jewish life is inextricably linked to access to positions of religious authority and ritual recognition of partnership relations that challenge heterosexist norms. But most lesbian and gay Israelis regard themselves as secular, and are more likely to campaign for civil rights and freedoms more broadly defined. Aviv and Shneer summarise the distinction as follows:

> If queer American Jews want to know when the first Israeli queer synagogue is going to open, many queer Israelis want to know when all Israeli citizens will have civil rights, when the intifada will end, and when Palestinians will have a home and state to call their own.[40]

These varying approaches to identity have led to the opening up of a gap between the expectations and ideals of Jews in Israel and Jews elsewhere. In contrast to the period before and immediately following 1948, many secular and religious Jews in the diaspora no longer regard Israel as a model state, spiritually or socially. Whereas early Zionists like Mordecai Kaplan believed that the survival of Jewish identity could only be guaranteed by a Jewish state, for many Jews today, particularly those who are not Ashkenazi Orthodox, that same state is now seen as potentially threatening Jewish identity, especially its religious aspects.

Noting these differences, it is perhaps no longer helpful or accurate to conceptualize Jewish life globally in terms of a binary – Israel/diaspora or Jewish home/Jewish homelessness – model. The extent of political, ethnic and religious divisions is such that many Jewish Israelis do not feel themselves to be unequivocally 'at home' in Israeli society. Equally, many diaspora Jews do not feel Israel to be their 'home'. Despite the relative ease with which one can travel and relocate today, they choose to remain elsewhere, for a variety of reasons.[41] How far these trends will continue in the future is a critical issue not just for the study of Judaism but for the future character of Judaism and Jewish identity.

Online religion

As touched on in Chapter 3, the internet provides a space within which people are able to engage freely in debates about questions of belief and practice. Online chat rooms and instructional texts and videos are now key sites of knowledge production. At the same time, an increasing number of online advertisers offering goods and services has contributed to a new degree of commodification of Jewish religious commitment – especially its Orthodox observant forms. In these and other ways, a 'new Judaism' – or perhaps more accurately, 'new Judaisms' – are in the making. For some Jews, new online forms of Judaism are the principle ways in which they identify and express their religiosity. These include online global prayer groups, online religious study opportunities (including online conversion courses) and online multi-user religious rituals.

OurJewishCommunity.org, an interactive website developed by Congregation Beth Adam in Loveland, a suburb of Cinncinnati, Ohio, is one example of such a development. Amongst other things, it streams a live *Shabbat* service every Friday night. The service is a loosely structured mixture of *Shabbat* readings and rituals such as the lighting of candles and *kiddush*, and chatty conversation reflecting on the nature of *Shabbat*, current affairs and other issues. The experience is led by the members of the rabbinical team (one of whom was hired specifically to serve the online community), but those accessing online can watch and listen, and are encouraged to share their personal news and responses to the discussion topics via email, Facebook and Twitter.

Such developments may fundamentally alter the character and experience of Judaism – according to some commentators, they are already doing so. Most obviously, they weaken the role that geographical location plays in religious identity and observance, and transform the experience of a ritual. In many respects OurJewishCommunity.org's Shabbat is very much an American Jewish experience. Beth Adam is an independent, unaffiliated synagogue: its rabbis trained at the Reform movement's Hebrew Union College–Jewish Institute of Religion in Cincinnati, the synagogue's literature describes its approach as humanistic, and members develop and use their own liturgies, which do not contain traditional references to God. The free-flowing on-camera conversation reflects American concerns and events. But the rabbis acknowledge that some participants, including military personnel, are based elsewhere, and the online *Shabbat* service may be viewed and experienced around the world, throughout the subsequent week.

For some religious Jews, online Judaism represents 'a profound contradiction of the human sociability' at the heart of traditional rituals based around the synagogue and home.[42] Certainly, many of the aspects of ritual that are memorable to participants, and/or are typically of interest to students of religion – sight, sound, smell, touch, taste – are absent from or transformed by the online environment. Yet it also remains the case that online experiences are of profound significance for some. In one of the first book-length accounts of online religion, Brasher describes how participation in a Cyber-Seder ultimately led one American woman to convert to Judaism.[43]

It is perhaps this aspect of the future of Judaism that is hardest to predict. Like the *havurah* movement referred to in Chapter 2, aspects of online Judaism influence the offline Jewish religious world. Graham and Vulkan have written recently of the difficulties associated with the production of accurate synagogue membership figures because of changing modes of affiliation, which are increasingly 'highly fluid, informal and transient' – all characteristics typically associated with online communities.[44] Aside from modes of affiliation, it is even harder to speculate about what the rise of online religion will mean for the content of Judaism.

Practitioners of religious studies are only now beginning to develop the tools required for the conduct of virtual ethnography. Helland summarises some of the challenges that scholars face as follows:

> What action or online activity can be considered a genuine religious action? How is it possible to determine if the people practising forms of online religion are in fact … having genuine religious experiences? … [I]t is not merely the action that makes an activity religious, rather it is the intent behind the action that gives it its religious significance … [L]ighting a candle may or may not be considered a religious event; it is dependant upon the situation and also the interpretation of the participants. The same holds true for clicking hyperlinks on websites. People may or may not be undertaking the activity to obtain a true religious experience. In many ways, evaluating the activity focuses upon the authenticity of the event and this is something that is extremely problematic to determine.[45]

While many of these problems would apply to the study of ritual in general, the lack of verbal and non-verbal cues in much online religious activity makes it especially hard to interpret and evaluate, and finding new ways of doing this will be a critical issue for the future study of Judaism. To these practical questions, ethical ones might also be added: it is relatively easy for a researcher to gather data covertly online, and it may be argued that some online environments like chatrooms are 'public' rather than 'private' spaces, but ethical norms in research generally require that the informed consent of subjects be sought. When and how should this be done by virtual ethnographers? Discussion of these and other methodological issues associated with online research will be a critical issue for the study of Judaism in the future.[46]

Further study

You may have arrived at these final paragraphs without having read all of the material that proceeds them, perhaps because you have found some of the chapters and issues more or less appealing or pertinent than others, or because your reading has been constrained by the rigours of a particular course schedule. But even if you have simply skimmed the chapter and section headings, or glanced at the exercises, text-boxes or photographs, this will have given you a sense of the range of methods, subjects and questions that are entailed in the study of Judaism. The notes and bibliography cite other books, articles and websites that can help you to pursue topics further, by providing factual information or by presenting theories and analyses that you may wish to apply or challenge.

Like its series companions, this book is intended to be suggestive rather than exhaustive in nature, to encourage rather than to close-down intellectual exploration. For this reason it does not close with a conclusion but with an invitation to further study.

Notes

Series Preface Endnotes

1 Or, as Smart (1968) put it, 'the study of man is in an important sense participatory – for one has to enter into men's intentions, beliefs, myths, desire, in order to understand why they act as they do – it is fatal if cultures including our own are described merely externally, without entering into dialogue with them' (104).

2 As Religious Studies (RS) becomes more participatory, concerned with the faith in people's hearts, practitioners who self-identify with a faith tradition will inevitably explore questions about the status of their own faith in relation with others, thus treading on what might be regarded as theological ground. As RS professionals become involved in personal encounter, the distinction between RS and Theology becomes blurred. For some, this compromises RS as a neutral discipline. Others point out that RS can evaluate the plausibility of arguments or theological stances regarding the status of different religions without adjudicating whether they are true or false, thus remaining neutral. A confessional theologian, for his or her part, might declare a certain view correct and that others are heretical, or suspect.

Chapter 1 Endnotes

1 de Lange (2010), 1.

2 Neusner (2003a), 3.

3 Strassfield and Siegel (1973), 12.

4 The Enlightenment was an originally philosophical, but later wide ranging European cultural movement, characterized by a confidence in reason, truth and progress.

5 Johnson et al. (2004), 18. For further discussion of some of the issues raised in this section, see Chapter 10.

6 See Chapter 8. On religious law, see Chapter 3.

7 Nye (2008), 20.

8 Nye (2003), 24. The second edition of Nye's book revises this passage in a manner that evidences an increasing de-centring of religion in favour of culture more broadly conceived: 'a critical study of culture ... can include not only the "great" works of art, literature and music (religious or otherwise), but also the less great (or more *popular*) works' (2008, 26–7).

9 Cort (1996), 631.

10 Satlow (2006b), 9.

11 See also Steinweis (2006), 18–22.

12 Geertz (1999), 52.

13 For a discussion of his life and work, see *Mennonite Quarterly Review* 47 (April 1974).

14 Yovel (2009), 379. On Marranos, see Chapter 10 of this book. For another example of the Academy's influence on Jewish self understanding, see the discussion of Kaufmann Kohler's definition of Judaism in Chapter 2.

15 See Chryssides (2007b), 228–30 for more on this topic.

16 Smart (1989), 12–21.

17 Smart (1996), 289.

18 For a fuller discussion of this issue, see Chapter 11.

19 Said (1985) [1975], 13, and Highmore (2009), 110–20 offer useful discussions of the notion of beginnings in relation to cultural studies.

Chapter 2 Endnotes

1 For examples and a brief discussion of the issue, see Jacobs (1995) and Werblowsky and Wigoder (1997), v.

2 For additional textbook discussions of the etymology of the term 'Judaism', see de Lange (2003), 1–4; Wright (2003), 1–2; Hoffman (2008), 2, 6 and Segal (2009), 1–7.

3 Note, however, that 2 Macc. was written in Greek.

4 For a discussion of the term *dati* in contemporary Israeli, see Katz (2007), 166–7.

5 Kohler (1902), 359–60.

6 Satlow (2006a), 842.

7 Satlow (2006a), 843.

8 Nesbitt (2002), 110.

9 Wright (2003), 4.

10 Satlow (2006b), 6.

11 Warburton (2001), 68–9.

12 Satlow (2006b), 4–16.

13 On the history and historiography of the 'Trefa Banquet,' see Sussman (2005). Highland House was a fashionable entertainment and dining venue in Mount Adams, Cincinnati. It was destroyed by fire in 1895.

14 See http://reformjudaism.org (accessed 1 September 2009).

15 See 'Progressive Judaism in Israel', available at http://www.reform.org.il/Eng/About/ProgressiveJudaismInIsrael.asp (accessed 1 September 2009).

16 Hirsch (1995).

17 See Soloveitchik (1983).

18 Heilman (1992, 26).

19 Louis Finkelstein, quoted in Klein (1979), xxii.

20 Waxman (2005), 138.

21 *Halakhically*, a Jew is someone who is born of a Jewish mother, or has undertaken an acceptable conversion including immersion in a ritual bath, male circumcision, and an interview with a rabbinic court. The American Reform movement (and Liberal Judaism in Britain) accept patrilineal as well as matrilineal descent, and adopt a more flexible approach to conversion. Consequently, there are a number of people affiliated to Reform and Liberal synagogues who are not seen as Jewish, and whose religious lives would not be regarded as Judaism by Orthodox authorities. See Chapter 10.

22 Freud-Kandel (2005), 89—90; Holtschneider (2010).

23 People who have undergone non-Orthodox conversions to Judaism or who are Jewish by patrilineal descent alone are not regarded as Jews by Orthodox religious authorities.

24 Levine (2001), 56–65.

Chapter 3 Endnotes

1 Geller (2004), 2032.

2 Walzer, Lorberbaum and Zohar (2000), 112.

3 Ibid., 169.

4 Fishbane (1985) terms this kind of activity, 'inner biblical exegesis'.

5 Walzer, Lorberbaum and Zohar (2000), 248.

6 Quoted in Walzer, Lorberbaum and Zohar (2000), 346–7.

7 See further Zohar (2005), 186.

8 Ben-Menachem and Hecht (1999), xii.

9 Schwarzfuchs (1993), 35–49.

10 Schwarzfuchs (1993), xi-xii and 146.

11 Alpert and Staub (1997), 82.

12 *Millet* means 'nation' in Turkish.

13 Civil marriages performed in other countries are recognized in Israel. For this reason, many Israelis travel abroad if they wish to contract a marriage that would not be acceptable to religious authorities (this might include marriage to a member of another religion or (in the case of Kohanim) marriage to a divorcee or convert). A similar situation applies in other countries in the region, including Syria and Lebanon.

14 For summaries of Weber on authority, see Gerth and Wright Mills (1991), 245-8; Weber/Parsons (1968), 130–2, 328–33, 341–4; and excerpts in McIntosh (1970), 165–75.

15 Hannah Rachel Verbermacher (1815–1888) of Ludmir (now Volodymyr-Volynskyi, Ukraine) was, uniquely, a female Hasidic leader who accepted prayer requests and held a Sabbath *tish* (meal, literally 'table') at which she taught her followers. She was pressured by male religious leaders to marry and assume the traditional role of a Hasidic woman (see Chapter 6); in later life, she emigrated to Jerusalem, where she continued to attract followers.

16 Kellner (1996), 1–2.

17 Bourdieu (1987), 129–31.

18 'Internet for Religious Studies' by Meriel Patrick. Available online at http://www.vts.intute.ac.uk/tutorial/religiousstudies/?sid=1355700&itemid=12021 (accessed 2 June 2010).

19 Na'aman (2006).

20 Campbell (2010), 30.

21 Stolow (2006), 86–7.

22 Round (2010), 3. The mitzvahapp is no longer in circulation and its web presence has ceased. There are several other apps with a similar aim, however.

Chapter 4 Endnotes

1 Sacks (2007), 75.

2 Movement for Reform Judaism (2008), 75.

3 Segal (2009), 138.

4 Bell (1998), 207.

5 Smart (1989), 21.

6 Bunis (2005), 60.

7 Bell (1998), 207.

8 Ochs (2007), 141.

9 Heilman (1976), 140.

10 Alpert and Staub (1997), 22.

11 Sacks (2007), xxix.

12 Levy, Levinsohn and Katz (1997), 7. A follow–up study conducted in 1999, after the arrival of nearly a million immigrants from the former Soviet Union, found that more than half of Israelis celebrated the arrival of *Shabbat* (Katz 2007, 159).

13 On the social functions of festivals in Israel, see Levy, Levinsohn and Katz (1997), 11.

14 Satlow (2006), 176.

15 See Chapter 7.

16 Sheinson and Touster (2000).

17 Feldman (2008), 135–6.

18 For a more extended discussion of these ideas, see Eisen (1999), especially 247.

19 The Baghdadis are communities of Jews who moved from the Middle East to India in the 1700s.

20 Needel (2008), 69.

21 Magnier (2009).

22 *Kol Nidre* asks God to annul all vows that an individual makes to God in the coming year. It is intended to avert any punishment that might result from failure to keep such a vow. Anti-Jewish polemicists have sometimes cited *Kol Nidre* as evidence of the untrustworthiness of Jews and, as a result, it was removed it from the *Yom Kippur* liturgies used by Reform Jews in Europe and America in the nineteenth century.

23 Levy, Levinsohn and Katz (1997), 12.

24 Kaplan (1934), 448–51.

25 Dan (2006), 54–5.

26 Dan (2006), 102. Dan's study is noteworthy for its brevity and its even-handed treatment of the shifting contours and meanings attached to *kabbalah* by Jews and non-Jews.

27 Ibid., 111.

28 Einstein (2007), 150.

29 Ibid., 172.

30 See Alexander (2002) for a relatively recent discussion of the historiography of Jewish mysticism, including Scholem's contribution.

Chapter 5 Endnotes

1 Smart (1989), 17.

2 Although the label 'Orthodox' might seem to imply emphasis on correct belief or doctrine, it is important to note that this term originated in Christian discourse and was first used negatively by Jewish reformers to refer to their opponents. See further Chapter 2.

3 Jacobs (1965), 139.

4 See Rabbi Louis Jacobs' obituary in *The Telegraph* newspaper. Available online at http://www.telegraph.co.uk/news/obituaries/1523257/Rabbi-Louis-Jacobs.html (accessed 1 September 2009).

5 Werblowsky and Wigoder (1997), 205.

6 Levy, Levinsohn and Katz (1997), 25.

7 Brown (1988), 72.

8   See also Chapter 10.

9   Maybaum (1949), 162.

10 Maybaum (1949), 155–6.

11 Plaskow (1991), 135.

12 Plaskow (1991), 122.

13 Samet (1988), 257.

14 See Cantor and Swetlitz (eds) (2006) for explorations of different aspects of the relationship between Judaism and evolutionary theory.

15 See further Dan (2006), 38–9.

16 Klapper (1999), 71.

17 Jacobs (1995), 429f.

18 Rosenzweig quoted in Glatzer (1998), 246.

19 Text from a Chabad-Lubavitch pamphlet, quoted in Caplan (2002), 146.

20 Maybaum (1965), 200.

21 Rubenstein (1992), 250.

22 Levy, Levinsohn and Katz (1997), 25.

23 Chryssides and Geaves (2007), 84–5.

24 Marcus (2004), 51.

25 See Berger (2001).

26 Kravel-Tovi describes various ways in which this *rebbe*'s followers construct a ritual space for his virtual presence: 'Three times a day, one of the yeshiva students uncovers the Rebbe's empty armchair just before prayers and then covers it again after prayers are completed… . On the Sabbath and other days on which the Torah is read, the Rebbe's Torah scroll is placed on the lectern in front of his empty armchair. At special ceremonial gatherings when the Rebbe used to sing with his followers, sermonize to them, and distribute wine and the Sabbath loaf … the same artifacts are still used: the Hasidim lay the Rebbe's place at the table, set his armchair by it, place food and drink on the table… . At the end … one of the … elders carefully and very reverently distributes the wine and the halla among the crowd.' (2009, 255).

27 Berger (2001), Ehrlich (2004).

28 Marcus (2001).

29 Freud (2001b), 273–4.

30 Freud (2001a), xv.

Chapter 6 Endnotes

1   Ethiopian Jews are the only Jewish community, ancient or modern, known to have practiced female circumcision. The practice has been largely abandoned following the migration of the majority of Ethiopian Jews to Israel. See Cohen (2005), 59.

2 Hearn and Morgan (1990), 7.

3 Hearn and Morgan (1990), 5.

4 Freud's story cited in Boyarin (1998), 63.

5 Boyarin (1998), 63.

6 Berman (1990), 63.

7 Boyarin (1998), 64, 76.

8 Oakley (1974).

9 See Smart (1996), 21, which refers to but does not discuss 'new perspectives and questions' raised by women's studies. Not unusually, the terms 'men' and 'gender' are absent from the index to Hoffman (2008), while 'women' is listed, suggesting that female experience is important but supplementary to a normative male experience.

10 Chryssides and Geaves (2007), 314–42. See Chapter 2 of this book for a brief discussion of the problems linked to essentialist approaches to religion.

11 Schüssler Fiorenza (1992), 57.

12 For an example of this kind of approach, see Feldman (2003).

13 Sezgin (2005), 222.

14 See Chapter 3, note 15.

15 Benor (2004).

16 Sered (1992), 3.

17 Sered (1992), 9.

18 Sezgin (2005), 223.

19 Berman (1973), 16.

20 Segal (2009), 259. Note that Segal's point depends in part on a clear sex-gender dichotomy, and that it places both biology and somewhat puzzlingly, economics, in a realm apart from culture.

21 Meiselman (1975), 56.

22 Grossman (2004), 180–1.

23 Meiselman (1998), 24.

24 For more on Jonas, see von Kellenbach (1994).

25 Baskin (2010), 377–8.

26 Judith Kaplan quoted in Marcus (2004), 107.

27 Family or surnames became common amongst Sefardi Jews in the medieval period, and later on amongst Ashkenazim. Most Jews continue to also have a Hebrew name which is used in a number of religious contexts, for example in a text of the *ketubah* (marriage contract). They take the form 'X son/daughter of Y'. The Hebrew name of Moses Maimonides is, for example, Moshe ben Maimon (Moshe son of Maimon).

28 Levy, Levinsohn and Katz (1997), 14.

29 See Ochs (2007), 21–4.

30 Marcus (2004), 56.

31 Benor (2004), 165.

32 Fader (2006), 217.

33 Silbiger (2001), 4-5.

34 Hartman (2007), 95.

35 Amongst other things Baumel-Schwarz (2009) finds evidence of the limitations of Orthodox women's education and the influence of feminism, as well as a tendency towards increased stringency in *halakhic* practice, in her study of Orthodox women's internet forums.

36 Wolowelsky (2002).

37 Sered (1992), 106.

38 Sered (2005), 165.

39 *Tzniut* is absent from Hoffman (2008), Segal (2009), and Wright (2003), and receives the briefest of mentions in De Lange (2010), 114.

40 Falk (1998), 38, 103, 563.

41 Tamar Elor, quoted in Levertov (2008).

42 Ginsburg in Kasnett (1996), 76–7.

43 Polygamy persisted within some Jewish communities living in Islamic countries into the twentieth century. For example, some Yemeni and Iranian migrants to Israel in the 1950s and 1960s were party to polygamous marriages.

Chapter 7 Endnotes

1 Smart (1996), 289–95.

2 The definitions of politics are drawn from Walzer, Lorberbaum and Zohar (2000), xxi–xxii.

3 Smart (1996), 293–5.

4 Herbert (forthcoming 2012).

5 See further Chapter 3.

6 Stessel (1995), 96–102.

7 See Chapter 3.

8 Walzer, Lorberbaum and Zohar (2000), 431.

9 Israeli settlers are civilians who live in territories occupied by the State of Israel during the Six Day War.

10 See further Shapira and Lichtenstein (2007), which also considers whether departing Jews may demolish synagogues in order to prevent their being vandalized.

11 Singer (2000), 25–7.

12 Della Pergola (2007).

13 See also the discussion of pilgrimage in Chapter 9.

14 Herzl [1896] (2006), 204, 16. Not all early advocates of a Jewish state believed that it must be in Palestine. Herzl's book mentions Argentina as a possible homeland: at the time, the country had an open-door immigration policy and was attracting Jewish migrants from Europe, Morocco and the Ottoman Empire. In 1903, the British government offered its colony, Uganda, as a homeland for Russian Jews fleeing persecution.

15 Kessler (2002), 143.

16 Kaplan (1934), 273.

17 See also the discussion in Chapter 11.

18 Masada is an ancient fortress overlooking the Dead Sea. Several hundred Jews committed suicide there rather than surrender to Roman troops at the end of the Jewish revolt against Rome in the first century CE. In the 1920s Zionist youth groups began pilgrimages to Masada, and for many years new Israeli soldiers swore their oaths of allegiance there.

19 Liebman and Don Yehiya (1983).

20 Anti-Zionism and the elimination of religion were both policies of the Soviet Union (1922–1991). Religious education and the Hebrew language were suppressed. Jews were recognized as a separate ethnic minority, and were subject to negative discrimination, most notably under Joseph Stalin.

21 Riesebrodt and Konieczny (2005), 129–31.

22 Shabi (2008), 10–12.

23 These statistics are taken from Ben-Rafael and Peres (2005), 78.

24 Gilman (2006), 183.

25 Ben-Rafael and Peres (2005), 148.

Chapter 8 Endnotes

1 Williams [1976] (1983), 11–14.

2 Clifford (1988), 10.

3 Biale (2002), xvii.

4 Abrahams (1895), 77–8.

5 Smart (1996), 288.

6 See, for example, de Lange (2003), 38, 50 and Hoffman (2008), 149–51, which discuss *tallit* and *tefillin* in chapters on worship and prayer respectively.

7 Smith (2007), 107.

8 'Modest Clothing Doesn't Have to Be Dull!'. Available at http://www.tznius.co.uk/index.php (accessed 12 November 2009).

9 See further Fader (2009), 150–5.

10 Jeffay (2007), 15.

11 Joselit (1994), 171.

12 Pre-stunning renders an animal or bird non-*kosher*. *Halal* meat (produced according to Islamic dietary laws) is affected by the same legislation.

13 Wilson (2007), 289.

14 Kraemer (2007), 119.

15 Quoted in (Kraemer), 2007, 138.

16 Kraemer (2007), 139.

17 See further Wright (2003), 119.

18 Nye (2008), 55.

19 For a much fuller treatment of the issues raised in this section, discussing approaches and analyzing a contemporary American *pushke* or charity box in detail, see Wright (2011).

20 Bronner (2008), 4.

21 Sabar (2009), 135.

22 Quoted in Sabar (2009), 137.

23 Most *genizot* (archives, or more literally, 'hiding-places') were periodically emptied. The *genizah* in Ben Ezra Synagogue, Cairo, Egypt, was unopened for centuries and contained more than a quarter of a million documents, which were brought to Britain and the US just over a century ago, partly through the efforts of Solomon Schechter. The Maimonidean responsum in Fig. 3.1 is an example of a document from the Cairo *genizah*.

24 For example, note the absence of film, and paucity of references to visual culture more generally, in de Lange (2010), Hoffman (2008) and Segal (2009).

25 See Chapter 11.

26 Gruber (2001).

27 On Judaism in film, see Wright (2009), and on religion and film more generally, Wright (2007), especially 11–31 (on theory and method) and 129–41 (on *Keeping the Faith* [Edward Norton, 2000] a romantic comedy featuring Jewish and Christian characters).

Chapter 9 Endnotes

1 Marcus (2004), 193.

2 An *ohel* may be built over the grave of a prominent religious figure, see Chapter 2, Fig. 2.1

3 Children who are not yet *bar* or *bat mitzvah* are not obligated to mourn.

4 In Israel, it is the customary to erect a memorial stone at the end of the thirty day period.

5 See, for example, the Yizkor site operated by ORT, an educational and training charity founded in Russia in 1880 (http://yizkor.ort.org:8081/index.html), or the Memorial Archives at OurJewishCommunity.org (http://www.ourjewishcommunity.org/lifecycle/memorial-archives/) (both accessed 9

June 2010). The ORT site includes the text and audio recordings of the main memorial prayers.

6 Marcus (2004), 235.

7 Fishbane (1995).

8 http://www.motl.org/ (accessed 6 June 2011).

9 http://www.birthrightisrael.com/site/PageServer (accessed 6 June 2011).

10 See, for example, the discussion in Kugelmass (1992).

11 Gitlitz and Davidson (2006), 143ff.

12 Nora (2001), vii. For Halbwachs' obituary, see Friedmann and Mueller (1946), 509–17.

13 See also the discussion of Emil Fackenham in Chapter 5.

14 Finkelstein (2000).

15 Young 1995, 302.

16 http://www.library.yale.edu/testimonies/ (accessed 29 May 2011).

17 Abramson (2005), 293.

18 Abramson (2005), 295.

19 Abramson (2005), 296.

20 Caplan (2002), 145.

21 http://www.jewishmuseum.org.uk/ground-floor-displays (accessed 29 March 2010).

22 See, for example, the Chamber of the Holocaust project, which focuses explicitly on the religious commemoration of the murdered Jews through traditional ritual: http://www.diaspora.org.il/The_Chamber/ (accessed 29 May 2011).

23 http://www.mjhnyc.org/ (accessed 29 May 2011).

24 http://www.jewishmuseum.org.pl/en/cms/home-page/ (accessed 29 May 2011).

25 http://www.sztetl.org.pl/en/cms/the-project/ (accessed 29 May 2011).

26 See, for example, http://www.tabletmag.com/arts-and-culture/68204/out-of-the-ghetto/?print=1 (accessed 25 May 2011).

27 Gitlitz and Davidson (2006), 212.

Chapter 10 Endnotes

1 Paden (2005), 208.

2 See Paden (2005) and Roscoe (2006) for accounts by advocates of comparativism.

3 Paden (2005), 217.

4 Nissimi (2007), 33.

5 Yovel (2009), 379.

6 Nissimi (2007), 121.

7 Jewish forced converts to Christianity and their descendants were variously known by a range of derogatory terms including *Marranos* (often thought to be derived from a Spanish word for a pig), *Conversos* (converts) and New Christians. The Hebrew term for forced converts is *anusim*.

8 Yovel (2009), 381.

9 Stewart and Shaw (1994), 1–26.

10 On biblical and rabbinic attitudes to other religions, see further Goldenberg (1997).

11 Rabban Gamliel (also known as Gamliel the Elder or Gamliel I) was head of the *Sanhedrin* (see Chapter 3). Rabbinic texts credit him with various reforms including measures to remedy the situation of some potential *agunot* (see Chapter 6 and *m.Yevamot* 16.7). He died circa 50CE and is mentioned in the New Testament (Acts 5.34–40; 22.3).

12 Acco (also Akko/Acre) is a town in northern Israel.

13 Gamliel, intentionally or otherwise, misinterpreted the statue's function. Not all images or statues were regarded as sacred artefacts but formal and vernacular religious rituals did take place in bathhouses.

14 Toner lists activities associated with bathhouses in this period as 'meeting, cleansing, exercise, health, relaxation, education, talking, eating, ostentation and awe' (1998, 53).

15 See *Mishneh Torah* XIV: Judg. 8.10–11 in Twersky (1972), 221.

16 Goldenberg (1997), 83–4.

17 See, for example, http://www.noahide.org/ the website of the Institute of Noahide Code (accessed 6 July 2010).

18 Bill to designate March 26, 1991 as 'Education Day, U.S.A.', 102nd Cong., H. J. Res 104.

19 Graetz [1894], (Vol 3), (2009), 235.

20 Flesler and Pérez Melgosa (2010).

21 Kinzig (2003), 275.

22 The term anti-Semitism is first used in a political sense by radical activist Wilhelm Marr (1879). Bibliographer and lecturer Moritz Steinschneider used it in 1860 when discussing Ernest Renan's hostility towards Jews (Levy 2005, 24).

23 Kinzig (2003), 280.

24 Exclusivist theologies hold that there is only one valid means of relationship with God.

25 Supersessionism, also known as replacement theology, holds that the Christian church has taken the place of the Jews as God's chosen people.

26 Jacobs (1995), 75.

27 Heschel (1967), 8.

28 Washofsky 2001, Chapter 7.

29 For the full text of the statement, see http://www.jcrelations.net/en/?item=1014 (accessed 5 June 2011).

30 See http://www.jcrelations.net/en/?item=1014 (accessed 5 June 2011).

31 Levenson (2001).

32 Soloveitchik (1964), 24.

33 Berkovits (1973), 47.

34 Like Islam (and, less equivocally, Christianity) Sikhism is generally regarded by religious Jews (as by Sikhs themselves), as monotheistic, and thus less problematic than Hinduism. Buddhism's non-theism and its understanding of suffering as an inevitable aspect of existence are generally held by Orthodox Jews to contradict fundamental aspects of Judaism. However, Buddhist ideas and practices such as meditation have proven popular amongst some Jews in North America and Israel, and have influenced the Jewish Renewal movement.

35 See Est. 1.1, 8.9 where Ahaseurus' kingdom is described as stretching from India to Ethiopia.

36 The field began with studies of Jewish communities in India, notably those published in the 1970s and 1980s by Nathan Katz and Shalva Weil. Bibliographies of relevant work appear frequently in the *Journal of Indo–Judaic Studies*, which was launched in 1998.

37 Egorova (2006), 105.

38 Needel (2008), 73–6.

39 Needel (2008), 59–60.

40 Egorova (2006), 113.

41 Hayes (2002), 25.

42 Adolphe Thiéry, quoted in Hyman (1998), 21.

43 Alba (2006).

44 Fenster (1998).

45 Fenster (1989), 186.

46 McGinity (2009), 4–5.

47 DellaPergola (2009), 6.

48 Egorova (2006), 111.

49 'Cairo Court Rules on Egyptian Men Married to Israeli Women' BBC News, http://www.bbc.co.uk/news/10247437 (accessed 5 June 2011).

50 Hoffman (2010), 126.

51 McGinity (2009), 201–2.

52 McGinity (2009), 169–70.

Chapter 11 Endnotes

1 Fearn and Francis (2004), 5. Male and female students expressed similar levels of interest in these issues with the exception of religion and the media, which appealed more strongly to females. There were no significant religious differences in the levels of interest shown in the various topics.

2   Cush (2010), 87.

3   Harvey (2010), 1.

4   Holtschneider (2010), 173–93.

5   Graham and Waterman (2005), 94. The total British Jewish population has been estimated to be approximately 293,000.

6   Vulkan and Graham (2008), 14.

7   In 2010, it was announced that the 2011 UK Census will be available in Yiddish, in an attempt to count the Haredi community more fully, but this does not address the issue of Hebrew-speaking Israeli migrants to the Anglo-Jewish community.

8   Gitlitz and Davidson (2006), 211.

9   Goldscheider (2010), 505, estimates that seven and a half million Jews transferred out of Europe through immigration.

10 Kurdish Jews are Jews with roots in the region of Kurdistan, which covers parts of modern day Iran, Iraq, Syria and Turkey.

11 Needel (2008), 65.

12 Lowenthal (1998), 6.

13 Graham and Vulkan (2010), 4.

14 Heilman (2006), 47.

15 Amongst other things, '*kosher* investment' requires that Jewish-owned companies are Sabbath observant and interest is not earned on loans between Jewish investors and Jewish-owned corporations.

16 Buck 2010, 11.

17 Katz (2007), 160.

18 Dromi (2008), 15.

19 Barenblat (2010), http://www.religiondispatches.org/archive/sexandgender/2340/sara_hurwitz%E2%80%99s_%E2%80%98ra bba%E2%80%99_title_sparks_orthodox_jewish_condemnation (accessed 7 June 2011).

20 http://www.rabbis.org/news/article.cfm?id=105554 (accessed on 7 June 2011).

21 Traditionally, many educated Haredi women found paid employment in teaching and administration. Increased levels of education, and the growth in Haredi population, has led to an emerging shortage of such jobs within some communities, meaning that more women pursue qualifications and employment within more secular environments, with as yet unknown consequences in the social and religious spheres.

22 For detailed discussion of the imposition of the death penalty in Judaism, see Rapoport (2004), 137–9. Same-sex relations did of course take place between two Jews and between Jews and non-Jews. Ben-Naeh (2005) discusses evidence of same-sex relations involving Jews in the Ottoman Empire, the *halakhic* questions that arose, and the attempts by authorities to limit opportunities for same-sex encounters by circumscribing the employment of young apprentices by unmarried males, and requiring that young men be chaperoned when going out at night, even when travel was for the purposes of religious study or celebration.

23 According to the Talmud and later rabbinic literature, Jews should also forfeit their lives rather than commit murder or idolatry (see further Chapter 10). Maimonides' *Mishneh Torah* and Karo's *Shulhan Arukh* describe the extension of this concept, stating that, in circumstances where Jewish communities are under pressure to abandon Judaism en masse, individuals are obligated to sanctify God's name and die as martyrs rather than violate *any* of the *mitzvot*.

24 Early rabbinic literature is interested in identifying the gender of individuals only insofar as this has implications for permitted and prohibited acts (including all areas of ritual life, not just sexual relations). In addition to male and female, it categories some individuals as androgynous or *tumtum* (see Chapter 6). The literature on these issues is an important source for religious Jews seeking a *halakhic* grounding for contemporary responses to transssexualism, intersexualism and transgenderism.

25 *Keshet* is the Hebrew word for 'rainbow'.

26 Fishman (2000), 106–9; Schnoor (2006).

27 'Mission Statement' available online at http://www.jonahweb.org/index.php (accessed 18 May 2010).

28 Rapoport (2004), 135.

29 Greenberg (2004), 227.

30 Greenberg (2004), 203.

31 See Chapter 6.

32 For example, Hoffmann suggests that 'questions about the acceptability of homosexual relationships do not arise' in Orthodox Judaism and that 'Reform Jews wrestle with these questions'. Much of the paragraph that follows is concerned primarily with questions concerning Christianity and homosexuality (2008, 120). De Lange deals with biblical prohibitions and modern attitudes in two paragraphs (2010, 90 and 110).

33 Tatchell (2006),http://www.guardian.co.uk/commentisfree/2006/may/24/moscowbansgayprideparade (accessed 7 June 2011); Baird (2007), 112.

34 Earis (2010), 141.

35 The reasons for the conflict remain disputed, with Arab states and their allies condemning Israel's actions as an aggressive bid for territorial enlargement, and Israel arguing that the airstrikes were necessary defensive acts, initiated in response to military intelligence warning of imminent Arab attacks. On the impact of the War on diaspora Jewry, see Lederhendler (2000).

36 Katz (2007), 158; National Jewish Population Survey 2001–2002, http://www.jewishfederations.org/page.aspx?id=33650 (accessed 1 July 2011); Jewish College Students (2004), 19, http://courses.washington.edu/judaism/Readings/2004HillelSurvey.pdf (accessed 1 July 2011).

37 Elazar (2001), 327–8.

38 The curriculum consists of Sayings of the Fathers (a tractate of the *Mishnah* which, unusually, is a compilation of ethical sayings), the weekly Torah

portion, Orthodox Jewish liturgy, and one of the key early texts of Zionism, Theodor Herzl's utopian novel *Altneuland* (Kashti 2010).

39 Katz (2007), 165–6.

40 Aviv and Shneer (2004), 136. See also Earis (2010).

41 Aviv and Shneer (2005), xvi, 19–20.

42 Brasher (2001), 77.

43 Brasher (2001), 77.

44 Graham and Vulkan (2010), 4.

45 Helland (2005), 6.

46 Ess, Charles, and the AoIR Ethics Working Committee, 'Ethical decision-making and Internet research: Recommendations from the Association of Internet Resarchers (AoIR) Ethics Working Committee', November 27, 2002. Available online: www.aoir.org/reports/ethics.pdf (accessed 2 June 2010).

Bibliography

Abrahams, B. Lionel (1895) 'The Condition of the Jews of England at the Time of Their Expulsions in 1290', *Transactions of the Jewish Historical Society of England*, 2, 76–105.

Abramson, Henry (2005) 'A Double Occlusion: Sephardim and the Holocaust' in Zohar, Zion ed., *Sephardic and Mizrahi Judaism From the Golden Age of Spain to Modern Times*, New York: New York University Press, 285–99.

Alba, Richard (2006) 'On the Sociological Significance of American Jewish Experience: Boundary Blurring, Assimilation, and Pluralism', *Sociology of Religion*, 67, 4, 347–58.

Alexander, Philip (2002) 'Mysticism' in Martin Goodman (ed.), *The Oxford Handbook of Jewish Studies*, Oxford: Oxford University Press, 705–32.

Alpert, Rebecca T., and Jacob J. Staub (1997) *Exploring Judaism: a Reconstructionist Approach*, Wyncote: The Reconstructionist Press.

Aviv, Caryn, and David Shneer (2005) *New Jews: The End of The Jewish Diaspora*, New York: New York University Press.

Baer, Yitzhak (1961) *A History of the Jews in Christian Spain 2*, Philadelphia: Jewish Publication Society.

Baird, Louise (2007) *The No-Nonsense Guide to Sexual Diversity*, London: New Internationalist Publications.

Baskin, Judith R. (2010) 'Jewish Private Life: Gender, Marriage, and the Lives of Women' in Judith R. Baskin and K. Seeskin (eds), *The Cambridge Guide to Jewish History, Religion, and Culture*, Cambridge: Cambridge University Press, 357–80.

Baumel-Schwarz, Judy Tydor (2009) 'Frum Surfing: Orthodox Jewish Women's Internet Forums as a Historical and Cultural Phenomenon', *Journal of Jewish Identities*, 2, 1, 1–30.

Bell, Catherine (1998) 'Performance' in Mark C. Taylor ed., *Critical Terms for Religious Studies*, Chicago: University of Chicago Press, 205–24.

Ben-Menachem, Hanina, and N. S. Hecht (1999) *Authority, Process, and Method: Studies in Jewish Law 2*, Newark: Harwood Academic.

Ben-Naeh, Yaron (2005) 'Moskho the Jew and His Gay Friends: Same-Sex Sexual Relations in Ottoman Jewish Society', *Journal of Early Modern History*, 9,1, 79–108.

Ben-Rafael, Eliezer and Yochanan Peres (2005) *Is Israel One? Religion, Nationalism, and Multiculturalism Confounded*, Leiden: Brill.

Benor, Susan Bunin (2004) '*Talmid Chachams* and *Tsedeykeses*: Language, Learnedness, and Masculinity Among Orthodox Jews', *Jewish Social Studies*, 11,1, 147–69.

Berger, David (2001) *The Rebbe, The Messiah and the Scandal of Orthodox Indifference*, London: Littman Library of Jewish Civilization.

Berkovits, Eliezer (1973) *Faith after the Holocaust*, New York: KTAV.

Berman, Saul J. (1973) 'The Status of Women in Halakhic Judaism', *Tradition*, 14, 2, 5–28

Biale, David ed. (2002) *Cultures of the Jews: A New History*, New York: Schocken.

Biale, Rachel (1984) *Women and Jewish Law: The Essential Texts, Their History, and Their Relevance for Today*, New York: Schocken.

Bleich, J. David (2010) 'Survey of Contemporary Halakhic and Legal Literature', *Tradition*, 42, 4, 58–95.

Bourdieu, Pierre (1987) 'Legitimation and Structured Interests in Weber's Sociology of Religion' (trans. Chris Turner) in Scott Lash and Sam Whimster (eds), *Max Weber, Rationality, and Modernity*, London: Allen and Unwin, 119–36.

Boyarin, Daniel (1998) '*Goyim Naches*: The Manliness of the *Mentsh*' in Bryan Cheyette and Laura Marcus (eds), *Modernity, Culture and 'the Jew'*, Cambridge: Polity, 63–87.

Brasher, Brenda E. (2001) *Give Me That Online Religion*, San Francisco, CA: Jossey Bass.

Brick, Michael (2004) 'There's Something in the Water and It May Not Be Strictly Kosher' *New York Times*. 1st June 2004. Available online at http://www.nytimes.com/2004/06/01/nyregion/01water.html (accessed 1 July 2011).

Bronner, Simon J. (2008) 'Introduction. The chutzpah of Jewish Cultural Studies' in Simon J. Bronner ed. *Jewishness: Expression, Identity, and Representation*, Jewish Cultural Studies Volume 1, Oxford: Littman, 1–26.

Brown, Laurence (1988) *The Psychology of Religion: An Introduction*, London: SPCK.

Buck, Tobias (2010) 'Israelis savour rise in kosher investments', *Financial Times*, March 2, 11.

Bunis, David M. (2005) 'Judaeo-Spanish Culture in Medieval and Modern Times' in Zion Zohar ed. *Sephardic and Mizrahi Judaism From the Golden Age of Spain to Modern Times*, New York: New York University Press, 55–76.

Burman, Rickie (1990) 'Jewish Women and the Household Economy in Manchester, c. 1890–1920' in David Cesarani (ed.), *The Making of Modern Anglo-Jewry*, Oxford: Basil Blackwell, 55–75.

Campbell, Heidi A. (2010) *When Religion Meets New Media*, London: Routledge.

Cantor, Geoffrey, and Marc Swetlitz (eds) (2006) *Jewish Tradition and the Challenge of Darwinism*, Chicago: University of Chicago Press.

Caplan, Kimmy (2002) 'The Holocaust in Contemporary Israeli Haredi Popular Religion', *Modern Judaism*, 22, 142–68.

Chryssides, George D. (2007a) 'The Tools of the Trade' in George D. Chryssides and Ron Geaves (eds), *The Study of Religion: An Introduction to Key Ideas and Methods*, London and New York: Continuum, 1–34.

Chryssides, George D. (2007b) 'Phenomenology and Its Critics' in George D. Chryssides and Ron Geaves (eds), *The Study of Religion: An Introduction to Key Ideas and Methods*, London and New York: Continuum, 210–37.

Chryssides, George D., and Ron Geaves (eds) (2007) *The Study of Religion: An Introduction to Key Ideas and Methods*, London and New York: Continuum.

Clifford, James (1988) *The Predicament of Culture: Twentieth Century Ethnography, Literature, and Art*, Cambridge, Mass.: Harvard University Press.

Cohen, Mark R. (1995) *Under Crescent and Cross: The Jews in the Middle Ages*, Princeton, NJ: Princeton University Press.

Cohen, Shaye J. D. (2005) *Why Aren't Jewish Women Circumcised? Gender and Covenant in Judaism*, Berkeley, CA: University of California Press.

Cort, John (1996) 'Art, Religion, and Material Culture: Some Reflections on Method', *Journal of the American Academy of Religion*, 64, 3, 613–32.

Cush, Denise (2010) 'Engaged Religious Studies: Some Suggestions for the Content, Methods and Aims of Learning and Teaching in the Future Study of Religions', *Discourse*, 4, 2, 83–103.

Dan, Joseph (2006) *Kabbalah: A Very Short Introduction*, Oxford: Oxford University Press.

de Lange, Nicholas (2010) *An Introduction to Judaism*, second edition, Cambridge: Cambridge University Press.

de Lange, Nicholas (2003) *Judaism*, Oxford: Oxford University Press.

Della Pergola, Sergio (2007) 'World Jewish Population, 2007' in *American Jewish Yearbook Vol. 107*, New York: American Jewish Committee, 551–600.

Dromi, Uri (2008) 'Jerusalem is the Key', *Jewish Quarterly*, 209, 14–17.

Earis, Rosalind (2010) 'Gay Pride in Jerusalem', *The Point*, 2, 141–4.

Egorova, Yulia (2006) *Jews and India. Perceptions and Image*, London: Routledge.

Ehrlich, M. Avrum (2004) *The Messiah of Brooklyn. Understanding Lubavitch Hasidism Past and Present*, Jersey: KTAV.

Einstein, Mara (2007) *Brands of Faith: Marketing Religion in a Commercial Age*, London: Routledge.

Eisen, Arnold M. (1999) *Rethinking Modern Judaism: Ritual, Commandment, Community*, Chicago: The University of Chicago Press.

Elazar, Daniel J. (2001) 'Changing Places, Changing Cultures: Divergent Jewish Political Cultures' in Deborah Dash Moore and S. Ilan Troen (eds), *Divergent Jewish Cultures: Israel and America*, New Haven: Yale University Press, 319–31.

Elazar, Daniel J. (2002) 'Judaism as a Theopolitical Phenomenon' in Jacob Neusner and Alan J. Avery-Peck (eds), *The Blackwell Companion to Judaism*, Oxford: Blackwell. Available online at http://www.blackwellreference.com/ subscriber/tocnode?id=g9781577180593_chunk_g978157718059324 (accessed 3 April 2009).

Fader, Ayala (2006) 'Learning Faith: Language socialisation in a community of Hasidic Jews', *Language in Society*, 35, 2, 205–29.

Fader, Ayala (2009) *Mitzvah Girls: Bringing Up the Next Generation of Hasidic Jews in Brooklyn*, Princeton, NJ: Princeton University Press.

Falk, Pesach Eliyahu (1998) *Modesty – An Adornment for Life: Halachos and Attitudes Concerning Tznius of Dress and Conduct*, Gateshead: Feldheim Publishers.

Fearn, Mike, and Leslie J. Francis (2004) 'From A-Level to Higher Education: Student Perceptions of Teaching and Learning in Theology and Religious Studies', *Discourse*, 3, 2, 58–91.

Feldman, Aharon (2003) 'Communications', *Tradition*, 37, 2, 93–4.

Feldman, Emanuel (2008) 'The odd and instructive habits of non-observant Jews: A look at *Berit Milah* and *Pesah*', *Tradition*, 41, 2, 127–37.

Fenster, Tovi (1998) 'Ethnicity, Citizenship, Planning and Gender: The Case of Ethiopian Immigrant Women in Israel', *Gender, Place and Culture*, 5,2, 177–89.

Finkelstein, Norman G. (2000) *Holocaust Industry: Reflections on the Exploitation of Jewish Suffering*, London: Verso.

Fishbane, Michael (1985) *Biblical Interpretation in Ancient Israel*, Oxford: Clarendon.

Fishbane, Simcha (1995) 'Jewish mourning rites: a process of resocialization' in Jack N. Lightstone and Frederick B. Bird (eds), *Ritual and Ethnic Identity: A Comparative Study of the Social Meaning of Liturgical Ritual in Synagogues*, Waterloo, Ont.: Wilfrid Laurier University Press, 169–84.

Fishman, Sylvia Barack (2000) *Jewish Life and American Culture*, New York: SUNY Press.

Flesler, Daniela, and Adrian Pérez Malgosa (2010) 'Hervás, *convivencia* and the heritagization of Spain's Jewish past', *Journal of Romance Studies*, 10, 2, 53–76.

Freud, Sigmund (2001a) 'Totem and Taboo' in James Strachey and Anna Freud (trans. and eds), with Alix Strachey and Alan Tyson, *The Standard Edition of the Complete Psychological Works of Sigmund Freud*, Vol. 13, New York: Vintage.

Freud, Sigmund (2001b) 'Address to the Society of B'nai B'rith Vienna' in James Strachey and Anna Freud (trans. and eds), with Alix Strachey and Alan Tyson, *The Standard Edition of the Complete Psychological Works of Sigmund Freud*, Vol. 20, New York: Vintage.

Freud-Kandel, Miri (2006) *Orthodox Judaism in Britain Since 1913: An Ideology Forsaken*, London: Vallentine Mitchell.

Freud-Kandel, Miri (2005) 'Modernist Movements' in Nicholas de Lange and Miri Freud-Kandel (eds), *Modern Judaism: An Oxford Guide*, Oxford: Oxford University Press, 81–92.

Friedmann, Georges and Mueller, John H. (1946) 'Maurice Halbwachs, 1877–1945', *American Journal of Sociology*, 51, 6, 509–17.

Geertz, Clifford (1999) '"From the native's point of view": On the Nature of Anthropological Understanding', in Russell T. McCutcheon (ed.), *The Insider/Outsider Problem in the Study of Religion*, London: Cassell, 50–63.

Geller, Stephen A. (2004) 'The Religion of the Bible' in Adele Berlin and Marc Zvi Brettler (eds), *The Jewish Study Bible*, Oxford: Oxford University Press, 2021–40.

Gerth, Hans Heinrich, and Charles Wright Mills (1991) *From Max Weber: Essays in Sociology*, London: Routledge.

Giddens, Anthony (1990) *The Consequences of Modernity*, Cambridge: Polity.

Gilman, Sander (2006) *Multiculturalism and the Jews*, London: Routledge.

Gitlitz, David M., and Linda Kay Davidson (2006) *Pilgrimage and the Jews*, Westport, CT: Praeger Publishers.

Glatzer, Nahum (1998) *Franz Rosenzweig: His Life and Thought*, New York: Hackett Publishing.

Goldenberg, Robert (1997) *The Nations That Know Thee Not: Early Jewish Attitudes Towards Other Religions*, Sheffield: Sheffield Academic Press.

Goldscheider, Clara (2010) 'The Future of World Jewish Communities' in Judith H. Baskin and Kenneth Seeskin (eds), *The Cambridge Guide to Jewish History, Religion and Culture*, Cambridge: Cambridge University Press, 494–509.

Goodman, Martin ed. (2002) *The Oxford Handbook of Jewish Studies*, Oxford: Oxford University Press.

Graetz, Heinrich (2009) [1894], *History of the Jews (in 6 volumes): Vol. 3*, (ed. Bella Löwy), New York: Cosimo.

Graham, David, and Stanley Waterman (2005) 'Underenumeration of the Jewish Population in the UK 2001 Census', *Population Place and Space*, 11, 89–102.

Graham, David and Daniel Vulkan (2010) *Synagogue Membership in the United Kingdom in 2010*, London: The Board of Deputies of British Jews and the Institute of Jewish Policy Research.

Greenberg, Steven (2004) *Wrestling with God and Men: Homosexuality in the Jewish Tradition*, Madison: University of Wisconsin Press.

Grossman, Avraham (2004) *Pious and Rebellious: Jewish Women in Medieval Europe*, Waltham, Mass.: Brandeis University Press.

Gruber, Ruth Ellen (2001) *Virtually Jewish: Reinventing Jewish Culture in Europe*, Berkeley, CA: University of California Press.

Hartman, David (2007) 'The Religious Significance of Religious Pluralism' in Moshe Halbertal and Donniel Hartman (eds), *Judaism and the Challenges of Modern Life*, London: Continuum, 95–104.

Hartman, Tova (2007) *Feminism Encounters Traditional Judaism*, Waltham, Mass.: Brandeis University Press.

Harvey, Graham ed. (2010) *Religions in Focus: New Approaches to Tradition and Contemporary Practices*, London: Equinox.

Hayes, Christine (2002) *Gentile Impurities and Jewish Identities: Intermarriage and Conversion from the Bible to the Talmud*, New York: Oxford University Press.

Hearn, J., and D. Morgan (1990) *Men, Masculinities and Social Theory*, London: Unwin Hyman.

Heilman, Samuel C. (1976) *Synagogue Life: A Study in Symbolic Interaction*, Chicago: The University of Chicago Press.

Heilman, Samuel C. (1992) *Defenders of the Faith: Inside Ultra-Orthodox Jewry*, New York, Schocken Books.

Heilman, Samuel C. (2006) *Sliding to the Right: The Contest for the Future of American Jewish Orthodoxy*, Berkeley: University of California Press.

Helland, Christopher (2005) 'Online Religion as Lived Religion: Methodological Issues in the Study of Religious Participation on the Internet', *Online – Heidelberg Journal of Religions on the Internet*, 1, 1, 1–16. Available online at http://www.ub.uni-heidelberg.de/archiv/5823 (accessed 17 March 2010).

Herbert, David (forthcoming 2012) 'Theorising Religion and Media in Contemporary Societies: an Account of Religious "Publicisation"', *European Journal of Cultural Studies*, 14, 6.

Herzl, Theodor (2006) [1896], *The Jewish State*, Raleigh: Hayes Barton Press.

Heschel, Abraham J. (1967) 'From Mission to Dialogue', *Conservative Judaism*, 21, 1, 1–11.

Highmore, Ben (2009) *A Passion for Cultural Studies*, London: Palgrave Macmillan.

Hirsch, Samson Raphael (1995) *The Nineteen Letters*, (trans. J. Elias), Jerusalem: Feldheim.

Hoffman, Christine M. (2008) *Teach Yourself Judaism*, London: Hodder Education.

Holtschneider, Hannah (2010) 'Jews' in Graham Harvey ed. *Religions in Focus: New Approaches to Tradition and Contemporary Practices*, London: Equinox, 173–93.

Hyman, Paula (1998*) The Jews of Modern France*, University of California Press, Berkeley CA.

Institute for Jewish Policy Research (2010) *New Conceptions of Community*,
    Institute for Jewish Policy Research: London.
Jacobs, Louis (1965) *We Have Reason to Believe*, third edition, London:
    Vallentine Mitchell.
Jacobs, Louis (1987) 'God' in Arthur A. Cohen and Paul Mendes-Flohr (eds),
    Contemporary Jewish Religious Thought, New York: The Free Press, 291–8.
Jacobs, Louis (1995) *The Jewish Religion: a Companion*, Oxford: Oxford
    University Press.
Jacobs, N. (2001) *Yiddish: A Linguistic Introduction*, Cambridge: Cambridge
    University Press.
Jeffay, Nathan (2007) 'Strictly Orthodox and Style-Conscious', *The Jewish
    Chronicle*, 3 August 2007, 15–16.
Johnson, Richard, Deborah Chambers, Parvati Raghuram and Estella Tincknell
    (2004) *The Practice of Cultural Studies*, London: Sage.
Joselit, Jenna Weissman (1994) *The wonders of America: Reinventing Jewish
    culture 1880–1950*, New York: Hill and Wang.
Juschka, Darlene M. (2005) 'Gender' in John Hinnells ed. *The Routledge
    Companion to the Study of Religion*, London: Routledge, 229–42.
Kaplan, Mordecai M. (1934) *Judaism as a Civilization: Toward a Reconstruction of
    American-Jewish Life*, New York: Thomas Yoseloff.
Kashti, Or (2010) 'Israel to Introduce Revamped Jewish Studies Curriculum in
    State Schools', *Haaretz*, 24 June 2010. Available online at http://www.haaretz.
    com/news/national/israel-to-introduce-revamped-jewish-studies-curriculum-in-
    state-schools-1.297957 (accessed 27 July 2010).
Kasnett, Yitzchak (1996) *The World That Was. Volume 1. Lithuania*, Cleveland,
    Ohio: Hebrew Academy, Cleveland.
Katz, Elihu (2007) 'Two Dilemmas of Religious Identity and Practice among
    Israeli Jews', *Contemporary Jewry*, 27, 1, 157–69.
Kaufmann, Eric (2007) 'Shall the Religious Inherit the Earth?', *Jewish Quarterly*,
    207, 24–7.
Kellner, Menachem (1996) *Maimonides on the 'Decline of the Generations' and
    the Nature of Rabbinic Authority*, New York: State University of New York
    Press.
Kessler, Edward (2002) *An English Jew: The Life and Writings of Claude
    Montefiore*, revised edition, London: Vallentine Mitchell.
Kinzig, Wolfram (2003) 'Closeness and Distance: Towards a New Description of
    Jewish-Christian Relations', *Jewish Studies Quarterly*, 10, 274–90.
Klapper, Robert (1999) 'Review Essay. Meta-Halakhah by Moshe Koppel',
    Tradition, 33, 4, 70–80.
Klein, Isaac (1979) *A Guide to Jewish Religious Practice*, New York: Jewish
    Theological Seminary.
Knott, Kim (2001) 'The Sense and Nonsense of "Community": A Consideration
    of Contemporary Debates About Community and Culture by a Scholar of
    Religions', *British Association for the Study of Religions Occasional Paper 22*,
    Leeds: British Association for the Study of Religions.
Kohler, Kaufmann (1904) 'Judaism', *The Jewish Encyclopedia*, New York: Funk
    and Wagnalls, 359–68.
Kraemer, David (2007) *Jewish Eating and Identity Through the Ages*, London:
    Routledge.

Kravel-Tovi, Michal (2009) 'To See the Invisible Messiah: Messianic Socialization in the Wake of a Failed Prophecy in Chabad', *Religion*, 39, 248–60.

Kugelmass, Jack (1992) 'The Rites of the Tribe: American Jewish Tourism in Poland' in Ivan Karp, Christine Mullen Kreamer and Steven D. Lavine (eds) *Museums and Communities: The Politics of Public Culture*, Washington, DC: Smithsonian Institution Press, 382–427.

Kunin, Seth (1998) *God's Place in the World: Sacred Space and Sacred Place in Judaism*, London: Cassell.

Lederhendler, Eli ed. (2000) *The Six Day War and World Jewry*, Bethesda: The University Press of Maryland.

Leigh, John (1999) *The Search for Enlightenment. An Introduction to Eighteenth-Century French Writing*, London: Duckworth.

Levenson, Jon D. (2001) 'How not to conduct Jewish-Christian Dialogue', *Commentary*, December 2001. Available online at http://www.commentarymagazine.com/article/how-not-to-conduct-jewish-christian-dialogue/ (accessed 5 June 2011).

Levenson, Jon D. (2004) 'The Agenda of Dabru Emet', *Review of Rabbinic Judaism*, 7, 1–26.

Levertov, Michael (2008) 'Unveiled, the Israeli women in "burkas"', *The Jewish Chronicle*, 31 January 2008. Available online at http://website.thejc.com/home.aspx?AId=57786&ATypeId=1&search=true2&srchstr=tzniut&srchtxt=0&srchhead=1&srchauthor=0&srchsandp=0&scsrch=0 (accessed 31 March 2009).

Levine, Joel L. (2001) 'Why People in the Sunbelt Join a Synagogue' in David E. Kaplan ed. *Contemporary Debates in American Reform Judaism: Conflicting Visions*, London: Routledge, 56–65.

Levy, Richard S. (2005) 'Antisemitism, etymology of' in Richard S. Levy (ed.), *Antisemitism: A Historical Encyclopedia of Prejudice and Persecution*, vol. 2, Santa Barbara, CA: ABC Clio, 24–5.

Levy, Shlomit, Levinsohn, Hanna, and Elihu Katz (1997) 'Beliefs, Observances and Social Interaction Among Israeli Jews,' in Charles S. Liebman and Elihu Katz (eds), *The Jewishness of Israelis: Responses to the Guttman Report*, New York: State University of New York, 1–37.

Lichtenstein, Aharon (1989) 'Religion and State,' in Arthur A. Cohen and Paul Mendes-Flohr (eds), *Contemporary Jewish Religious Thought*, New York: The Free Press, 773–8.

Liebman, Charles S., and Elihu Katz (eds) (1997) *The Jewishness of Israelis. Responses to the Guttman Report*, New York: State University of New York.

Lifshitz, Hefzibah, and Rivka Glaubman (2004) 'Caring for People with Disabilities in the Haredi Community: Adjustment Mechanism in Action', *Disability and Society*, 19, 5, 469–86.

Lowenthal, David (1998) *The Heritage Crusade and the Spoils of History*, Cambridge: Cambridge University Press.

Magnier, Mark (2009) 'Afghan Jew a one man upholder of tradition', *Los Angeles Times*, September 20, 2009. Available online at http://articles.latimes.com/2009/sep/20/world/fg-afghan-lastjew20 (accessed 30 November 2009).

Marcus, Ivan (2004) *The Jewish Life Cycle: Rites of Passage from Biblical to Modern Times*, Washington: University of Washington Press.

Marcus, Joel (2001) 'The Once and Future Messiah in Early Christianity and Chabad', *New Testament Studies*, 47, 3, 381–401.

Masliyah, Sadok (1994) 'The Bene Israel and the Baghdadis: Two Indian Jewish Communities in Conflict', *Judaism*, 43, 3, 279–93.

Maybaum, Ignaz (1949) *The Jewish Mission*, London: James Clarke and Co.

Maybaum, Ignaz (1965) *The Face of God after Auschwitz*, Amsterdam: Polak and Van Gennep.

McGinity, Keren R. (2009) *Still Jewish: A History of Women and Intermarriage in America*, New York: New York University Press.

McIntosh, Ian ed. (1997) *Classical Sociological Theory: A Reader*, Edinburgh: Edinburgh University Press.

Meiselman, Moshe (1975) 'Women and Judaism: A Rejoinder', *Tradition*, 15, 3, 52–68.

Meiselman, Moshe (1998) 'The Rav, feminism and public policy: an insider's overview', *Tradition*, 33, 1, 5–30.

Mecklenburger, Ralph (2007) 'In An Age of Broken Myths: Preliminary Thoughts toward a Liberal Jewish Theology of Christianity', *CCAR Journal: A Reform Jewish Quarterly*, 3, 25–38.

Movement for Reform Judaism (2008) *Forms of Prayer*, London: Sternberg Centre for Judaism.

Na'aman, Yated (2006) 'Agudath Israel Convention at New Location', *Dei'ah veDibur*. Available online at http://chareidi.shemayisrael.com/aagudalch67.htm (accessed November 1, 2009).

Needel, Yale M. (2008) 'Rethinking "Sephardic": Rosh Hashanah and Yom Kippur Observances Among the Jews of Bombay', *Shofar: An Interdisciplinary Journal of Jewish Studies*, 26, 2, 59–80.

Nesbitt, Eleanor (2002) 'Ethnography and Religious Education' in Lynne Broadbent and Alan Brown (eds), *Issues in Religious Education*, London: Routledge, 106–16.

Neusner, Jacob (2003a) 'Defining Judaism' in Jacob Neusner and Alan Avery-Peck (eds), *The Blackwell Companion to Judaism*, Oxford: Blackwell.

Neusner, Jacob (2003b) 'The Religion, Judaism, in America: What has Happened in Three Hundred and Fifty Years?', *American Jewish History*, 91, 3–4, 361–9.

Nirenberg, David (2002) 'What Can Medieval Spain Teach Us About Jewish-Muslim Relations?', *CCAR Journal: A Reform Jewish Quarterly*, 2, 17–36.

Nissimi, Hilda (2007) *The Crypto-Jewish Mashhadis: The Shaping of Religious and Communal Identity in their Journey from Iran to New York*, Brighton: Sussex University Press.

Nora, Pierre (2001) 'General introduction' in *Rethinking France: Les Lieux de Mémoire, Vol.1 the State*, (trans. Richard C. Holbrook), Chicago: University of Chicago Press, vii–xii.

Nye, Malory (2003) *Religion: The Basics*, London: Routledge.

Nye, Malory (2008) *Religion: The Basics*, second edition, London: Routledge.

Oakley, Ann (1974) *Housewife*, London: Allen Lane.

Ochs, Vanessa (2007) *Inventing Jewish Ritual*, Philadelphia: Jewish Publication Society.

Paden, William E. (2005) 'Comparative Religion' in John Hinnells ed. *The Routledge Companion to the Study of Religion*, London: Routledge, 208–25.

Plaskow, Judith (1991) *Standing Again at Sinai: Judaism from a Feminist Perspective*, San Francisco: Harper.

Polak-Sahm, Varda (2009) *The House of Secrets: The Hidden World of the Mikveh*, Boston: Beacon Press.

Rapoport, Chaim (2004) *Judaism and Homosexuality: An Authentic Orthodox View*, London: Vallentine Mitchell.

Ray, Jonathan (2005) 'Beyond Tolerance and Persecution: Reassessing Our Approach to Medieval Conviviencia', *Jewish Social Studies*, 11, 2, 1–18.

Riesebrodt, Martin, and Mary Ellen Konieczny (2005) 'Sociology of Religion' in John Hinnells ed. *The Routledge Companion to the Study of Religion*, London: Routledge, 125–43.

Ringelbaum, Joan (1996) 'Preface to the study of women and the Holocaust', *Contemporary Jewry*, 17, 1, 1–2.

Roscoe, Paul (2006) 'The Comparative Method' in Robert A. Segal (ed.), *The Blackwell Companion to the Study of Religion*, Oxford: Blackwell, 25–46.

Round, Simon (2010) 'Mitzvah mobile puts a spy in your pocket', *The Jewish Chronicle*, 26 February 2010, 3. Available online at http://archive.thejc.com/search/pagedetail.jsp?origin=16&gofrom=null&goto=null&issue=February%2026%202010&refno=/archive/output/2010/2010_0226_03c.gif&pgn=03 (accessed October 14, 2011).

Rubenstein, Richard (1992) *After Auschwitz: History, Theology, and Contemporary Judaism*, second edition, Baltimore: John Hopkins University Press.

Sabar, Shalom (2009) 'Torah and Magic: The Torah Scroll and Its Appurtenances as Magical Objects in Traditional Jewish Culture', *European Journal of Jewish Studies*, 3, 1, 135–70.

Sacks, Jonathan (2003) *The Dignity of Difference: How to Avoid the Clash of Civilizations*, London and New York: Continuum.

Sacks, Jonathan and The United Synagogue (2007) *The Authorised Daily Prayer Book of the United Hebrew Congregations of the Commonwealth*, London: Collins.

Said, Edward (1985) [1975], *Beginnings: Intention and Method*, New York: Columbia University Press.

Samet, Moshe (1988) 'The Beginnings of Orthodoxy', *Modern Judaism*, 8, 3, 249–69.

Satlow, Michael L. (2006a) 'Defining Judaism: Accounting for "Religions" In the Study of Religion', *Journal of the American Academy of Religion*, 74, 4, 837–60.

Satlow, Michael L. (2006b) *Creating Judaism: History, Tradition, Practice*, New York: Columbia University Press.

Schnoor, Randall F. (2006) 'Being Gay and Jewish: Negotiating Intersecting Jewish Identities', *Sociology of Religion*, 67, 1, 43–60.

Schüssler Fiorenza, Elisabeth (1992) *But She Said: Feminist Practices of Biblical Interpretation*, Boston: Beacon Press.

Schwartz, Shuly Rubin (2006) *The Rabbi's Wife: The Rebbetzin in American Jewish Life*, New York: New York University Press.

Schwarzfuchs, Simon (1993) *A Concise History of the Rabbinate*, Oxford: Blackwell.

Segal, Eliezer (2009) *Introducing Judaism*, London: Routledge.

Sered, Susan Starr (1992) *Women as Ritual Experts: The Religious Lives of Elderly Jewish Women in Jerusalem*, Oxford: Oxford University Press.

Sered, Susan Starr (2005) 'The Ritualized Body: Brides, Purity, and the *Mikveh*' in Esther Fuchs ed. *Israeli Women's Studies: A Reader*, New Brunswick: Rutgers, 150–68.

Sezgin, Pamela Dorn (2005) 'Jewish Women in the Ottoman Empire' in Zion Zohar ed. *Sephardic and Mizrahi Judaism From the Golden Age of Spain to Modern Times*, New York: New York University Press, 216–35.

Shabi, Rachel (2008) 'Mizrahi', *Jewish Quarterly*, 212, 10–12.

Shapira, Avraham, and Aharon Lichtenstein (2007) 'A Rabbinic Exchange on the Gaza Disengagement', *Tradition*, 40, 1, 17–44.

Sheffer, Gabriel (2003) *Diaspora Politics: At Home Abroad*, Cambridge: Cambridge University Press.

Sheinson, Yosef Dov and Touster, Shaul (2000) *A Survivor's Haggadah*, Philadelphia: Jewish Publication Society.

Silbiger, Auriel (2001) *Bread, Fire and Water: Laws of Niddah, Candlelighting and Separating Challah*, (trans. S. Cymerman), Gateshead: Feldheim Publishers.

Singer, Peter (2000) *Marx: A Very Short Introduction*, Oxford: Oxford University Press.

Smart, Ninian (1989) *The World's Religions: Old Traditions and Modern Transformations*, Cambridge: Cambridge University Press.

Smart, Ninian (1996) *Dimensions of the Sacred: An Anatomy of the World's Beliefs*, Berkeley, Ca.: University of California Press.

Smith, Mark M. (2007) *Sensory History*, London: Berg.

Soloveitchik, Joseph D. (1964) 'Confrontation', *Tradition*, 6, 2, 5–29.

Soloveitchik, Joseph D. (1983) *Halakhic Man*, (trans. L. Kaplan), Philadelphia: Jewish Publication Society.

Sombart, Walter (2001) *The Jews and Modern Capitalism*, (trans. M. Epstein), Kitchener: Batoche Books.

Steinweis, Alan E. (2006) *Studying the Jew: Scholarly Antisemitism in Nazi Germany*, Cambridge, Mass.: Harvard University Press.

Stessel, Zahava Szász (1995) *Wine and Thorns in Tokay Valley: Jewish Life in Hungary: the History of Abaújszántó*, Madison, NJ: Farleigh Dickinson University Press.

Stewart, Charles, and Rosalind Shaw (1994) *Syncretism/anti-syncretism: The politics of religious synthesis*, London: Routledge.

Stolow, Jeremy (2006) 'Communicating Authority, Consuming Tradition: Jewish Orthodox Outreach Literature and its Reading Public' in Birgit Meyer and Annelies Moors (eds), *Religion, Media and the Public Sphere*, Bloomington: Indiana University Press, 73–90.

Strassfield, Michael and Richard Siegel (1973) *The First Jewish Catalog: A Do-it-yourself Kit*, Philadelphia: Jewish Publication Society of America.

Sussman, Lance J. (2005) 'The Myth of the Trefa Banquet: American Culinary Culture and the Radicalization of Food Policy in American Reform Judaism', *American Jewish Archives Journal*, 57, 1/2, 29–52.

Toner, Jerry P. (1998) *Leisure and Ancient Rome*, Cambridge: Polity Press.

Twersky, I. (1972) *A Maimonides Reader*, West Orange, NJ: Behrman House.

von Kellenbach, Katharina (1994) 'Fräulein Rabbiner Regina Jonas (1902-1945): Lehrerin, Seelsorgerin, Predigerin', *Yearbook of the European Society of Women in Theological Research*, Kampen: Kok Pharos, 97–102.

Vulkan, Daniel, and David Graham (2008) 'Population Trends Among Britain's Strictly Orthodox Jews', Report of the Community Policy Research Group of the Board of Deputies of British Jews, London. Available online at http://www.boardofdeputies.org.uk/file/StrictlyOrthodox.pdf (accessed 1 July 2011).

Walzer, Michael, Menachem Lorberbaum and Noam J. Zohar (eds) (2000) *The Jewish Political Tradition. Volume One. Authority*, New Haven: Yale University Press.

Warburton, Nigel (2001) *The Art Question*, London: Routledge.

Washofsky, Mark (2001) *Jewish Living: A Guide to Contemporary Reform Practice*, New York: URJ Press.

Waxman, Chaim I. (2005) 'American Jewry' in Nicholas de Lange and Miri Freud-Kandel (eds), *Modern Judaism: an Oxford Guide*, Oxford: Oxford University Press, 129–43.

Weber, Max (1968) *Max Weber. The Theory of Social and Economic Organisation*, (ed. T. Parsons), New York: Free Press.

Weber, Max (2001) [1930], *The Protestant Ethic and The Spirit of Capitalism*, London: Routledge.

Weller, Paul (2008) *Religious Diversity in the UK: Contours and Issues*, London: Continuum.

Werblowsky, R. I. Zwi, and Geoffrey Wigoder (eds) (1997) *The Oxford Dictionary of the Jewish Religion*, Oxford: Oxford University Press.

Whitehead, Anne (2009) *Memory*, London: Routledge.

Williams, Raymond (1983) [1976], *Keywords: A Vocabulary of Culture and Society*, London: Fontana.

Wilson, Charles L. (2007) *Microbial Food Contamination*, second edition, New York: CRC Press.

Wistrich, Robert (1997) 'Israel and the Holocaust Trauma', *Jewish History*, 11, 2, 13–19.

Wolowelsky, Joel B. (2002) 'Rabbis, Rebbetzins, and Halakhic Advisors', *Tradition*, 36, 4, 54–63.

Woodward, Ian (2007) *Understanding Material Culture*, London: Sage.

Wright, Melanie J. (2003) *Understanding Judaism*, Cambridge: Orchard Academic.

Wright, Melanie J. (2007) *Religion and Film: An Introduction*, London: I. B. Tauris.

Wright, Melanie J. (2009) 'Judaism' in John Lyden ed. *The Routledge Companion to Religion and Film*, London and New York: Routledge, 91–108.

Wright, Melanie J. (2011) 'Material Judaism: Interpreting the Pushke' in Daria Pezzoli-Olgiati and Christopher Rowland (eds.), *Approaches to the Visual in Religion*, Göttingen: Vandenhoeck & Ruprecht, 51–64.

Wulff, David M. (1997) *Psychology of Religion: Classic and Contemporary*, New York: John Wiley and Sons.

Yerushalmi, Yosef Hayim (1996) *Zakhor: Jewish History and Jewish Memory*, Seattle: University of Washington Press.

Young, James E. (1995) 'The U.S. Holocaust Memorial Museum: Memory and the Politics of Identity' in Linda Nochlin and Tamar Garb (eds), *The Jew in the Text: Modernity and the Construction of Identity*, London and New York: Thames and Hudson, 292–304.

Yovel, Yirmiyahu (2009) *The Other Within: The Marranos. Split Identity and Emerging Modernity*, Princeton: Princeton University Press.

Zohar, Zion ed. (2005) *Sephardic and Mizrahi Judaism From the Golden Age of Spain to Modern Times*, New York: New York University Press.

Zohar, Zion (2005) 'Sephardim and Oriental Jews in Israel: Rethinking the Sociopolitical Paradigm', in Zion Zohar (ed.), *Sephardic and Mizrahi Judaism From the Golden Age of Spain to Modern Times*, New York: New York University Press, 300–27.

Index